C000277174

HALLYU!

The Korean Wave

Edited by Rosalie Kim

With contributions from Youna Kim, Dal Yong Jin,
Soo-Man Lee, Darcy Paquet, Song Jong-hee,
So Hye Kim, Crystal S. Anderson, Mariam Elba, Lee Sol,
Lia Kim, Dasom Sung, Sun Lee, Joanna Elfving-Hwang,
Yoojin Choi, Gee Eun, Yunah Lee and InHae Yeo

V&A Publishing

Published to accompany the exhibition *Hallyu! The Korean Wave*
at the Victoria and Albert Museum, London,
from 24 September 2022 to 25 June 2023

Supported by

 Ministry of Culture, Sports and Tourism

GENESIS

With additional support from

 **BAGRI FOUNDATION**

 LG

netmarble
Healer.B

First published by V&A Publishing, 2022
Victoria and Albert Museum
South Kensington
London SW7 2RL
vam.ac.uk/publishing

Distributed in North America by Abrams, an imprint of ABRAMS

ISBN 9781 83851 033 6

10 9 8 7 6 5 4 3 2 1
2026 2025 2024 2023 2022

A catalogue record for this book is available from the British Library.

Designer: Marwan Kaabour
Copy-editor: Neil Stewart
Origination: DL Imaging
Index: Nic Nicholas
Printed in Italy by Printer Trento

MIX
Paper from
responsible sources
FSC® C015829

V&A Publishing

Supporting the world's
leading museums of art,
design and performance

Editorial note

We have used Korea to refer to South Korea (officially known as the Republic of Korea) except in cases of ambiguity, where South Korea is used in full. North Korea is used for the Democratic People's Republic of Korea.

The romanization throughout this book follows the guidance set out by the National Institute for the Korean Language, known as the Revised Romanization 2000, the most recent version of which can be found on their website (kornorms.korean.go.kr/m/m_regltn.do?regltn_code=0004#a).

While we have broadly followed the guidance on the romanization of personal names found there as of May 2022, exceptions have been made in the following circumstances:

- Where the named individual has a specific preferred romanization
- Where family names have widely used conventional romanizations, e.g., Kim rather than 'Gim', Park rather than 'Bak', etc.
- Where the named individual has a public profile associated with a particular romanization in any language that uses the roman alphabet, e.g., Bong Joon-ho, Park Chan-wook, etc.
- Where the romanization of an individual's name is an integral part of their professional identity, e.g., they have a mononymous stage name with a particular romanization, they exhibit their work using a particular romanization of their name, or use a particular romanization of their name as brand name, etc.
- Where a particular romanization is used to attribute authorship in text written in languages that use the roman alphabet, e.g., bylines in English-language journalism, French-language academic publications, etc.
- Where historic personages have conventionalized, non-standard romanizations of their names (e.g., Admiral Yi Sun-shin)

Cover image

The finger heart gesture, used to show love and appreciation, was popularized by K-pop and K-drama idols and their fans. It is used widely throughout Asia, and has more recently been taken up across the globe (see p. 35). This version was designed for the V&A by Steven Storm.

Captions, bled images

p. 5	Gwon Osang's sculpture of K-pop idol G-Dragon, *Untitled GD*, 2015
p. 7	Model Han Eu-ddeum is photographed by Hyea W. Kang wearing hanbok on a segway in Dongdaemun Design Plaza, Seoul, for *Vogue Korea*, January 2014
p. 8	Detail of the iconic staircase from *Squid Game*, 2021
p. 10	Detail of image pp. 124–5
pp. 14–15	Shin Gwang, Internet Made Studio, 'We live in Seoul' posters, 2017
pp. 38–9	Tourists and locals in Seoul are encouraged to wear traditional Korean hanbok in return for discounts to the five royal palaces, as seen in this 2018 photograph at Gyeongbokgung Palace
pp. 198–9	K-pop fans at a public K-Pop concert, Seoul, August 2015
p. 201	Tuk-tuk drivers, with their vehicles decorated with banners of K-pop idols, wait for customers in Bangkok, Thailand, 2021
p. 203	Photograph from the set of *Parasite*, 2018. Production design by Lee Ha-jun

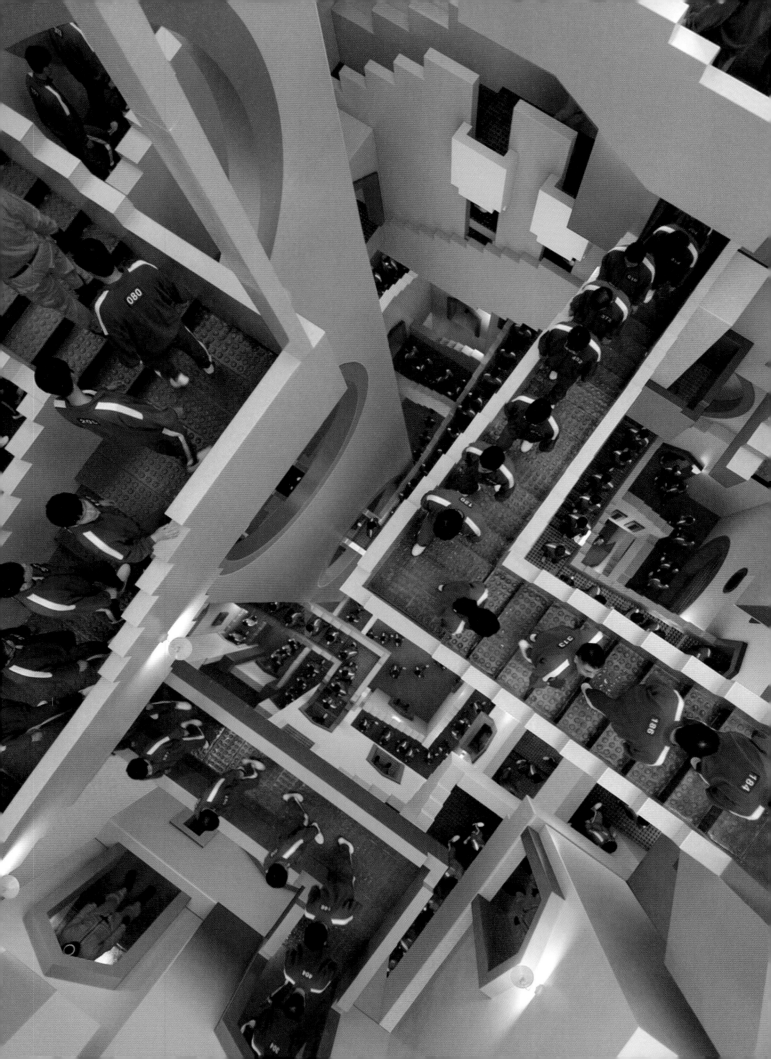

Contents

Hallyu! The Korean Wave is the first major exhibition about Korea at the V&A since 1961, when it hosted the seminal *National Art Treasures of Korea*, introducing the concept of South Korea as an independent country to a European public for the first time. It is also the first of its kind to explore hallyu – the Korean Wave – a term that captures the meteoric rise of South Korea's vibrant popular culture around the world. It posits Korea as a leading cultural powerhouse in the era of social media and digital culture.

The exhibition and this accompanying publication delve into hallyu through the lenses of drama and cinema, K-pop and its fans, and beauty and fashion, examining how the hybrid nature of each sector has been shaped by Korea's compressed modern history and by the spheres of influence to which the country was subjected across the twentieth century. They highlight the seminal role of fans across the world, who use social media platforms to engage publicly in political, social and environmental issues, raising the profile and relevance of hallyu internationally.

The publication expands on these themes through the voices of cultural historians, industry insiders and fans, unravelling the synergy between government strategy, innovative technology and media platforms that put Korea firmly on the cultural map.

I would like to thank Rosalie Kim and the curatorial and exhibitions teams for assembling a complex show in a compressed time span, as well as our many lenders and exhibition supporters, especially the Ministry of Culture, Sports and Tourism Republic of Korea; Genesis; The Bagri Foundation; LG Electronics & LG Display; and Netmarble Healer.B, without whom the breadth of this joyful, energetic exhibition would not have been possible.

Tristram Hunt
Director, V&A

Sponsor's Foreword
Ministry of Culture, Sports and Tourism
Republic of Korea

The Ministry of Culture, Sports and Tourism Republic of Korea, was established to preserve, promote and share Korean culture both domestically and on the world stage. In the decades since, we are proud that hallyu (the Korean Wave) has evolved from a regional development into a global phenomenon, much to the delight and enjoyment of fans around the world. The UK has welcomed hallyu with open arms, and Korean words, restaurants, beauty products, pop music, film and television have now become part of the everyday cultural landscape.

In 2019 the Ministry of Culture, Sports and Tourism initiated a five-year partnership with the V&A by making a major grant that not only supported the important development of this exhibition but also facilitates an expansive programme dedicated to Korean contemporary culture. In the years to come, this partnership will raise awareness of Korean culture across the breadth of the Museum's programming, including an artist residency, a series of publications and new learning programmes, such as workshops, seminars, and conferences. Leading creatives from Korea will also have the opportunity to showcase their work to V&A audiences through existing and popular events including Fashion in Motion and Friday Late.

The V&A was the first museum in London to open a dedicated gallery for art and design objects from Korea. This outstanding collection now spans from the fourth century to the present day and is notable as one of the largest and most prestigious holdings of contemporary craft and design outside Korea. It is therefore fitting that we now proudly sponsor this exhibition, the first of its kind. We hope it plays a part in further fostering international dialogue and exchange and introducing broad new audiences to both Korean cultural history and the V&A.

Genesis was born in 2015 in Korea with a mission to create a whole new luxury automotive experience. Genesis is inspired by the best of contemporary Korean culture and has a bold ambition to challenge automotive conventions.

This mindset is at the very heart of what we do and who we are.

Inspired by Korean design and hospitality, we take great pride in treating our customers as valued guests and respect their greatest luxury of all – their time. At Genesis, you do not have to spend your time coming to us; we come to you.

We share Korea's enthusiasm for technology and innovation and aspire to be one of the first car brands to go fully electric by 2025. It is our ambition to create a new, more sustainable luxury automotive experience that is mindful, human and future facing.

We combine the highest aesthetic ambition with meticulous Korean craftsmanship. Our design is inspired by the beautiful tension of Korean modernity and deep-rooted traditions – audacious, yet timeless; athletic, yet elegant; sophisticated, yet simple: form with function.

As a Korean brand that is part of the Korean Wave we are immensely proud to support this exhibition at the V&A, the beating heart of design and culture in Europe. Bringing modern-day Korea to a London audience feels like a natural part of our DNA, which is so deeply rooted in both east and west.

We sincerely hope that this exhibition will inspire you, just like it inspired us.

Introduction:
The Hallyu Origin Story
한류의 시작

Rosalie Kim

PSY performs his massive global hit 'Gangnam Style' on NBC's *Today* programme, New York, 2012.

Within living memory, South Korea has experienced a meteoric rise, from a country ravaged by war in the mid-1950s to a leading cultural powerhouse by the dawn of the twenty-first century. Its vibrant and colourful popular culture has captured the imagination and attention of a global audience in the past two decades. Published to coincide with a major V&A exhibition, this book explores hallyu – literally the 'Korean Wave' – which refers to this phenomenal surge of popular culture from South Korea (hereafter Korea).

This is the story of a country whose trajectory from 'rags to riches' is marked by potentially risky strategies and innovations paired with a *ppalli-ppalli* ('quick-quick') ethos, where speed is of the essence. Beginning in the late 1990s with the increasing popularity of Korean TV dramas and cinema across Asia, hallyu gained worldwide momentum in the mid-2000s through the remarkable success of the Korean music industry, which coincided with the global rise of the internet, social media and the birth of Gen Z. Korea's cultural gamble – to regain its economic confidence by investing in information and communication technologies (ICT) and culture industries – led to the growth of its international standing through the 'soft power' of culture, with the support of the Korean government and finance from the private sectors. Hallyu has become 'the world's biggest, fastest cultural paradigm shift in modern history' as noted by writer Euny Hong.[1] It is a story told here not only through the voices of cultural historians, but also through industry insiders who have played a role in propelling hallyu forward. Divided into sections, the first highlighting transformations in politics, technology and business models, and the others exploring K-drama and film, K-pop and its fandoms, and

K-beauty and fashion, this book reveals how *Parasite* and *Squid Game*, BTS and BLACKPINK have come to dominate the global consciousness.[2] But first, it is important to paint a picture of the origins of the Korean Wave, to underline both the threads of continuity from which hallyu sprung and the dramatic contrast with what came before.

Oppan Gangnam Style

On 15 July 2012 Park Jae-Sang, a South Korean singer, songwriter and producer better known as PSY, made history when his catchy tune 'Gangnam Style' launched on YouTube. His adrenaline-fuelled, technicolour music video and quirky horseriding dance moves went viral overnight, breaking multiple sales and viewing records, inspiring numerous parodies and gathering prestigious awards and global followers in its wake. By May 2014 the song had clocked over two billion views on YouTube, forcing its owner Google to recalibrate its play counter: '[We] never thought a video would be watched in numbers greater than a 32-bit integer ... that was before we met PSY.[3] Despite coming under fire for playing up to a western racial stereotype as the goofy, Asian sidekick[4] and being dismissed as 'a freak incident'[5] by North American media, PSY 'put South Korea on the map for people around the world'.[6]

Beyond its global popularity, the song is foremost a socio-cultural commentary on Korea's materialistic pursuits, particularly of those 'posers and wannabes' longing to be part of the glitzy Gangnam clique. Nowadays, Gangnam – a district of Seoul located south of the Han river – is the most glamorous and affluent area of the city, and it is easy to forget that 40 years earlier this area was a poor, desolated rice paddy field, bordered

Jun Min Cho's photograph captures old scenes of Apgujeong-dong in 1978 Gangnam, before urban development.

by the empty concrete shells of the apartment blocks that dotted the banks of the river.

From Japanese to American cultural imperialism
In the space of two generations, much of Korea's rural land and scenery has been supplanted by the concrete high-rise buildings of tech-driven cities, reflecting the country's rapid move from an economy relying on agriculture, forestry and fishery to a digital, service-based economy. Nowadays, Korean society boasts many subcultures, where cutting-edge technology and plastic surgery coexist with centuries-old shamanistic and Confucian rituals. In the early 1990s Chang Kyung-Sup, Professor of Sociology at the Seoul National University, coined the term 'compressed modernity' to explain how these paradoxes and anachronisms resulted from a modernization process that was condensed and abrupt rather than a gradually maturing.[7] The long-established socio-cultural, economic and political values based on Neo-Confucian ideology inherited from more than 500 years of Joseon dynasty rule (1392–1910) were confronted overnight with new norms and alien policies that Korean society had little time to digest and embrace in earnest.

Instead, the twentieth century in Korea was marked by a long and rapid succession of disastrous events, starting with the asymmetrical Treaty of Ganghwa Island with Japan (1876), followed by the Japan–Korea Protectorate Treaty (1905–10), which led to the colonial period (1910–45). This was a time of socio-political subjugation and forced assimilation to Japanese cultural frameworks under the pretext of bringing Korea up to speed with the modern world. After its liberation at the end of the Second World War, Korea once again fell victim, this time to the Cold War. In 1945 its territory was arbitrarily divided by the Allies along the 38th parallel, with the North under the trusteeship of the Soviet Union and the South that of the Americans. Cold War antagonism fed into the outbreak of the Korean War (1950–3), which turned into a gruesome battle of ideology by proxy that devastated the peninsula.[8] As no peace treaty has yet been reached, North and South Korea remain technically at war today.[9] Despite the 58 countries involved, 2.5 million lives lost, and the first military intervention by the newly established United Nations Command, the Korean War was dubbed the Forgotten War due to media censorship by the US military at the time, the public's fatigue following the Second World War, and its eclipse by the Vietnam War (1954–75).

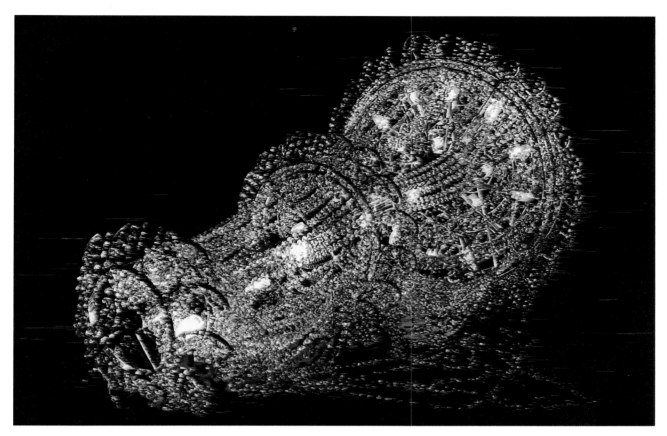

(Above)
What you see is the unseen/Chandeliers for Five Cities SR 01-03, 2015, a large needlework designed by South Korean artist Kyungah Ham and made by anonymous embroiderers from North Korea. The fallen chandelier offers a metaphor for the arbitrary decision taken by the Allies to divide the country in two.

(Below)
US soldiers check refugees for contraband before allowing them to cross the 38th parallel bridge during the Korean War, 8 December 1950. Today, many Korean families are still separated as a consequence of the territorial division.

A photograph taken in the 1920/1930s of the Bonjeong/Honmachi shopping district in Seoul/Keijo, which was emblematic of the modernity and consumerist culture introduced during the Japanese colonial period. Its western-style architecture, department stores, cafés and theatres drew in a Korean and Japanese crowd in 'modern' dress, kimono and hanbok.

Against this dramatically shifting backdrop, the local folk culture that had been enjoyed by the masses during the Joseon dynasty was gradually supplanted by alternative forms of entertainment that provoked both fascination and disdain. During the colonial period, Japanese versions of modern Euro-American music – collectively referred to as jazz[10] – spread across Korea, as did Japanese ryūkōka (popular song). Those foreign melodies were emulated and given translated or mixed lyrics (in a fashion not dissimilar to K-pop today) or new words entirely, later spawning a Korean musical genre known nowadays as teuroteu ('trot') or ppongjjak.[11] This new soundscape was promoted by the establishment of the first Korean radio station, JODK, in 1927 and the first Korean music recording studio, Okeh, in 1933, alongside the proliferation of the much-coveted gramophones throughout the 1930s.

Motion pictures, first introduced from America in the late nineteenth century, also gained traction in the 1910s and 1920s with the increase in commercial movie theatres, mainly screening imported Euro-American films and propaganda materials locally produced by Japanese-owned companies. This period saw the emergence of movies featuring, directed by and made for Koreans based on folktales or local narratives. One such example was Arirang (1926), directed by Na Un-gyu, which galvanized the local audience with its patriotic tone and Na's anti-colonial stance.[12]

These new forms of entertainment expanded Korea's worldview and triggered an awareness of colonial modernity by mirroring the real changes that were affecting the lives of many Koreans at the time. From the proliferation of electricity and motor vehicles to coffee houses and department stores, cities were transforming radically, while 'modern girls and boys'

adopted western garments and hairdos, and enjoyed a lifestyle deemed frivolous and decadent by a vast majority of Korean society still swayed by Neo-Confucian ethics. The new popular culture was thus embraced with varying degrees of enthusiasm, reflecting complex attitudes towards a colonial modernity introduced by Japan.[13]

By the outbreak of the Second World War in 1939, western music and films were prohibited by the colonial government, which reinforced Japan's status as the main sphere of cultural influence on the peninsula until its liberation in 1945. Following the end of colonial rule, South Korea endeavoured to reclaim its identity and culture amid strong anti-Japanese sentiment. In 1945 it introduced a ban on Japanese cultural imports such as films, music and manga, which only began to be lifted over half a century later, in 1998.[14]

America took over as the main cultural influence in South Korea through performances at its military bases and via its broadcasting service, the American Forces Korea Network (AFKN). To boost the morale of US troops, the United Service Organization (USO) arranged various public movie screenings and concerts, from Hollywood celebrity Marilyn Monroe performing for the US Eighth Army in 1954[15] to Louis Armstrong inaugurating the Walker Hill Resort in 1963 in front of '800 ROK and US military dignitaries'.[16] This military entertaining circuit also provided Korean performers with a regular income and a springboard from which to launch a musical career locally and internationally. They serenaded the crowd with cover versions of western songs, pronouncing words they sometimes barely understood. The Kim Sisters illustrate this stellar trajectory from GI camps to Las Vegas, as they won the American audience over with their 'exoticized' East Asian look and their outstanding

(Above)
Marilyn Monroe performing on her USO tour to entertain the American Forces stationed in Korea, February 1954.

(Below)
The Kim Sisters found enormous success in the US. They are seen here advertising National Electric guitars in a 1966 edition of *Life* magazine.

In his ink painting *Quiet Listening*, 1934, Kim Ki-Chang (known as Woonbo) shows multiple facets of modernity in colonial Korea, including a gramophone, which transformed the way music was consumed.

(Above)
The Mymy (1982), Korea's first portable mini-cassette player, quickly became one of the most coveted items among students, reflecting the growing profile of pop music in 1980s Korea. This advertisement is from c.1987.

(Below)
In 1959 the A-501 became the first radio manufactured in Korea. It was designed by Park Yong Gui for Goldstar, better known today as LG Electronics.

A military police officer cuts a young man's hair in front of others. In 1973 the Park Chung-hee government adopted the Minor Offenses Act banning men from having long hair.

In 1980 student-led pro-democratic demonstrations in Gwangju were brutally suppressed by Chun Doo-hwan's forces in what became known as the Gwangju Massacre.

musical talents. The band was also a conduit for bolstering the US government's efforts to rally public opinion in support of its military objective in Korea by showcasing successful outcomes resulting from its presence. Nevertheless, early bands like the Kim Sisters, Korean Kittens and Add 4 were pioneers who paved the way for future generations of Korean artists to find success abroad.[17]

The 1950s also ushered in the golden age of Korean cinema. Films were a source of much-needed escapism and entertainment, and in 1954 domestic studios received financial incentives from the government to boost production and attendance figures.[18] The measure proved to be popular: an increasing number of movies were released, attracting record audiences, and more studios and cinemas were built to sustain demand. Young directors engaged with contemporary themes such as cultural malaise, social inequality and women's emancipation, experimenting with a freedom that Korea had not enjoyed for over 50 years. A classical canon of Korean cinema was shot between 1953 and the early 1960s, including the daring *Madame Freedom* (Han Hyeong-mo, 1956); *The Housemaid* (Kim Ki-young, 1960), heralded as the forerunner to Bong Joon-ho's *Parasite*; *The Aimless Bullet*, a portrait of alienated vulnerability (Yu Hyun-mok, 1961); and the humanist *The Coachman* (Kang Dae-jin, 1961). The latter became the first Korean film to be recognized abroad, winning the Silver Bear for the Extraordinary Jury Prize at the 1961 Berlin Film Festival.

It was also during this period that cinemascope and colour technologies merged to give the audience a vibrant and immersive experience.[19] Shin Sang-ok used these techniques for the first time to shoot *Seong Chun-hyang* (1961), based on a beloved folktale about morals and faithful love, bringing to life its colourful costumes and set. The film's blockbuster success established a popular and lucrative genre that engendered a plethora of historical epics which continued to be produced throughout the 1960s.[20]

Military rule and cultural protectionism

The Korean War ushered in an era of political unrest and economic instability, which provided fertile ground for the coup d'état orchestrated by Major General Park Chung-hee in 1961, inaugurating two decades of dictatorship. When he took over South Korea it was considered a Third World country in ruin, poorer than its North Korean counterpart, with a GDP per

capita 'lower than that of Haiti, Ethiopia and Yemen, and 40% below India's'.[21] Park's military regime pressed for the rapid modernization and economic recovery of South Korea, which built upon some of the remaining Japanese colonial businesses, with financial and infrastructural support from Europe and the USA as well as Japan, with whom relationships were resumed in 1965.[22] The government quickly opted for an export-oriented, heavy industry-based economy to compensate for a weak and limited domestic market, while also identifying a select number of companies it deemed reliable and sustainable enough to support its ambition. It was during this period that *chaebol* – large family-owned conglomerates such as Samsung, LG and Hyundai – rose to prominence. They benefited from fiscal advantages and political ties, which attracted foreign capital and expanded their trade. These companies became the engine of the rapid modernization and industrialization of Korea from the 1960s to the 1980s: the 'Miracle on the River Han'.

As modernization proceeded apace, Park's government implemented the Cultural Heritage Protection Act in 1962.[23] Sites, monuments and skills considered of 'high historical and artistic significance' to Korea were protected and given the titles of Important In/tangible Cultural Property. Beyond merely preserving Korean cultural heritage, this set of policies aimed to rebuild a Korean identity free from Japanese colonial influence and to restore pride in Korean culture and history, while at the same time validating the authority of Park's regime. These ambitions are best symbolized by the 17-metre-tall statue of Admiral Yi Sun-shin unveiled in 1968 as the first commission of the Committee for Erecting Patriotic Forefathers. This naval figure is one of the most celebrated war heroes in Korean history, revered for defeating the larger Japanese fleet during the Imjin War (1592–9). Park requested that 'the statue of the figure most feared by the Japanese'[24] be situated on the Sejong-ro, the large central road leading to the Gyeongbok Royal Palace, once cradle of the Joseon royal authority, then appropriated and monopolized by the Japanese during the colonial period. Park was making the connection between himself, a Korean military leader standing up to Japan, and Admiral Yi.

In Park's view, popular culture was for the promotion of moral and patriotic values, not for entertaining the public. He disapproved of the growing influx of Euro-American popular music and its associated hippy culture, whose 'debauched'

The opening ceremony of the 1988 Summer Olympic Games in Seoul was the source of great national pride.

Actor Choi Min-su attends a 1999 rally in protest against the government's policy to reduce the screen quota system.

visuals and messages not only threatened local culture but also challenged his own authority. Seeking to avoid dissidence at a volatile time brought about by the Vietnam War, the resuming of economic relationships with Japan and the rising inequalities that arrived with the growth of consumer culture, Park hastily announced a wave of ethics committees and censorship regulations from 1962 to 1975, aiming to stifle freedom of expression and anti-state behaviour.[25] These included the Minor Offenses Act, which outlawed long hair for men and short miniskirts for women, and the banning by the Korean Broadcasting Ethics Committee of a string of so-called provocative songs and lyrics.[26] In parallel, movie productions became mass-production factories closely monitored by the state. A quantity-over-quality approach fuelled a rise in low-budget films but also a wider variety of genres, including comedies and literary adaptations. Growing restrictions stemming from the Yusin Reform (1972–9), which ruthlessly suppressed opposition and established Park's tenure for life, the subsequent mandatory inclusion of propaganda elements, combined with the advent of the TV era, all contributed to the demise of the golden age of Korean cinema in the early 1970s.

The 1960s and 1970s saw the mass dissemination of radios and TVs in Korea. The ruling regime saw these technologies as the perfect means to control and propagate their anti-Communist and modernization agenda, while audiences enjoyed them as a source of home entertainment amid improvements in living conditions such as round-the-clock access to electricity.[27] The affordable Goldstar A-501, the first radio designed and produced locally since 1959, became a crucial device, allowing people to be kept informed of the fast-changing socio-political landscape at the time. Radios were also airing gripping audio dramas like Camellia Lady (1963), which went on to spawn an equally successful film and soundtrack.

Initially an emblem of wealth, TV sets increased in number throughout these decades, from 8,000 in 1962 to almost 6 million by 1980,[28] while numerous public and commercial TV broadcasting companies, including KBS (Korean Broadcasting System) and MBC (Munhwa Broadcasting Corporation), emerged throughout the 1960s.[29] The TV took centre stage in the living room, as families gathered around state-approved variety shows, American series and Korean dramas and films.[30] Korean dramas had begun to gain momentum in the

1970s following the lifting in 1969 of a ban that prevented broadcasters benefiting from advertising.[31] The quality of TV production subsequently improved, as did the competition between broadcasting companies. One of the highlights of the time was Assi (Tonyang Broadcasting Company, 1970), a melodrama that followed the arduous life of a woman in a patriarchal society against the backdrop of the colonial and post-war periods. It became so popular that a warning line asked the audience 'to view the episode after checking that the door is properly locked to avoid theft, and water turned off'.[32] It is noteworthy, however, that very few dramas at this time engaged with unconventional or progressive subjects, in order to avoid governmental censorship on moral grounds.

By the end of the 1970s, the field of electronics was emerging as a dominant export industry. It benefited from governmental support because it was perceived to be a competitive and higher value-added sector that would be lucrative in the long run.[33] The 1980s liberalization of the economy saw a progressive shift towards production of the more refined, technology-intensive goods used in industrial electronic sectors (such as semi-conductors). At the same time, chaebol like Samsung, Hyundai and LG and universities grew the R&D in the field,[34] which later helped make Korea one of the leading producers and consumers of cutting-edge technology.

Seoul to the world – on the path to democracy

Park's military regime ended abruptly with his assassination in October 1979, but was promptly replaced by another dictatorship led by Major General Chun Doo-hwan. One of the most traumatizing moments of his brutal reign, and one that has been burnt into the Korean collective memory ever since, was the infamous Gwangju Uprising of May 1980, better known as the Gwangju Massacre. With the tacit approval of the US military,[35] Chun's armed paratroopers viciously suppressed pro-democratic demonstrations, led by students and labour unions who called for democratic reform and an end to martial law. Freedom of the press and human rights were severely suppressed, while anti-American sentiment spread among the Korean population. It would take another seven years and the landmark June Uprising protest of 1987, overwhelmingly backed by the middle class, to defeat autocratic rule, gradually remove censorship and firmly set Korea on the path to full democracy.

Office workers protest against the measures imposed by the International Monetary Fund (IMF) during the Korean economic crisis of the late 1990s.

To recover from the disastrous image that marked the beginning of his tenure, Chun's regime looked to popular culture. More than a propaganda vehicle, popular culture was now to become a deflection device, keeping public scrutiny away from politics as well as providing an outlet for the population to vent their frustration. Apart from measures including the lifting of curfew and a return to hairstyling freedom, the government implemented a set of cultural policies branded 3S, referring to Sports, Sex and Screen.[36] The 1980s witnessed the birth of Professional Sports Leagues in 1982 and the hosting of the 10th Asian Games in 1986, which was perceived as a dress rehearsal for the seminal 24th Summer Olympic Games in 1988.[37] Despite accusations of corruption, and an aggressive urban regeneration plan in Gangnam that led to mass homelessness during the preparation for the Games, the event was a turning point in Korean modern history and propelled the nation onto the international stage for the first time as a democratic and economically developed country. Ultimately, the 1988 Summer Olympics were a source of pride and cause for celebration, and projected a radically new image of the country, far from the rubble of the Korean War.

These games and sport events were closely watched on colour TVs, whose sales grew exponentially after 1980. Their advent accelerated a budding culture of consumerism with lush, technicolour adverts tempting consumer pockets. The artistic quality of TV dramas also improved, with more vibrant sets and costumes as well as colourful make-up launching new trends. The same period saw the rise to prominence of VCRs in many households, a rise echoed by the flourishing of video rental shops and a booming market in illegal videotapes. As Chun's regime was more lenient about sex, erotic films came to dominate the VCR and film industries in an otherwise moribund period, with some produced straight-to-video.[38] However, the situation started to shift in the second half of the 1980s as Korean cinema saw some important changes in legislation, the most impactful of which was the liberalization of the foreign film market. From 1986, Hollywood companies were allowed to directly distribute an unlimited number of their films in Korea, rather than go through local intermediaries, risking the livelihood of an already weakened domestic industry.[39]

On the music front, teenagers were the new cultural consumers, wielding power through their vocal, organized fandoms. Cho Yong-pil was the first artist to boast such a fandom in Korea, the fans naming themselves Oppa-Budae (Oppa's Troop) – a name reminiscent of today's BTS ARMY. Cho dabbled in different musical genres from retro rock to trot, ballad to jazz, sang his songs in Japanese for his Japanese audience and held concerts overseas, including in China and New York.[40] With the convergence of youth culture, colour TV and the portable cassette player, the 1980s saw the explosion of dance music. Popular variety or contest-based TV shows introduced young, attractive and stylish singers with great dancing skills that particularly appealed to teenagers. Synchronized choreography, modern fashion and a sound based on an American pop template rejuvenated the concept of *gayo*, the Korean word for 'popular song', previously referring to trot, rock or folky ballad. These dynamic performances were a far cry from those of previous generations of *gayo* performers, who would sing or play instruments while remaining in the same place onstage. Sobangcha, a boy band trio, led the pack, together with artists like Kim Wan-sun, invariably labelled the 'Korean Madonna', 'Dancing Queen' or 'Sexy Diva'. Unlike many of her peers, Kim was trained by her aunt, a famous talent agent, for three years before debuting at the tender age of 17 in 1986, a precursor to contemporary K-pop trainees. At this time, more educated and skilled women in Korea began to join the workforce, including the growing electronics sector, yet discrimination and inequality were rife.[41] In this context, the image of a female singer (and, by extension, of Korean women generally) was often designed to fit the non-threatening and subservient roles pre-set by a patriarchal society. Kim's branded image, and a repertoire that ranged from demure to sexy, shattered the norm and paved the way for more diversity among female singers, though it also drew criticism for its objectification of women, as did the growing culture of erotic movies.

Prelude to Hallyu: oppressed, repressed, expressed

Twentieth-century Korea was marked by a succession of violent oppressions and maddening suppressions. Once freed from occupation and military rule, the country underwent a rapid modernization that inevitably affected its cultural identity. Against the backdrop of growing middle-class consumerism, the country navigated through traditional values, unresolved imagery of modernity and subversive neo/colonial cultural influences to shape a new self.

In this context, local governments played a proactive role in the formation of Korea's cultural identity and the development of its industries, just as they had engineered the country's rapid economic recovery. Park's military regime established a series of rolling five-year plans and policies founded on cultural protectionism, with censorship as a key tool for monitoring production. Plans and policies were later amended or unpicked, and censorship gradually lifted by subsequent governments according to their political or economic agenda. Despite the maturing of Korean democracy and the growing neoliberalization of its economy in the 1990s, the state continued to intervene in the cultural sector, this time shifting its position from governing body to one supporting the global ambitions of the private sector.

In parallel, cultural industries such as music, drama and cinema began to expand in the wake of new artistic freedoms, a rise in urbanites' purchasing power and the flourishing of domestic electronics goods such as portable music players, TVs and PCs. In 1994 the news that the box office from Steven Spielberg's film *Jurassic Park* had outperformed the profits from the sale of 1.5 million Hyundai cars was not lost on Kim Young-sam's administration, the first civilian government in 30 years.[42] It acknowledged the huge economic potential and export value provided by the cultural industries, the opportunity they offered to raise the country's profile abroad, and their use as leverage in advancing Korea's cultural diplomacy. Having experienced and learned first-hand from America's deployment of soft power, Korea recognized that influence could be exercised through appeal rather than force.

Around the same time, the internet, previously reserved for universities and research institutions, became accessible to all. Driven by the belief that colonial occupation emanated from too slow an embrace of the Industrial Revolution in the late nineteenth century,[43] Korea was eager to embrace the Digital Revolution and invested in the internet and information and communication technology (ICT) early on. Between 1996 and 2001, governmental focus was on expanding high-speed internet infrastructure, providing free internet training to 30 per cent of the population throughout the country, and developing R&D around mobile communication technology to establish the foundation of its ICT industries. When the Asian Financial Crisis blew the Korean economy to pieces in 1997, a new generation of unemployed diverted their effort and knowledge into IT-based businesses, leading ultimately to a rapid recovery from the crisis.

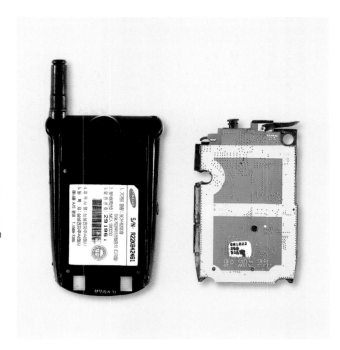

This Samsung mobile SCH-6200 1999 has 'The belief we can do it' engraved on the microchip, an example of hopes for a rapid recovery from the economic crisis of the late 1990s.

Repaying its US$58 billion International Monetary Fund bailout loan in full in 2001, ahead of schedule, Korea was simultaneously heralded as a benchmark model for high-speed internet technology among OECD countries, leading 'in both quantity and quality of internet use.'[44]

In the wake of the crisis, Kim Dae-jung's government reassessed its economic and financial operational models. The government began to move away from manufacturing industries, due to the competitive labour market from emerging countries, and prioritized instead the internet-, knowledge- and skill-based economy, alongside a focus on cultural industries, with the proactive aim to 'quadruple exports in cultural industries.'[45]

Korea's biographical trajectory charts a tumultuous twentieth century that led the country to cultivate its remarkable resilience. It learned to adapt fast to evolving situations, driven by a desire to survive and thrive. Hallyu emerged from this context, at a time when cultural policies, creative industries and digital technologies converged, sowing the seed for its development into a tech-savvy cultural powerhouse that would lead the field in an era of social media and digital culture by the dawn of the twenty-first century. Breaking conventions, mixing influences and making its own rules, Korea now spearheads a movement that challenges the global currents of popular culture, strengthening along the way its soft power.

K-Culture And Soft Power
K-문화와 소프트 파워

In September 2020, hallyu reached a milestone. Membership of hallyu fanclubs worldwide surpassed 100 million for the first time, reflecting an increase from 2019 of 30 per cent in America, 25 per cent in Europe and an impressive 270 per cent in Africa and the Middle East.[1] This equated to a 16.3 per cent annual rise in the export of Korean cultural content in 2020, a rare feat amid the adverse effect of the Covid-19 pandemic on all other export and domestic markets.[2] These cultural industries are branded under the banner 'K-' (K-pop, K-drama, etc.) to carve a distinctive status within the cultural globalization of the digital age. The Korean government's post-IMF strategic investments in ICT and entertainment industries, once seen as a risky gamble, seem in hindsight to have been a bold visionary move in view of social distancing, lockdowns and the contactless lifestyle developed during the pandemic.

Nowadays, high-profile K-pop idols increasingly take on goodwill ambassadorial roles for noble causes, from BTS's *Love Myself* UNICEF campaign promoting self-esteem and well-being to BLACKPINK's call for climate actions at COP26. K-pop fandoms mirror these good deeds through constructive activism, further propagating the philanthropic image of their idols. K-drama and cinema invariably boost tourism, Korean food and fashion, but also attract hordes of students to Korean language courses. In 2021, 26 Korean words – from hanbok to *daebak* and *dongchimi* – were added to the Oxford English Dictionary, demonstrating the international influence of hallyu. Beyond the commodification of culture, these entertainment industries are an underdog success story, having radically transformed the image of Korea overseas, from a once colonized country to an aspirational cultural trendsetter (see Youna Kim, pp. 32–9).

This shift in perception and a subsequent rise in soft power were amplified by technological innovations, which have been proven historically to be instrumental in triggering new patterns of cultural production and consumption. Korea was quick to explore this prospect in the wake of the high-speed internet rollout in the post-IMF era. The release of the world's first commercial MP3 player, MPMan F10 from Saehan Information Systems (1998), was swiftly followed by the first commercial satellite TV-mobile phone, SCH-M220 from Samsung (1999), and the first capacitive touchscreen mobile phone, LG KE850, also known as LG Prada (see p. 41). With the growth in household PCs from the mid-1990s, new digital entertainment in the form of social networking services and esports (initially online PC games) also gained prominence and completely redefined interactions in Korea. Social gatherings and idea exchanges were displaced from the real world to a myriad of virtual 'rooms' or 'cafés' where diverse topics could be discussed freely and anonymously. The prototypical social media site Cyworld (1999), for instance, presented webpages where users could share their blogs, photos and thoughts. By 2001, Cyworld had developed a playful and personal digital environment called 'miniroom', populated with customizable avatars, music playlists and digital decorations, all purchased online with dotori, the Cyworld's virtual currency. Wildly popular, by 2009 two-thirds of the country owned a miniroom. By the time Facebook, YouTube and Twitter emerged in the mid-2000s, Korea was familiar with, and recognized the potential of, social media and streaming platforms.

K-pop industries in particular were quick to adopt these channels as a conduit for strategically distributing and promoting their creative content, while simultaneously nurturing a worldwide fandom. Aware of the domestic market's limitations, Soo-Man Lee, founder of SM Entertainment – the powerhouse behind H.O.T., Girls' Generation, EXO, Red Velvet and NCT – devised in the mid-1990s a K-pop promotion system he termed Culture Technology (CT).[3] Its core principle was to transcend cultural diversity in order to expand K-pop's appeal across the world (see Soo-Man Lee, pp. 48–53). This was achieved by combining culture and technology with an underpinning system that localized K-pop's content and delivery to encourage its reception and bolster its fandom abroad. CT strategies included language classes for idols, recruitment of trainees at a global scale, and collaborations with international practitioners and partners. Social media was promptly incorporated to boost interactions and intimacy between idols and fans, and streaming platforms and fans-turned-producers were called upon for a rapid and effective online dissemination of K-pop. Despite criticism about the profit-oriented nature of its scheme, and the hybridized and manufactured nature of the resulting artistic output, CT gained credentials following the huge overseas success of SM's artists. Other entertainment companies quickly adopted the same approach, and the Korean star system was born.

Mini Room (Above) and *MD03/Min Ji Jo* (Below) from Emil Goh's series of digital prints 'MyCy', 2005. The artist explored the similarities and differences between people's real rooms and those they posted to Cyworld's Minihome site.

To remain competitive, CT needed to stay ahead of the game in technology. The next priority was the pursuit of new realities, which would blend AR/VR/AI, innovations whose development accelerated as the emergence of the pandemic prevented tours and live events (see Dal Yong Jin, pp. 40–7). Korean entertainment companies developed joint ventures with STEM universities and research labs as they entered the global race for the coveted metaverse, a parallel universe set in an immersive, virtual environment that expands our sensorial experience beyond the real world with the use of headsets and other technologies.[4] In the metaverse, users' interactions are mediated via avatars that are controlled remotely, can participate in all sorts of activities and share an experience of online events. The pandemic provided the right contextual background for the testing of budding alternative visuals, experiences and storytelling devices, all of which will affect the next K-pop evolution phase. This period also saw a succession of livestream concerts and the launch of new virtual idols.[5] It is noteworthy, too, that the online PC gaming industries that originated in the late 1990s still today constitute the largest cultural export from Korea, dwarfing the income generated by the other entertainment industries combined.[6] In 2022, esports will reach a turning point in their history as the Asian Games formally integrate esports and athletic sports for the first time, further blurring the boundary between the real and virtual worlds.

The K-culture industries – ranging from K-drama to webtoons (Korean digital cartoons), cinema, music and esports – can cross-pollinate their digital content thanks to media convergence and transmedia storytelling. Collectively pushing boundaries, they form a creative ecosystem that boosts growth and strengthens the 'K-' nature of their output while building a wider fandom along the way. These industries are further interconnected through their diversified portfolios: K-pop companies often manage their own modelling and talent agencies, which work in the broadcasting and film sectors. They also invest in technology R&D, just as computer game developers enjoy shares in the K-pop industries. More recently, these companies have also begun to venture into K-beauty, with music mogul Park Jin-young (JYP Entertainment) introducing a cosmetics line in collaboration with beauty brand Sioris, and mobile game giant NetMarble launching Healer.B cosmetics with Coway. These entertainment companies are quickly turning into the new beacon of the Korean export and cultural economy.

Hallyu:
Soft Power and Politics

Youna Kim

The 2016 K-pop festival KCON, held in Paris, attracted huge crowds.

Since the late 1990s South Korea (hereafter Korea) has emerged as a new centre for global popular culture, referred to as the 'Korean Wave' or 'Hallyu'. Initiated by the spread of television drama, hallyu includes K-pop music, film, animation, online games, smartphones, fashion, cosmetics, food and lifestyles. A key feature of the rise of hallyu is the active role of the nation-state in focusing on the creation of a cool national brand, reinforcing a commercialized pop nationalism or cultural nationalism that appropriates popular culture to promote political and economic interests. Popular culture has become an effective way to sell a dynamic image of the nation through soft power.[1] Through globalization and digitalization, hallyu is building a bridge of cultural connectivity to become Korea's strongest form of soft power, albeit with limitations. This chapter addresses the development of hallyu and its complex implications for soft power and cultural nationalism in the digital age. Hallyu is one facet of the decentralizing multiplicity of global cultural flows today, and its significance can be seen as a conscious (and often intentional) way to counter the threat and insensibility of the western-dominated cultural market within the context of global inequalities and uneven power structures. Korea, as a postcolonial and somewhat peripheral nation, has strengthened its national culture industry to compete with the dominant flow of western media products, while consolidating a rapidly growing position in the regional market and beyond.

The Korean culture industry was developed for socio-economic, cultural and political reasons in the late 1990s.[2] Following the 1997 IMF financial crisis, the Korean government thoroughly re-examined the process of modernization and identified the export of popular media culture as a new economic initiative, one of the major sources of foreign revenue vital for the country's economic survival and advancement.

Trade experts called for the nation to shift its key development strategy to fostering overseas marketing for culture and digital technology and services, including films, TV programmes, popular music, online games and distribution services. The government has striven to capitalize on Korean popular culture, giving it the same national support in export promotion once provided to electronics and cars. Hallyu started from the efforts of the private sector, but state-led developmentalist nationalism has played a key role in the speed of growth.

The Korean culture industry has been developed as a national project competing within globalization, not against it. The government, along with the private sector and academia, has worked on the re-creation of its national image and cultural identity.[3] The globalization policy of Kim Young-Sam's government (1993–8) started to respond to neoliberalism and regulatory practices imposed by the west. Kim Dae-jung's government (1998–2003) provided financial support to the culture industry: focusing on content, creativity and culture, it encouraged colleges to open culture industry departments. Roh Moo-Hyun's government (2003–8) advocated cultural diversity as well as creativity, and Lee Myung-Bak's government (2008–13) promoted 'Brand Korea', which aimed to enhance the nation's image through popular culture in a wide range of areas from K-pop to K-food. In 2016, to celebrate the 130th anniversary of diplomatic ties between Korea and France, the world's largest K-pop festival was held in Paris; attended by President Park Geun-hye, it attracted 13,500 hallyu fans and hugely boosted the visibility of Korean culture. And in 2017, President Moon Jae-In revealed his plan to increase the number of global hallyu fans to 100 million in the future.[4]

Today, policy discussions continue to utilize culture as a transnational commodity and capital. The Ministry of Culture,

Production still for Season 1 of KBS series, *Winter Sonata* (dir. Yun Seok-ho). First aired in 2002, the series became a particular hit in Japan.

Sports and Tourism and the Korea Trade-Investment Promotion Agency set aside budgets for programmes to promote the national image. Hallyu, with the active participation of the nation-state, is a pronounced example of the crossover of culture, economy and politics, exemplifying a neoliberal capitalist approach in the era of globalization.

Hallyu began to have a major impact with the export of television dramas that were less sexualized and violent than American dramas. Engaging with modernity and tradition, Korean dramas are self-reflexive and emotionally powerful.[5] Hallyu reached a peak in Japan when the romance drama *Winter Sonata* (2002) became a national phenomenon, and another with the airing of the historical drama *Jewel in the Palace* (2003); recent successes in K-drama include the historical supernatural thriller *Kingdom* (2019–20), co-produced by Netflix. Popular culture, once considered emotional and lowbrow in 'fast modernizing, highly educated neo-Confucian Korea', is now a potent export force providing significant underpinning for the generation of high value and meaning for the nation.[6] Amateur subtitling, known as 'fan-subbing', has been critical to the growth of hallyu, as dispersed fans contribute their linguistic knowledge and time for the greater good of the collective. This organic, collaborative culture of linguistic translations, for a language that holds a peripheral status in the global media industry, indicates the extent of fans' affective investment in K-drama.[7]

Korea's music industry – the sixth largest in the world – is a vital source of revenue for the national economy. The success of such K-pop bands as BLACKPINK is a direct outcome of the Korean 'star system', which uses intense training to deliver a polished and easily identifiable product with international appeal. Following the historic success in 2012 of unconventional Korean musician PSY, whose track 'Gangnam Style' unexpectedly became a global sensation, the K-pop boy band BTS debuted in 2013 and grew into a global phenomenon that is widely recognized and influential; the band has topped the *Billboard* album charts and became the first K-pop group to speak at the UN, helping to launch UNICEF's 'Generation Unlimited' campaign, promoting education, employment and empowerment for young people globally. While its member states have agreed to create development goals designed to overcome poverty, inequality and other international issues, the UN has also noted that 'most Heads of State coming to the General Assembly are sixty plus years old'[8] and stressed the need for younger generations to get involved; the invitation to BTS reflected the group's ability to attract and influence the global youth community by means of fast-moving digital technologies and networked communications. All over the world, the group's devoted fans, BTS ARMY, promote and spread their idols' stories and values via social media. Hallyu is emerging not only as a core component of Korea's economic competitiveness, but also as a powerful resource for social influence and cultural diplomacy at a global level.[9]

Korea has the fifth largest film industry in the non-western world. The development of a cinematic industry modelled on Hollywood was facilitated in the 1990s by the government's state-capital power and the capital investment of conglomerates (*chaebol*). *Shiri* (1999), Korea's first big-budget Hollywood-style thriller, attracted 5.8 million viewers – more than the 4.7 million who saw *Titanic* (1997) in Korea. Korean cinema marked its 100th anniversary in 2019; the global success that year of *Parasite* represented the culmination of the centennial development of the film industry into an international cultural powerhouse. *Parasite*'s historic victory at the Academy Awards was not really the moment Korean cinema finally made it, but rather the first time Hollywood and the west decided to take notice.[10] All along, the creative energy and attractive power of popular culture has been heightening Korea's visibility and capturing the imagination of new generations.[11]

The unprecedented historic success of hallyu has shone an unfamiliar spotlight on Korea, for centuries colonized or overshadowed by powerful countries. The Korean government now recognizes popular culture as an effective way to create and sell a dynamic image of the nation to international audiences through 'soft power'. Soft power – the ability to make others act in a way that advances preferred outcomes through attraction, rather than threat or coercion, and without the use of military or economic force – can achieve goals through long-term diffuse effects rather than by immediate or short-term actions.[12] Although the concept was introduced in the field of international relations focusing on states, soft power applies to a much wider range of actors and contexts: it can be 'high', directed at elites in a country, or 'low', aimed at the general public, and it can stem from governments and non-governmental actors including businesspeople and popular culture celebrities.[13] The soft power of any country rests primarily on three resources: the attractiveness of its culture, its political values when it lives up to them at home and abroad, and its foreign policies when they are seen as legitimate and having moral authority.[14] A country's popular culture can thus increase its overall attractiveness and its potential influence on the global stage, albeit in unquantifiable, often commercial and even paradoxical ways. Popular culture amounts to something more than mass-produced capitalistic entertainment and leisure activity, since relations of power and politics are inescapably interwoven with a cultural and ideological landscape that is always subject to negotiation, contestation and tension.

Hallyu is not just a cultural phenomenon, but fundamentally about the creation of soft power, nation branding and

BTS meet US President Joe Biden at the White House in June 2022. The finger heart gesture, popularized by Korean pop idols, underlines their anti hate crime message.

sustainable development through transnational meaning-making processes.[15] Going beyond traditional state-centric diplomacy, the Korean government has promoted hallyu to create positive dispositions towards the nation, and utilized the cultural diplomacy of celebrities to provide a multitude of connections to global audiences and global public spheres through digital media. The traditional definition of diplomats as agents of the state and the national interest excludes celebrities, just as it does all non-state actors, although in recent times celebrities have gained significant recognition as actors in global affairs.[16] In a nation with very low trust in politicians and political institutions, celebrities are more likely to fill the void in public trust vacated by the political classes; accordingly, hallyu celebrities may be employed by the government to play a supporting role in the realm of diplomacy among world leaders, and are appointed as honorary ambassadors for the country to use their brand power in cultural promotion abroad. They help the state to soften diplomatic tensions, refashioning the nation as a 'cool Korea' brand for the global public.

The popularity of hallyu celebrities has triggered an increase in foreign audiences visiting locations where favourite dramas and movies have been filmed. For avid audiences, locations become 'must see' places and their visits represent the mobile self.[17] As cities compete with others for global tourists, the identity of each city (or nation) is reconfigured in the hyper-spatial world – where space/time is stretched to accommodate the flows of capital and desires that characterize neoliberal capitalism.[18] Hallyu has become an integral part of Korea's attention economy, which is built around affective relationships and digital connections with audiences to shape desires and aspirations.

For example, the government provided the television drama *Winter Sonata* free of charge to broadcasters in Iraq and Egypt, in a move intended to generate positive feelings towards Korean soldiers stationed in Iraq and to improve the image of Korea in countries that had little understanding of or exposure to its culture.[19] For the first time in the Middle East, hallyu began spreading the non-economic side of its soft power to the political sphere. Following the broadcast, thousands of fan letters arrived at the Korean Embassy in Egypt. Viewers launched a hallyu fan club and website in the Arabic cultural sphere, expressing their new interest in Korean culture and desire to visit Korea.

Similarly, hallyu has stimulated young people around the world to engage with Korean studies and the Korean language. The government has appointed celebrities as cultural and tourism ambassadors, as well as hosting events for hallyu fan clubs overseas. The Ministry of Culture, Sports and Tourism promotes Korea through *Visit Korea* campaigns and a website that provides hallyu information including storylines, filming locations and celebrities: for instance, global fans of *Jewel in the Palace* are encouraged to visit the historical drama's shooting site, Jeju Folk Village, and experience traditional culture such as *hanbok* (traditional clothing), *hanok* (traditional housing) and *hansik* (traditional food). Sponsored events overseas such as 'Korea Day' or 'Korea Week' aim to enhance the country's international standing and change the image of its economic hard power that far outweighs its soft power in the eyes of the global community.

Hallyu! The Korean Wave

For the 2021 'Feel the Rhythm of Korea' campaign, released on YouTube, the Korea Tourism Organization worked with artists such as the *pansori* band Leenalchi and the Goblins dance team from Ambiguous Dance Company to create dynamic scenes in cities across Korea.

A 2006 photograph shows an Asiana Airlines passenger jet emblazoned with images of actress Lee Young-ae from the series *Jewel in the Palace* (2003–4).

In today's digital age, collaborative creativity 'from above' (nation-states, institutions, media industries) and 'from below' (digital fans as grassroots intermediaries, producers-consumers, publics) can appropriate popular culture to make its origin nation, language and culture attractive to international audiences and to open possibilities for soft power. Voluntary and affective participation – such as 'fan-subbing' – play a significant role in spreading popular culture and mediating soft power, although the 'from below' actors do not necessarily operate in predictable ways or coherently with top-down governmental or media actors. Digital technologies have ushered in affective politics, new strategies for mobilizing and capturing affect and emotion that have become central engines driving media culture and politics in the digital age, contrary to the traditional dogma of rational political actors.[20] The politics of emotion, or propaganda by other 'soft' means, are not new, but they have become strikingly apparent in digital diplomacy, especially when they involve popular culture or the symbolic meaning of celebrities.

With the active involvement of the government, hallyu has been largely constructed within nationalistic discourses and policies, and imagined as cultural nationalism: a form of hegemony masked in soft power. As a soft power resource that emerged from a postcolonial nation, hallyu can generate a new version of cultural imperialism that is deeply embedded in cultural nationalism and an ideological position that – ironically – undermines cultural diversity and soft power principles.[21]

Globalization and its associated digital technologies have made possible new forms of global nationalism that spread far beyond the borders of traditional nation-states,[22] and the historical traumas of the past animate global nationalism today.[23] The dialectic nature of globalizing and nationalizing forces is a key feature of popular culture, given the centrality of the nation-state to the promotion of cultural flows across national boundaries.

The heightened visibility of hallyu has been criticized by the mass media and the public overseas as a quasi-colonial cultural invasion on Korea's part. For some, hallyu is a subversive contraflow to service the diverse consumer market against a one-way flow from the west to the peripheral rest. In other communities, by contrast, its increasing volume and velocity has generated a sense of discontent and tension, giving rise to a backlash of anti-Korean sentiment in East Asia[24] and Southeast Asia.[25] Here, non-consumer online communities reinforce reactive nationalist discourses, with the complicity of local media productions and the state. However, a paradox is that the floating signifier of Korean cultural nationalism – newly expressed self-confidence, pride, cultural authenticity, inner passion and energy through popular culture – is also the reason that hallyu has powerful appeal across the digitalized, porous world.[26] This is a reflection of Korea's yearning for an independent cultural force, a particular speaking position in the struggle for national cultural identity amid the threatening presence of the mediated sphere of the west and its increasing vulnerability to western-style globalization.[27] Korea is reimagining and relearning its identity and future through alternative, decentralized cultural flows such as hallyu. This imagining and reflexivity is not just a sign of a newfound self-confidence, but also of heightened anxiety in a globally mediated world.

Digital Korean Wave: From Esports to K-pop

Dal Yong Jin

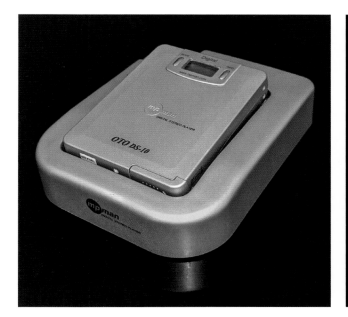

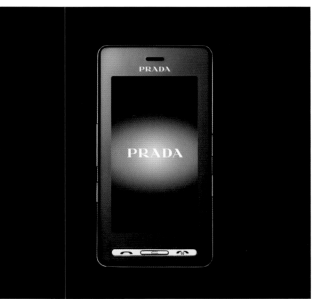

The world's first commercial MP3 player, the MPMan F10 (shown here together with its charging station), was created by Saehan Electronics in 1998.

The LG Prada KE850 smartphone, Korea's first touchscreen phone, was released in May 2007.

Since Korea rolled out high-speed internet in the late 1990s, digital technologies such as smartphones and digital gaming, as well as internet portals like Naver, Daum and Kakao, have become hallmarks of Korean society. Over the past two decades, the country has developed a variety of digital technologies and digital cultures that have had a fundamental impact on not only people's daily lives but also their cultural activities. In this chapter, I explore the entwined relationship between the advent of digital technologies and changes in Korean popular culture. After briefly documenting the rapid growth of digital technologies in the mid-1990s, I explain the ways in which the internet and social media have influenced the soaring popularity of hallyu content, including digital gaming and esports, and K-pop in the global cultural sphere. I also explore how internet portals such as Naver and Daum (now Kakao) – which are themselves turning into digital platforms – as well as mobile messaging services like KakaoTalk and Line have advanced new digital cultures. Finally, I discuss the recent growth of various cutting-edge digital technologies, including artificial intelligence (AI) and the metaverse, and their influence on the world of K-pop.

The emergence of digital technologies in Korea

Since the mid-1990s, Korea, once small and peripheral in the information technology (IT) sector, has rapidly advanced a handful of digital technologies to become one of the most significant areas for the national economy and youth culture. The Korean government first planned to transform the country into a knowledge-based economy by setting up the Korea Information Infrastructure (KII) in March 1995. It understood that 'the national digital network in use did not have the capacity to handle the vast amount of multimedia data that would be transmitted in the 21st century, and that Korea's future therefore depended on the implementation of an advanced information infrastructure'.[1] The goal was to construct a nationwide infrastructure consisting of communications

networks, internet services, application software, computers, and information products and services.[2] The KII project aimed to build high-speed and high-capacity networks through market competition and private sector investment, as well as government policies, thereby supporting a variety of actors including the government, private companies and end users.[3] The original plan was to provide broadband networks to all households by 2015, but in 1999 this target was brought forward to 2010, at a total project cost of US$24.5 billion, with the government investment accounting for US$1.5 billion.[4] Building on this infrastructure, towards the end of the 1990s a couple of big *chaebol* (conglomerates) – Samsung Electronics and LG Electronics – were beginning to develop new phone and music technologies. By the time CDMA (code division multiple access service) technology was launched in the late 1990s, allowing multiple transmitters to send information simultaneously over a single communication channel so that users could share a band of frequencies, the LG Economic Research Institute had already conceptualized their own notion of the smartphone, which would combine a mobile phone with the internet and email.[5] Samsung Electronics' 1998 annual report also used the term 'smartphone', explaining: 'a smartphone is a mobile handset which includes several functions, including email and Internet search, while sharing data with PCs. The smartphone is most commonly defined as a phone with several functions, such as fax, email, pager, paperless notepad, address book, calendar, and calculator, as well as touchscreen with specific operation system (OS) to run these applications'.[6] The period saw gradual progress towards the smartphone era that would arrive in the second half of the 2000s, as the government and handset makers started to advance both technologies and concepts.[7] As a result, Korea's mega tech giants developed several mobile phones, including the LG Prada, the first mobile phone in Korea to have a capacitive touchscreen. Four icons at the bottom of the touch-sensitive screen allowed the user to make a telephone call, send a message or go to the main

The *StarCraft* Pro League finals at Gwangalli Beach in Busan, 2017, showing the huge spectatorship for esports in Korea.

menu. There were also buttons at the side for volume control, camera and MP3 player. The LG Prada was released in May 2007, a month before Apple's iPhone.[8] Both Samsung and LG continued to produce their own smartphones from 2009, although LG Electronics shut down its smartphone business in 2021.[9] Meanwhile, Naver and Kakao have become two major digital platforms, with many Koreans relying heavily on them for news, information, entertainment and webtoons (manga-style web comics, typically published online in chapters known as 'episodes') (see Rosalie Kim, pp. 72–81).[10] Naver Corp is a global digital company, providing the search portal Naver; its subsidiaries and affiliates supply services including the Line messenger, the Snow camera app, the digital comics platform Naver Webtoon, group social media platform Naver Band and metaverse platform Zepeto. Another Korean digital platform, Kakao, was established in 2010, and has developed several applications and services, including KakaoTalk and KakaoPage. These platforms have turned out to be the primary actors in establishing digital Korea as both user and producer.

Digital Korea has transformed not only the national economy but also people's cultural activities. By utilizing digital technologies to enjoy cultural content, Koreans have considerably increased their use of and reliance on new digital technologies. As the Organisation for Economic Co-operation and Development (OECD) points out, 'Korea is a top player in emerging digital technologies, with an outstanding digital infrastructure and a dynamic ICT sector'; it notes, too, that 'digital technologies offer opportunities to raise firms' productivity and the population's well-being'.[11] As we will see, this convergence of digital technologies and relevant cultures has greatly facilitated the success of digital hallyu.

Digital gaming and esports

Digital gaming has become one of the most significant cultural activities in many parts of the globe, and Korea has notably developed various digital games and relevant cultures, including its PC Bang gaming centres – mainly established around the time of the 1997 economic crisis – and esports. In 1997 the number of PC- and internet-equipped houses was low, but high-speed internet was becoming more established because of the government's infrastructure project, and PC Bang increased its visitor numbers dramatically as Koreans came to watch game play without video dropouts. Shortly afterwards, *StarCraft*, a game released by US-based Blizzard Entertainment in 1998, made its way to Korea. The sci-fi-themed online strategy game became a mainstay of Korean esports, and 'a boon for Korean digital gaming culture, arriving as it did at the height of PC Bang expansion. *StarCraft* became a pop culture sensation in Korean seemingly overnight'.[12]

With the expansion of PC Bang venues in tandem with the soaring popularity of *StarCraft*, the number of esports games also rapidly increased. In 1999 there were 25 esports games in Korea, increasing to 51 in 2000, even before the esports broadcasting era. As a reflection of esports' growing importance for youth culture and their potential as a tool for boosting corporate image, *chaebol* like Samsung and Hyundai Securities Co., as well as media firms such as Sport Seoul, Tooniverse, Digital Chosun and SBS (Seoul Broadcasting System), hosted esports games.[13] The success of *StarCraft* and subsequent esports drove game developers to create new online games as well: for example, NCSoft's *Lineage I*, an MMORPG (massively multiplayer online role-play game), became a big hit immediately upon its release in 1998, ushering in Korea's golden age of online game development.[14]

Players of *League of Legends* at a PC Bang tournament organized by Riot Games, at Lion Internet Café in Seoul, 2012.

Esports especially grew with the live broadcasting of game competitions among professional players on cable channels, followed by networks, which expedited the growth of esports and spectatorship. In 2001 MBC Game – a subscription-based Korean television station well known as one of the most popular esports channels – began 24-hour game broadcasting. Others followed, contributing greatly to the progression of esports spectatorship. Alongside this, Ongamenet specialized in broadcasting video-game-related information and matches, covering *StarCraft*, *Warcraft III*, *FIFA Series*, *Counter-Strike*, *Winning Eleven*, *Age of Empires III* and *Dead or Alive*. In response to the soaring popularity of esports, a handful of IT-related firms, including Samsung, SKT and KT, formed their own professional game teams to boost their corporate images.

Although technological developments were key to this flourishing of internet gaming and the unique model of spectatorship, socio-cultural factors relating to dynamism and mass play culture in Korea also had a role. As one of the most networked societies, Koreans are used to playing together and working together, and their desire to be part of the gaming process – to play communally in a spirit of competition and immersion – is an important factor in the growth of digital games.[15] Korea not only advanced esports nationally but also globally: in the 2000s the country developed the World Esports Game League, which became a crucial venue for global game players for many years.

From the creation and export of many online and mobile games to esports, the Korean digital game sphere has had a global impact much bigger than that of broadcasting, film and even K-pop. While Korea exported US$7,245 million worth of digital games in 2020, the broadcasting industry exported US$486 million in television programmes and the film industry exported only US$54 million.[16]

Social media and K-pop

While there is a handful of different reasons for the soaring popularity of K-pop, digital technologies such as social media, AI and the metaverse have contributed to its success around the globe. Seemingly a very traditional cultural form, as singers continue to sing and dance in front of mass audiences, K-pop has become a symbol of the convergence of popular culture and cutting-edge digital technologies.

To begin with, social media has been one of the most reliable components for the success of K-pop in the global music scene. From the early 2010s, it has rapidly replaced the role of traditional media, allowing users transnational access to K-pop content. The lack of availability and presence of Korean pop culture content in mainstream North American media may even have triggered the emergence of the social mediascape of the Korean Wave: many global fans noted that reliance on social media was inevitable since broadcast and cable media channels were not programming hallyu content on a regular basis, with the exception of a very limited number of satellite or cable channels.[17] From PSY's 'Gangnam Style' (2012) to BTS's 'Dynamite' (2020) and BLACKPINK's 'How You Like That' (2020), K-pop idol groups and single artists have utilized social media not only to release new songs and albums, but also to connect with global fans.

As Rosalie Kim discusses in her introduction to this section, K-pop idol groups' use of social media platforms has been common industry practice, and the perceived reciprocal engagement between fans and idols is now typical of contemporary music consumption. Many top-tier K-pop idols –

including EXO, BLACKPINK and TWICE – have extensively utilized social media to foster audiences for their music. BTS are particularly well known for their social media use, with their Top Social Artist awards between the late 2010s and the early 2020s directly related to their extensive engagement with fans, which is perceived as one of their primary strengths.[18]

Starting in the mid-2010s, the Korean music industry began to develop another form of media convergence, adapting AI in order to expand its cultural production and global reach (a phenomenon that Soo-Man Lee, founder of SM Entertainment, explores in the following chapter). Interestingly, one of the first examples of the convergence of K-pop and AI was in the realm of digital gaming. In 2018 Riot Games debuted a new group, K/DA, during the *League of Legends* championship game in Incheon, Korea. K/DA is made up of both real Korean and American singers (including two members of other K-pop groups) and avatars. These real and virtual performers work in rotation on stage, making an important leap in bridging the real and the virtual fields. While these were not the first such avatars on the scene, they clearly introduced an era of K-pop avatars.[19] Like online concerts, this new trend has been significant during the time of Covid-19, when people could not attend events in person. By participating instead in online music concerts, fans have been part of K-pop, and now enjoy virtual K-pop groups by connecting with them 'virtually'.

In October 2020 SM Entertainment created a new girl group, aespa, which combines real idol members and virtual 'ae' counterparts (see p. 52). Developers of synthetic universes such as augmented reality (AR), virtual reality (VR) and extended reality are most often considered metaverse-related businesses.[20] In other words, the metaverse can be considered as a combination of multiple elements of technology, including VR, AR and video, where users live within a digital universe. Although aespa's formation led to debate online over the potential for dehumanization, the band has become a success, having one of the biggest K-pop hits of 2021 with their single 'Next Level', and their EP 'Savage' debuting at number 20 on the US *Billboard* chart. Other acts go even further in incorporating virtual avatars in their musical projects: in March 2021 the 11-member girl group Eternity, formed by the Seoul-based tech start-up Pulse9, released their single 'I'm Real'. Each member of Eternity – said to be the first K-pop group created using only AI – has their own personality and biography, and they are even able to conduct video interviews.[21]

This is only the beginning. Other major K-pop companies are also now starting to develop new AI- and metaverse-based K-pop movements. In 2017 YG Entertainment began working with Naver to build a new global music service platform by pooling Naver's technologies (including AI), resources and global influence. Naver and YG's affiliate YG Plus is expanding its music database to include more diverse genres as well as K-pop tracks.[22] This is just one example of how Korean cultural industries have fundamentally shifted their norms, strategically and tactically developing their cultural content with the help of digital technologies.

In Korea, the new technologies of high-speed internet, smartphones, social media and AI have substantively replaced traditional media as the major tools of the public sphere. The increasing use of digital technologies in cultural activities has been especially prominent in the Korean context because it is one of the world's most networked countries. Advances in technology have not only created and developed popular culture and cutting-edge digital products but also brought about the convergence of these two distinctive areas in order to advance digital hallyu.

It is certain that the use of digital technologies will continue and that their influence will further intensify. For those born after 1990, who have been living with digital media since their childhood, increasingly influence national culture, their use of and reliance on these digital technologies is both common and practical. Regardless of the increasing role of US-based digital platforms such as Facebook and Netflix in the Korean market, digital hallyu has strengths that will allow it to flourish. Vitally, it has emerged from a convergence not only between domestically developed popular culture and digital technologies, but also between locally created cultural content and western-based digital platforms. With this mixture of fast-paced homegrown innovation and global adaptivity already galvanizing Korean pop culture, it is clear that an understanding of digital technologies as an integral part of hallyu is crucial to its future.

Single cover for K/DA's 'More', 2020, showing *League of Legends* champions and pop band members Akali, Ahri, Evelyn, Kai'Sa and guest artist Seraphine (second from left). Voiced by Madison Beer, (G)I-dle, Lexie Liu and Jaira Burns.

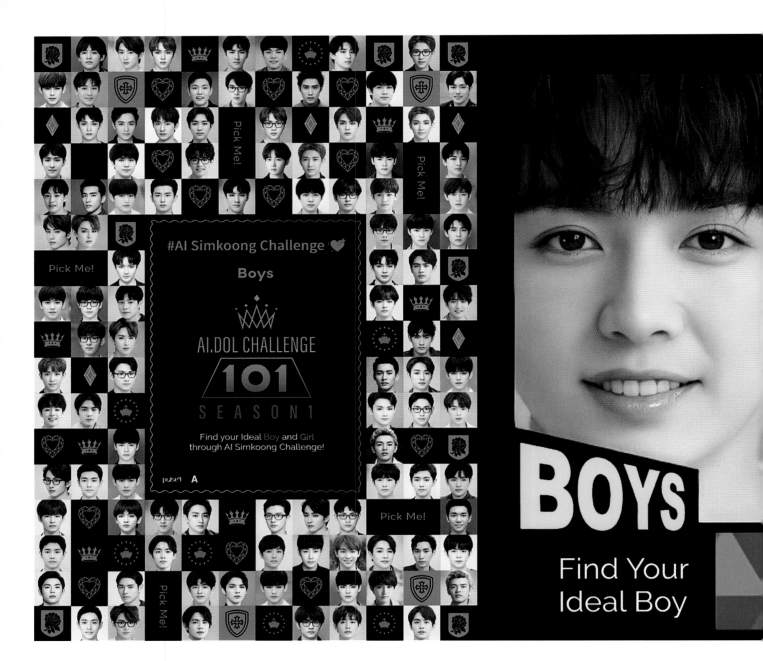

Poster for the 'AI Simkoong Challenge', December 2019, asking the public to vote for their favourite faces for a virtual K-pop band, and a photoshoot of the final line-up of Eternity, artificially created following the results.

GIRLS

Find Your
Ideal Girl

#AI Simkoong Challenge

Girls

AI.DOL CHALLENGE

101

SEASON 1

Find your Ideal Boy and Girl
through AI Simkoong Challenge!

ETERNITY

Culture Technology and the Future of Hallyu

Soo-Man Lee

Soo-Man Lee, who started out as a producer in the 1980s, pictured in the studio in 2018.

Hallyu is the future. The next hallyu, a metaverse where avatars, celebrities and global fandoms meet together, has already begun. This new history comprises performances in various fields such as K-pop, drama, film, beauty and fashion along with the growth and movement of the global fandom. Following the advent of ICT technology and social media in the 1990s, hallyu created a new paradigm through rapid shifts from analogue to digital, and now it has moved into an AI era. I have been producing K-pop before, at and after the birth of hallyu and have tried to build a new entertainment world that connects the world to culture, with the idea that when culture thrives so too will the economy: Culture First, Economy Next. I have also been responsible for advancing what I call Culture Technology (CT), which is the essential strength of the Korean Wave. Through this text, I would like to talk about the vision of the Korean Wave, CT and the potential of the Korean Wave to enrich our future.

Culture First, Economy Next

After a career as a singer and MC in the 1970s, I went to the United States in the 1980s to study computer engineering. During this period, I witnessed the birth of MTV, which led to my epiphany about a shift from 'music that is heard' to 'music that is seen' and revolutionary changes that would occur in pop music and society. I also realized that in order for Korea to enter the global market, a scientific and systematic producing system was needed. With the dream of globalizing Korean music, I returned home in 1989 and established SM Entertainment,

later SM Entertainment Co., Ltd., Korea's first company with a producing and management system fully aimed at fostering world-class artists.

The 1970s and 1980s were decades of 'Economy First, Culture Next', where the power of the economy led global culture. Yet I believed in the reverse: culture had the power to lead the world, and if you bring culture to the world, economic wealth will follow – 'Culture First, Economy Next'. I entered the world stage emphasizing the importance of the impact culture can have on the economy, with the belief that Korea would prosper if Korean culture became well known and loved.

From the start, the goal for K-pop was globalization. In order to find individuals with the potential to become global stars, I searched far and wide, not only in Korea, but also in New York and Los Angeles. My aim was to find the future star, one with great communication skills, personality and the ability to speak English, as well as having an understanding of global culture. With this in mind, I produced H.O.T. (High-five Of Teenagers), developed them into Korea's superstar group and announced their entrance into the global market in 1997. On 1 February 2000, H.O.T. held a concert in China, filling 12,000 seats in the Beijing Workers Gymnasium with passionate fans. With the newly coined word 'Hallyu' making headlines, Chinese media covered this as a social phenomenon. At the start of a new century H.O.T.'s concert in China became the catalyst for and commercialized the term. It was a moment of overwhelming gratitude for me.

Beijing Youth Daily was among many Chinese newspapers reporting on the huge impact of the H.O.T Beijing concert in 2000.

Soo-Man Lee and Steve Barnett, former Chairman and CEO of Universal Music's Capitol Music Group, join SuperM members for the band's debut in the United States in 2019.

Since then I have worked to make hallyu much more than the simple exporting and selling of albums, content or merchandise. I wanted to create a continuous movement of national prosperity through groups like H.O.T. (1996), S.E.S. (1997), SHINHWA (1998), FLY TO THE SKY (1999), BoA (2000), TVXQ! (2003), SUPER JUNIOR (2005), Girls' Generation (2007), SHINee (2008), EXO (2012), Red Velvet (2014), NCT 127 (2016), NCT DREAM (2016), WayV (2019), SuperM (2019) and aespa (2020). The main focus was on the creation of a global movement through a three-step strategy of export, collaboration and partnership. Through mutual exchanges with global markets and local partners, we aimed to create global movements that expanded the stage and boundaries of the Korean Wave to Asia, Europe and the United States.

The Future of Culture Technology

From the moment I started on this path as a producer, I have referred to the skill of producing culture as 'Culture Technology'. I firmly believe that since inception, Korea has had what the world praises as a 'skill of making culture'. Following in the footsteps of the potters of the Goryeo dynasty and the Joseon dynasty who created world-class artwork that is loved beyond its time and era, Korea today has the ability to produce dramas, movies, music and artists that are loved by the public. For K-pop, I have further developed a unique Culture Technology that has systemized artist casting, training, producing and management to aim for the global market. CT is the growth engine behind K-pop, and the fundamental operating system of SM Entertainment. I am working to advance CT by codifying and systematizing it still further to prevent it from disappearing, in order to pass it on to the next generation.

For the past 30 years SM and I have paid attention to new and upcoming technologies while making various attempts at incorporating them into culture. At an early stage, I set up an R&D team focused on 3D videos and we continuously experimented together. In 2000 we produced *Age of Peace* starring H.O.T., which became Korea's first 3D movie about idols. In 2010 SM joined with 3D film *Avatar* director James Cameron's production team and Samsung Electronics to establish a 3D Content Leadership Collaboration. This led to Girls' Generation's 3D music video, presented after long research and development. After that, with our experience of R&D, we were able to introduce

BoA and SUPER JUNIOR's 3D music videos as well. In 2012 we incorporated hologram and AR technology into content, creating a hologram live concert called 'V Concert' (virtual concert). After building a hologram-exclusive theatre with ICT Technology, we showcased the world's first hologram musical, *School Oz,* in 2015. With SK Telecom, the largest Korean wireless telecommunications company, we made an AI speaker that operated text-to-speech (TTS) technology using SM artists' voices. In 2019 we collaborated with Intel Studio on a project called 'Immersive Media 360: NCT 127-Superhuman', which was our attempt to activate a vision of new content that combines innovative technology with K-pop storytelling. By using volumetric capture and AR technology, we produced music videos that offered an experience of a 360-degree AR view of the artist's stage.[1]

In 2020 we presented the world's first online concert brand, 'Beyond LIVE', which aims to provide viewers with a fantastically immersive experience by applying AR and XR technology to concerts. Beyond LIVE was acclaimed by media around the world and announced as a 'new paradigm in the midst of a culturally stagnant world from Covid-19 that'll become the new concert model in a contactless era'[2], influencing the global entertainment industry. We are already expanding Beyond LIVE to provide a new cultural framework. Many people had doubts when I announced we would be stepping into the global market in 1997, and when I predicted in 2015 that 'the future will be a world for celebrities and AI' and we should therefore 'prepare a community that connects culture with celebrities'. In 2012 we announced a Virtual Nation together with the K-pop fandom. K-pop fans and SM artists gathered together at Jamsil's Olympic Stadium in Seoul, Korea's largest stadium, for the SMTOWN LIVE WORLD TOUR 2012. The event declared the global fandom community a Virtual Music Nation called 'SMTOWN', regardless of borders. MUSIC NATION SMTOWN PASSPORTS were made, and now, global fans who possess an analogue passport will get to own a virtual passport (MUSIC NATION SMTOWN META-PASSPORT) through blockchain in which all information is transparently recorded and proven. In SM's Metaverse, anyone can participate as a creator. Not only will they be financially rewarded for their activities, but they can also develop their natural creative capabilities. The entire process of a 12-year-old boy in a remote area becoming a super creator is revealed in real time worldwide. Phenomenal events like this will happen

H.O.T. *We Hate All Kinds of Violence*, album, 1996

BoA, *ID; Peace B*, album, 2000

Super Junior, *Mr. Simple*, album, 2011

Girls' Generation, *Gee*, album, 2009

SHINee, *Replay*, album, 2008

EXO, *Growl*, album, 2013

NCT, *Resonance Pt.2*, album, 2020

aespa, 'Next Level', single, 2021

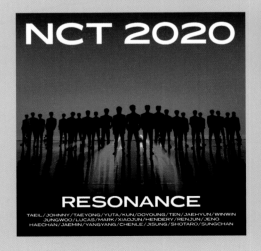

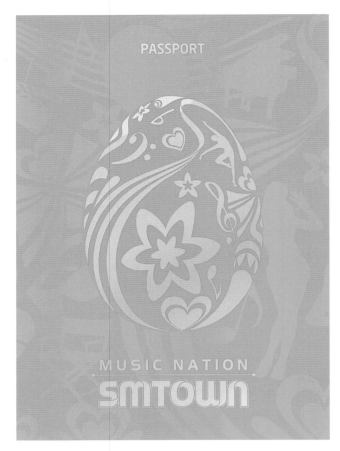

PASSPORT

MUSIC NATION
SMTOWN

The MUSIC NATION SMTOWN PASSPORT issued for the world tour in 2012. A virtual blockchain version known as the MUSIC NATION SMTOWN META-PASSPORT is in development.

Members of TVXQ!, EXO, Super Junior, Girls' Generation and f(x) carry the SM Nation Flag on the SMTOWN LIVE WORLD TOUR III in Seoul, 2012.

all the time. This is the reality that we are living in: technology is developing exponentially, faster than ever before, and in order to bring visions to life, constant effort and preparation are key. CT is innovation. The future of Culture Technology is 'preparing for the future one step ahead'. CT will evolve towards the future.

K-pop has always shown the future in a daring way, with aespa, in particular, opening the gates to the future of entertainment. Debuting in 2020, aespa became the first metaverse group, with artists in the real world coexisting with avatars in the virtual, encompassed within an expansive and developing narrative. With the start of aespa, the worldviews of different SM artists converged into SM Culture Universe (SMCU): a future entertainment era with unlimited content experiences going beyond the borders of the real and the virtual, which aims to connect the world through culture while transcending time and space.

The future of hallyu

This is the peak era of prosumers, the blockchain era. We are living in a metaverse where prosumers voluntarily re-create and expand content. The value of the original content is then maximized by its re-creation by these individuals, and within the metaverse such contents will become assets and further monetizable. So let us take a moment to imagine the day when cultural content becomes a form of currency. Will cultural content lead the prosumer's generation? Will it be accepted in a blockchain era in which the Creator Economy made by prosumers is most significant? These are important questions for the future of hallyu. I believe that this vision of the future is possible.

In 2021 SM and I announced a K-pop Generation with prosumers and promised to present 'an experience of our content infinitely expanding into Re-Creatable content of everyone': a content universe created together by producers and prosumers based off accumulated killer content. We knowingly designed the SM Culture Universe to allow the creation of an ecosystem in which prosumers can freely re-create and share content. SMCU is not a hallyu craze of a single generation, but a well-prepared worldview, vision and blueprint for content and future content to be loved without end.[3] This worldview is what I call a 'Metaversal Origin Story'. For a long time, we have been building the SM Culture Universe by creating the Origin Story and worldview of each artist. With EXO, we began to show specific details to the public (see p. 121), foreshadowing SM's metaverse SMCU. EXO were the new stars who came to Earth from an unknown planet, while the members of NCT sympathize with each other through dreams and become one with their music. Aespa move the story forward even further, with a worldview that coexists with avatars who clearly enact their Metaversal Origin Story. Soon, you will also be able to see EXO and NCT's Metaversal Origin Stories in detail. These will expand endlessly through prosumers' Re-created Content.

Each artist equals one world, and a producer creates worldviews. This world is then connected and expanded through limitless re-creation by fandoms and prosumers: a future entertainment metaverse where the world is connected through culture without the boundaries of real and virtual. This is SMCU's vision and the future we plan to create as our contribution to hallyu. It will become important for us to further embrace the influence of prosumers in all industries while pursuing a Bottom-Up Culture Movement.

Another vision I have for the future of hallyu involves the merging of science and entertainment. Components once considered irrelevant to entertainment such as AI, nanotechnology and biotech will be the factors that bring the greatest change to the future entertainment industry. Regardless of business area, many entrepreneurs will find themselves cooperating towards a new area of entertainment, creating not just new content but also moments that will revolutionize human life. A synergy from the combination of culture and scientific technology will become the driving force behind the future of

The real life and virtual members of aespa and ae feature in this promotional image for 2021's 'Next Level'.

hallyu globally. In a metaverse world, humanity will choose a direction that leads to a materially, culturally and mentally richer life.

We all have a desire for peaceful coexistence, happiness and culture. I believe that the convergence of culture and science to bring about a future in which mankind is connected through cultural richness without barriers is going to be the greatest vision and direction of hallyu.

Hallyu always aims for connection, convergence, coexistence and happiness. What is more surprising than the exponential evolution of technology is the deeply rooted humanity in hallyu and the explosive creativity of the fandoms and prosumers. I believe the future of hallyu lies with humanity and the creative dynamics of prosumers and producers. Play to Create! A prosumer's urge to re-create is a powerful human creative instinct. In a Creator Economy, a metaverse where anyone can embrace the joys of creation, everyone is a

prosumer. In coexistence with humanity, hallyu will awaken the essential and unique creative instincts of humankind through creations by fandoms and prosumers. It will enrich our future and bring forth a future entertainment world that anyone would want to live in.

At a time when the world is embracing K-pop and hallyu, I recognize that it is not only my greatest luck but also joy to have discovered outstanding artists while building hallyu alongside my remarkable fellow creators. With hallyu connecting people through culture, it appears the dream I had a long time ago has become a reality. A new time of creation has begun where everyone shares the joy of creation. Hallyu will provide a future for numerous artists, creators and prosumers who are striving to accomplish their dreams.

If we dream the same dream together, that will be the start of our future.

K-Drama, Webtoons and Film

K-드라마와 영화

The first hallyu wave rippled across Asia in the late 1990s, spearheaded by K-drama and cinema. Hallyu, a term deriving from the words *han* (Korea) and *ryu* (wave), was mentioned in 1999 by the *Beijing Youth Daily* (as 'Hanliu') in a report on the obsessive craze for Korean popular culture among Beijing youth, which was triggered by the growing influx of K-drama and K-pop music in China.[1] This enthusiasm was initially sparked by the success of *What is Love*, a family saga broadcast in 1997 on China Central Television (CCTV). K-drama went on to captivate Japan, Vietnam, Indonesia and other countries in the region before grabbing worldwide attention at the dawn of the twenty-first century thanks to the emergence of over-the-top (OTT) media services such as Amazon Prime, Netflix and Hulu. K-dramas reached dazzling heights during the Covid-19 pandemic when they provided a welcome escape from the unprecedented circumstances forcing many to isolate at home. The *Economic Times of India* noted a Netflix viewer increase of over 370 per cent for K-dramas from 2019 to 2020 alone.[2] Today, *Squid Game* and *All of Us Are Dead* have become household names around the world; *Squid Game* was the most viewed series on Netflix Global for ten consecutive weeks after its release in 2021,[3] while *All of Us Are Dead* shot to the top of the same chart upon release in January 2022,[4] respectively ranking first and second most-viewed series on Netflix Global.

This success results from the boom in a broadcasting industry that began to gain agency with the budding democracy of the late 1980s and early 1990s. TV was then perceived as the main source of entertainment, with the average daily viewing time reaching 3.2 hours in 1996.[5] The progressive lifting of state censorship translated into an increase of funds raised by advertising and, in 1991, the establishment of a new commercial TV station, SBS (Seoul Broadcasting System). With the introduction of cable television in 1995, 30 additional channels joined the Korean TV landscape. All of these factors fuelled viewership rivalry and contributed to the diversification of dramas' storylines and themes, alongside improvements in production quality.[6] It is in this context that the format of modern K-drama was shaped: blocks of 16–24 hour-long episodes, made on a live-shoot system,[7] which started to be exported throughout Asia at a competitive price at a time when Japanese popular culture was waning.[8]

K-dramas quickly gathered pace and fans. Series such as *Winter Sonata* (2002) or *Jewel in the Palace* (2003) resonated with Asian and Muslim communities due to their cultural proximity; plotlines underlined Asian sensibilities involving healthy familial, educational and moral values embedded in Neo-Confucianism,[9] while sex and nudity were eschewed in favour of pure and demure love. These socially conservative values by western standards contextualized in a globalized environment like Korea offered a relatable social construct for these regional audiences, articulating an image of Asian modernity navigating western and eastern experiences alien to Euro-American TVs.[10] Conversely, historical dramas called *sageuk* showcased elegant traditional architecture (*hanok*) and lavish clothing (*hanbok*) that offered novelty and contrast to their more familiar Chinese and Japanese counterparts.

The shows' global reach and success was accelerated through OTT, reaching millennial and Gen Z consumers whose inclusivity and appreciation for cultural diversity predisposed them to openly engage with and embrace marginal cultures. K-drama's shimmering cityscapes, cool fashion and attractive actors (including K-pop idols) pulled in a younger crowd, while emotionally charged local narratives chimed with historically disempowered minorities. Two primary sentiments can be seen as underpinning Korean culture and driving the plots of K-drama: used as a feel-good storytelling device, *jeong* refers to warm affection and collective bonding over a shared experience, while *han* alludes to bottled-up feelings of helplessness, deep sorrow and resentment provoked by relentless oppression and injustice – a feeling Korea acquired in the wake of its traumatic modern history. Balancing *jeong* and *han*, K-dramas not only provided entertainment but also comfort and wellbeing, particularly in the worldwide Asian diaspora. Recent clinical research led by Dr Van Ta Park shed light on K-dramas' potential as a mental health therapy and educational tool for Asian American youth.[11] A growing number of these series took on social issues including intergenerational friction within families and bullying encountered at school or in the workplace. Most importantly, they destigmatized mental health issues in their narrative, which brought hope and relief to many viewers.

Finally local narratives, like Hell Joseon[12] or North Korea, also constituted a great pull for the audience, and it is noteworthy that the representation of North

The Korean women's ice-hockey team playing Switzerland in the PyeongChang Winter Olympics, 2018.
North and South Korea fielded a united team for the event, as reflected by the emblem on their shirts (above).
The underlying political will for reunification was echoed in the K-drama *Crash Landing on You*, 2019 (below).

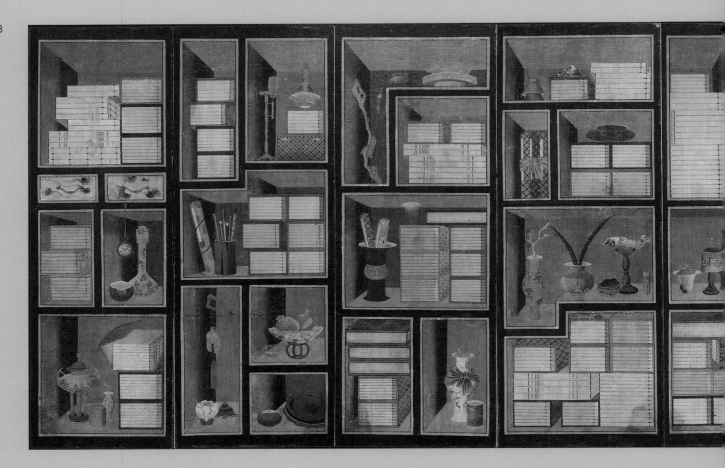

(Above)
Chaekkeori – a folding screen showcasing books, scholarly equipment and precious items – was emblematic of the knowledge, self-cultivation and refined taste of the scholar-gentleman during the Joseon dynasty (1392–1910). The same values are upheld in contemporary Korea, with academic pressure often represented in TV dramas.

(Oppsite)
Nam June Paik's *Mirage Stage*, 1986, a three-channel video shown on 33 TV monitors and 40 wooden TV carcasses. Paik witnessed the broadcasting revolution in both Korea and the west in the 1960s and recognized the massive socio-cultural impact this new communication tool represented.

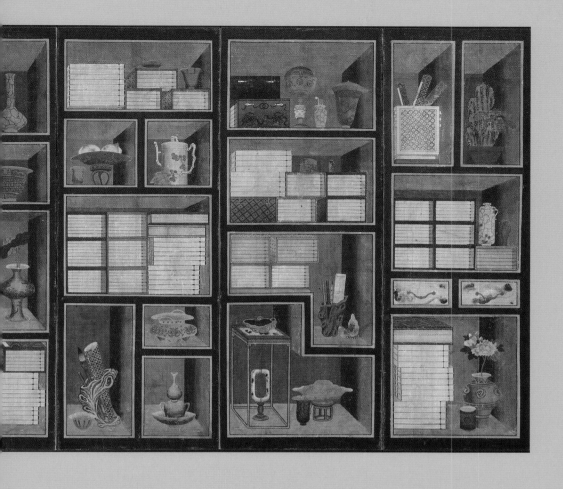

Koreans like those in *Crash Landing on You* (2019) chimed with the governmental stance on the reunification of the peninsula, which was encapsulated by the unified Korean women's ice-hockey team at the PyeonChang Winter Olympic Games in 2018.[13] In the past decade, many K-dramas and films have sourced their narratives from Korean digital cartoons called webtoons, much as Hollywood superhero films and series draw their inspiration from Marvel and DC comics. Cheap and fast to produce, webtoons constitute a boundless source of bold and original plotlines created by a wide pool of professionals and amateurs alike. Some enjoy a loyal fan-base that K-drama, cinema and online gaming industries can easily tap into.

In the late 1980s and early 1990s, the gradual relaxation of Motion Picture Laws initially set by military rule saw the growth of arthouse productions that dabbled with realism to critically portray the country's tumultuous past for the first time. These movies were conceived as a socio-political commentary on modern and contemporary Korea, which was a big departure from those of the previous decade. Yet Hollywood movies remained at the top of the box office across the nation. Following the 1988 Olympic Games in Seoul, a number of protests and acts of vandalism were staged across the capital in cinemas screening foreign films.[14] The protesters claimed that the 1986 Motion Picture Law allowing foreign companies to directly distribute in Korea had opened the gate to a glut of Hollywood movies that was drowning Korea's own output and pushing Korean cinema to the brink of extinction. At the same time, *chaebol* like Samsung and Daewoo started to diversify their portfolios by investing in the industry as a way of sourcing new content for their VCR divisions that had also been affected by the same law.[15] Driven by commercial success, the *chaebol* injected big budgets into filmmaking. They devised strategic approaches to film planning and production, before expanding their role further into distribution and screening by erecting multiplex cinemas across the country from 1998 onwards. *Chaebol* thereby had considerable power to shape and influence the 1990s Korean cinematographic landscape.

The renaissance in Korean cinema in the mid-1990s came about with the simultaneous rise of a new generation of young directors and screenwriters – many of whom had studied overseas and enjoyed access to a broad selection of films – and of the private investment funds that gradually overtook the *chaebol*. Aiming to attract a new audience to cinema, investors gave these filmmakers the financial support that enabled them to experiment without worrying about commercial pressures. It was an explosive combination, and a flurry of domestic and critically acclaimed blockbusters ensued, starting with *Shiri* by Kang Je-gyu in 1999. Drawing on local narratives with universal appeal, film repertoires were expanded by deftly mixing genres. Additionally, new aesthetics began to thrive thanks to a resourceful group of film creatives sharing the same desire to experiment, including colourists, production designers, costume designers, make-up artists and propmasters. This period also saw the proliferation of film festivals and specialized magazines in Korea, while film export increased, particularly around Asia.

By 2007 the experimental spirit and raw energy of Korean cinema of the late 1990s and early 2000s had exhausted itself both domestically and internationally. Production costs increased to the point of outweighing revenues, while online piracy – ironically amplified by the country's access to high-speed broadband internet – was rife, making the system unsustainable. The private investment funds soon dwindled, with the workforce following suit.[16] Meanwhile, video-on-demand (VOD) and OTT streaming services like Hulu and Netflix emerged in 2017 as a new form of entertainment, bringing cinema swiftly into the comfort of one's home. Film consumption patterns changed anew, sowing anxiety within the film industry – until 2019, when Bong Joon-ho's *Parasite* made history by becoming the first non-English-language film to win the Oscar for Best Movie. *Parasite* garnered an impressive collection of prestigious awards on the international film festival circuit in 2019 and 2020, bringing the world's attention back to Korean cinema. In the years following *Parasite*'s success, however, the Covid-19 pandemic caused film production worldwide to stall, with the film market moving substantially online. Nevertheless, the Korean Film Council recorded an increase of 43 per cent in the export of completed films in 2020, with Taiwan, Japan, China and Hong Kong as the main buyers.[17]

It is noteworthy that, since the mid-2010s, a young generation of female directors has gained prominence with independent short films and self-produced films released on social media platforms like YouTube, imparting a fresh outlook on what is yet to come in Korean cinema.

(Above) Still from *House of Hummingbird* (2019, dir. Kim Bora), praised for its immersive, realistic portrayal of a middle-school girl whose life is touched by tragedy. (Below) Still from *Maggie* (2018, dir. Yi Ok-seop), whose stylized, energetic comic style is underpinned by a serious message about the challenges faced by young people in Korea today. Both films exemplify new modes of storytelling coming from the next generation of Korean film directors.

The Road to *Parasite* (and Beyond)

Darcy Paquet

Han Suk-kyu and Choi Min-sik in action film *Shiri* (1999, dir. Kang Je-gyu), which was consciously positioned as a blockbuster.

In early 1999, director Kang Je-gyu and distributor Samsung Entertainment called a press conference in Seoul to announce the release of the upcoming film *Shiri*. Highlighting the film's scale, action sequences and starry cast, Kang described *Shiri* as a 'Korean blockbuster' that would compete head-to-head with big-budget Hollywood movies at the Korean box office.

Their tone may have struck some observers as overly ambitious, and some scepticism seemed warranted. South Korean films in the late 1990s generally struggled to attract viewers to the cinema, and were almost completely unknown abroad. In 1998, the year before *Shiri*'s release, James Cameron's *Titanic* set an all-time record with 1.97 million admissions in Seoul,[1] and eight of the top ten grossing films that year were from Hollywood. The only Korean films to crack the top ten were the melodrama *A Promise* (in fourth position, with 705,000 Seoul admissions) and horror film *Whispering Corridors* (sixth, with 620,000 admissions). These two films had targeted audiences in the traditional way: with emotionally charged stories that combined good acting with settings and situations to which local viewers could easily relate.

But *Shiri* promised to deliver spectacle, and no Korean film released to that point had ever succeeded with such a strategy. The plot centres around a group of North Korean special forces who break from their government and attempt to spark a second Korean War by staging an elaborately planned terrorist attack in Seoul. The film features gunfights, car chases, ticking bombs and exploding buildings. In terms of star power, the most popular actor of the day, Han Suk-kyu, was cast in the leading role of the South Korean agent trying to thwart the attack. The

rest of the cast was rounded out by respected actors primarily known for their supporting performances, though Choi Min-sik, Song Kang-ho and Kim Yunjin would all go on to become major leading stars in the near future.

Shiri was released to coincide with the Lunar New Year holiday in February 1999, and smashed expectations from the first day. It was the very definition of an event movie, with the whole nation discussing its innovations and themes, and an accompanying media frenzy picking the film apart from every possible angle. It remained in cinemas for an unusually long 17-week run, and easily surpassed *Titanic* to set a new all-time box office record with 2.45 million Seoul admissions. The nationwide tally was ultimately estimated to be 6.2 million tickets sold. Perhaps even more surprisingly, distribution rights for *Shiri* were sold to Japan, where it opened at number one in the box office charts, and to Hong Kong, where the film opened at number three. These were unprecedented achievements for a Korean film.

Shiri was a landmark in many respects, from its production values (to contemporary viewers it may seem light on spectacle, but from the perspective of audiences in 1999 it was a striking leap forward) to its distribution strategy. But more than anything else, what *Shiri* achieved was a recalibration of expectations and ambitions within the Korean film community. Prior to its release, few people working in the industry imagined it would be possible for a local film to outgross *Titanic*, particularly a film marketed as a big-budget genre movie. Nor did they imagine a day when a Korean film might sit atop the Japanese box office. Now that these things had come true, some filmmakers dared to dream even bigger.

Song Kang-Ho, Lee Byung-hun and Shin Ha-kyun in *Joint Security Area* (*JSA*) (2000, dir. Park Chan-wook), a new, more complex depiction of the relationship between North and South Korea.

Unexpectedly, it took only about a year and a half before another film duplicated *Shiri*'s success. *Joint Security Area*, or *JSA*, shared some things with its predecessor: it was also centred around the tense political relationship between North and South Korea, and billed itself as a blockbuster, though it had fewer gunfights and action sequences (*JSA*'s primary source of spectacle was a strikingly realistic-looking set of Panmunjeom, where North and South Korean soldiers face each other on either side of the border). And it too utilized local star power, with Lee Byung-hun, Lee Young-ae and Song Kang-ho all taking major roles.

In other ways, however, *JSA* was groundbreaking and unusual. Under the authoritarian rule of previous administrations, it was an unwritten rule that South Korean filmmakers should avoid humanizing North Korean characters to the degree that audiences might identify with them. The great director Lee Man-hui even spent two months in prison in 1966 for doing precisely that, in his now-lost war film *Seven Women Prisoners*. By the late 1990s, however, newly elected president Kim Dae-jung had announced a 'Sunshine Policy' of engagement with the North, and it was clear that new kinds of stories about North–South relations would be encouraged. *Shiri* had taken a small but significant step towards humanizing its North Korean character, but *JSA* would take this much further.

The film opens with reports of a shooting incident at the border city of Panmunjeom, with two North Korean soldiers killed and one South Korean soldier wounded. The North claims that the South Korean soldier crossed the border and carried out an unprovoked act of violence, while the South claims its soldier was kidnapped and had to fight his way back to the South. Through a neutral investigation carried out by a Swiss military officer, played by Lee Young-ae, the truth gradually emerges that the North and South Korean soldiers had in fact become friends, and would cross the border in secret to meet at night.

JSA captures one of the key contradictions of North–South relations, in that the tensions and divisions imposed from above do not erase the fact that, on a personal level, citizens on either side of the border have much in common. The film is a tragedy, clear-eyed about the grim reality of the political situation, while at the same time expressing hope for reconciliation. Such complex themes resonated strongly with audiences. Its final box office tally was broadly similar to that of *Shiri*: 2.5 million admissions in Seoul, and 5.8 million nationwide. The success also brought fame and recognition to the film's director, a previously little-known critic-turned-filmmaker named Park Chan-wook.

Box office success on this scale certainly justified the use of the word 'blockbuster' to describe *JSA* and *Shiri*. But in other respects, too, these works represented a new approach to filmmaking in the context of South Korean cinema. Transliterated directly from English into Korean, the word 'blockbuster' was closely associated with Hollywood cinema, so the use of the word itself implied a new willingness to challenge the world's most commercially successful film industry. The word also implied a promise to give the audience some measure of scale and spectacle, at least in relation to previous Korean films. Of course, Korean blockbusters were not able to compete solely

Cha Tae-hyun and Jun Ji-hyun in *My Sassy Girl* (2001, dir. Kwak Jae-yong), which was adapted from a series of blog posts that later became a novel, and which was hugely popular across Asia.

Lee Byung-hun in *A Bittersweet Life* (2005, dir. Kim Jee-woon), which took a subtler approach to the gangster movie genre.

on the basis of spectacle, given that their budgets were a small fraction of those of major US movies, but they could speak more directly to the Korean audience by touching on local themes such as the North–South conflict. Over the years, some 'Korean blockbusters' enjoyed great success, such as Kang Je-gyu's big-budget follow-up to *Shiri*, the Korean War film *Tae Guk Gi: The Brotherhood of War* (2004), which grossed over 10 million admissions. Other would-be blockbusters failed spectacularly, despite their extensive marketing campaigns.

But it was not only blockbuster projects like *Shiri* and *JSA* that achieved blockbuster-level success. The year 2001 was a collective breakthrough for Korean cinema, the first year that local films accounted for over 50 per cent of all ticket sales.[2] Six of the top seven highest-grossing films of the year were Korean, with only *Harry Potter and the Sorcerer's Stone* coming in at number four. But it was a diverse range of Korean movies that were finding success. The year's top-grossing title, Kwak Kyung-taek's coming-of-age gangster drama *Friend*, was a modestly budgeted work that had struggled to secure an investor. Yet it struck audiences as something decidedly exciting and new, in part because it was the first Korean film to look back on the 1980s in a strongly nostalgic light, and in part because it celebrated the dialect and local culture of Busan with such obvious affection. *Friend* ended up setting a new box office record with 8.2 million admissions.

Nonetheless, it was the second-highest grossing film of 2001 that fully embodied the future potential of Korean cinema. *My Sassy Girl* began life as an internet novel, published in serial format online by a writer who claimed to be basing it on his own experiences dating an especially ebullient (but often aggressive) woman. First spotted by the well-known film producer Shin Chul, adapted by writer/director Kwak Jae-yong and brought to life by the actors Jun Ji-hyun (aka Gianna Jun) and Cha Tae-hyun, *My Sassy Girl* became a sensation for the pointed and hilarious way it captured Korean youth culture and shifting gender norms. It sold 4.9 million tickets and made a star of Jun Ji-hyun, but its runaway success in other parts of Asia in particular eclipsed that of any other Korean film. It spent two weeks at number one at the Hong Kong box office, and was hugely popular in mainland China, where it never received an official release but circulated widely in pirated copies. (Five years later, a poll in China asked young

respondents to name several words or phrases that came to mind when they thought of South Korea, and 'My Sassy Girl' was one of the ten most common answers alongside such words as 'kimchi' and 'tae kwon do'.) In that sense, the film can be seen as a major contributor to the early development of the Korean Wave.

From today's perspective, *My Sassy Girl* also stands out as representative of how South Korea's dynamic internet culture has provided fertile source material for successful films. A particularly influential genre that would later emerge was the 'webtoon', which resembles a graphic novel formatted vertically for computer screens and mobile phones (see pp. 72–81). The huge number of webtoons published on internet platforms like Naver and Kakao have become an abundant source of ideas and stories for contemporary filmmakers: in that sense, too, *My Sassy Girl* was pointing towards the future.

Big-budget genre films and high-concept comedies were some of the key drivers of Korean commercial cinema in the early 2000s, but another group of directors including Bong Joon-ho, Park Chan-wook and Kim Jee-woon adopted a different approach. In one sense they were firmly committed to commercial cinema (in contrast to arthouse directors finding success on the festival circuit, such as Lee Chang-dong, Kim Ki-duk and Hong Sang-soo). They worked with medium to large budgets and targeted the widest audience possible. But even while working in the commercial sector, these filmmakers developed their own distinctive, individual directorial styles and broke with many of the established conventions of genre cinema. Their works showed the influence of a wide spectrum of different styles, ranging all the way from genre cinema to minimalist arthouse films. One might say they combined the energy of commercial filmmaking with the 'auteur' approach championed at major film festivals.

Park Chan-wook's international breakthrough *Oldboy* (2003), which won the Grand Prix at Cannes, is a consummate example. Liberally adapted from a Japanese manga, this tale of forced incarceration and desperate thirst for revenge challenges audience expectations at every turn. In contrast to the classical Hollywood approach to narrative, which strives to keep the viewer comfortably oriented within the story, *Oldboy* overwhelms the viewer by presenting a tremendous amount of information in nearly every scene, deliberately disorienting its audience. The result is a film that rejects standard approaches

Tilda Swinton in *Snowpiercer* (2013, dir. Bong Joon-ho), which was produced in Korea but features a mainly English-speaking cast.

to storytelling, but which was still a commercial hit thanks to its exuberant energy and thrilling style.

Kim Jee-woon's critically acclaimed *A Bittersweet Life* (2005) is another example of a film that looks on the surface to be a slickly directed genre film, but which in the course of its running time reveals hidden layers and complexities. Lee Byung-hun plays a cold, ruthlessly professional gangster whose organization ends up turning against him. Generally in commercial cinema, viewers have grown accustomed to decisive, dynamic lead characters whose actions are easy to understand and who naturally elicit our sympathies. But the motivations and inner psychology of Lee's character in *A Bittersweet Life* remain frustratingly vague to the very end of the story. It is as if the main character of a minimalist arthouse film has escaped into a big-budget action movie.

This nuanced approach to storytelling, which was also employed by Bong Joon-ho in his hugely successful second and third features *Memories of Murder* (2003) and *The Host* (2006), attracted notice well beyond the borders of South Korea, particularly in Europe and North America. The wide spectrum of works being produced by the Korean film industry appealed in various ways to viewers at home, in Asia and in other parts of the world. Optimism about the potential of South Korean cinema began to surge, especially after a string of films featuring popular hallyu stars secured record-breaking distribution deals with Japan. The future of Korean cinema seemed bright.

How were these films being financed? It is true that the South Korean government provided generous financial support to the local film industry, beginning in the late 1990s under President Kim Dae-jung. But the support policies drafted at the Korean Film Council were deliberately centred on developing infrastructure rather than investing directly in individual films. Instead, aside from sponsoring training programmes, supporting film festivals, providing loans to movie theatres and so on, the government contributed to film investment funds that were set up and run by venture capital firms. In this way, money flowed into the industry, but the government did not take part in choosing how it was spent. This, together with the financing provided by the film divisions of large conglomerates like CJ and Lotte, gave the film industry ample fuel to burn.

But then came the crash. After several years in which international sales (particularly to Japan) boomed and a string of film companies were listed on the stock market, a bubble had formed. Production budgets had risen quickly, and the number of films being shot rose even faster. A profitability crisis followed and, just as quickly, investors pulled their money from the industry. The years 2007 and 2008 were dark times for Korean cinema, with many production companies going bankrupt or barely managing to stay afloat.

The end result was a shift of power within the industry. Up until the crisis, a key role had been played by powerful producers such as Tcha Seung-jai (Sidus), Shim Jae-myung

Poster for zombie thriller *Train to Busan* (2016, dir. Yeon Sang-ho), an international success.

(Myung Films) and Kang Woo-suk (Cinema Service), who set up their own companies and showed a willingness to take risks on talented young directors. They often provided a kind of shelter where directors could experiment in various ways without feeling the direct pressure of investors and large distributors. The crisis hit such producers particularly hard, however, and after 2007 the industry became more and more dominated by the large local conglomerates CJ, Lotte and the Orion Group (Showbox). Under these corporations, the production process became streamlined, and large investors gained a greater say in what kind of movies were produced and how they were made.

The success of JK Youn's blockbuster *Haeundae* (2009), about a massive tsunami that strikes the port city of Busan, marked the end of the two-year crisis. It also became clear that the industry's ambitions would continue to grow during the second decade of Korean cinema's contemporary renaissance. *Haeundae* itself was a case in point: although in one sense it stayed true to the formula followed by previous Korean blockbusters, incorporating a strong local element (in this case, the culture and cityscape of Busan) into a genre-inflected story, the technological progress shown by local VFX companies meant that it was now possible to put visual spectacle at the very centre of a Korean film. In the coming years, such visual effects companies would contribute much to the steadily developing aesthetics of Korean cinema.

A milestone in terms of the industry's international aspirations came in 2013 with the release of Bong Joon-ho's *Snowpiercer*. Based on a French graphic novel about a train that carries the last remnants of humanity in a frozen apocalyptic world, Bong's film was targeted squarely at the global market. Shot in the Czech Republic with an international cast speaking mostly in English, *Snowpiercer* is nonetheless an entirely Korean production, financed in full by distributor CJ Entertainment. It was a strong commercial success in countries like France, China and its home market South Korea, although plans for a wide North American release were scrapped when the director refused to let local distributor Harvey Weinstein cut 20 minutes from the film. It is hard to know what might have happened if the film had been successful in English-speaking countries, but to date it remains a rare instance of a big-budget English-language film produced in Korea but targeted at international audiences.

Perhaps counterintuitively – or perhaps not – many of the top Korean directors found more international success with Korean-language productions than they did with films shot in English. Park Chan-wook made his Hollywood debut in 2013 with the mystery-thriller *Stoker*, starring Mia Wasikowska and Nicole Kidman. The film premiered at Sundance but ultimately never reached a wide audience in North America or international markets. In contrast, Park's 2016 Korean-language film *The Handmaiden* proved to be his most successful release since *Oldboy*. Adapting Sarah Waters's bestselling 2002 novel *Fingersmith*, Park shifted the setting from Victorian England to 1930s Korea under Japanese colonial rule, and wrote a new ending. Premiering at Cannes, the film was rapturously reviewed, sold widely around the world and became the first Korean production to win a BAFTA, for Best Film Not in the English Language.

Another major international success was *Train to Busan* (2016), a high-concept horror film about a group of passengers battling a zombie outbreak on a high-speed train. Directed by Yeon Sang-ho, who was making his live-action debut after directing several independent animated features, the film's clever use of genre conventions and elaborate staging of action in the space of the train made for a runaway hit. Penetrating all corners of the globe, it was particularly popular in other Asian markets, setting new box office records for a Korean film in Hong Kong, Singapore and Malaysia.

Without question, however, the most successful film of Korean cinema's renaissance has been Bong Joo-ho's *Parasite*, about a poor family who scam their way into working lucrative jobs for a rich family, with tragic consequences. Shot on the heels of Bong's bilingual Netflix project *Okja* (2017), *Parasite* premiered at Cannes in May 2019 to ecstatic reviews, becoming the first Korean film ever to carry home the festival's top prize, the Palme d'Or. It went on to enjoy an enormously successful commercial rollout across the world, particularly in North America. The combination of a well-structured screenplay, timely and relevant themes, cutting humour and cinematic flair helped *Parasite* cross language barriers and become a popular phenomenon. Enthusiasm for the film continued to grow through the Oscar awards season, until on 9 February 2020 *Parasite* achieved something that most Koreans assumed they would never see in their lifetimes: it won four Academy Awards, including Best Picture.

Just over two decades since the release of *Shiri*, the Korean film community once again found itself having to reassess what it is possible for locally made films to achieve. For the first time, a film produced in Korea had become a cultural touchstone for people all around the world. For those who remembered what the industry was like before *Shiri*, it seemed too incredible to be true. For a brief interval, the Korean film industry celebrated *Parasite*'s Oscar success, and tried to imagine what the future might hold.

Alas, it was only two weeks after the Academy Awards that South Korea was hit by a major outbreak of Covid-19 in the city of Daegu. Film distributors quickly postponed the season's major releases, hoping for a recovery in the coming months, but the pandemic would prove long-lived. Although theatres never completely shut down, box office takings for 2020 plunged 70 per cent year-on-year, and the situation in 2021 improved only slightly.

Looking ahead, it is too soon to say whether a return to older viewing habits might help to revive the film industry when the pandemic recedes. In 2019 South Koreans had a higher rate of theatrical attendance per capita than any other country in the world, so the industry does have some grounds for optimism. In recent memory, going to the theatre was deeply embedded in the social routines of younger and older Koreans alike.

As citizens forced to remain at home turned in ever greater numbers to Netflix and other over-the-top (OTT) platforms, a further power shift took place in the industry. It is not surprising that in the new media environment, production by OTT platforms greatly expanded, while traditional distributors cut back their investment in feature films. Correspondingly, much of the industry's talent – including not only actors and directors but also cinematographers, editors, production designers and other technicians – was pulled in by OTT content. Netflix's decision to invest US$500 million in Korean content in a single year alone did not exist in a vacuum, but had deep ramifications for the Korean film industry.

Nonetheless, an indication of how the world has changed for South Korean content creators was glimpsed in September 2021, with the release of the Netflix series *Squid Game* (see So Hye Kim, pp. 86–91). Directed by Hwang Dong-hyuk, who had already made several highly successful features in the film industry, the instantly meme-able *Squid Game* became a worldwide sensation. Whereas the release of *Parasite* had played out over months at selected film festivals and in carefully managed releases in countries around the world, it took mere days for *Squid Game* to become the most talked-about TV series on Earth. It was Netflix's distribution mechanism and broad subscriber base that enabled the speed of this success, but the phenomenon also suggested that the potential audience for Korean content was only growing larger.

What might the future hold? How many more times might Korean content achieve what was previously thought to be impossible? How big should this industry dream? It may be quite a few more years before these questions are fully answered.

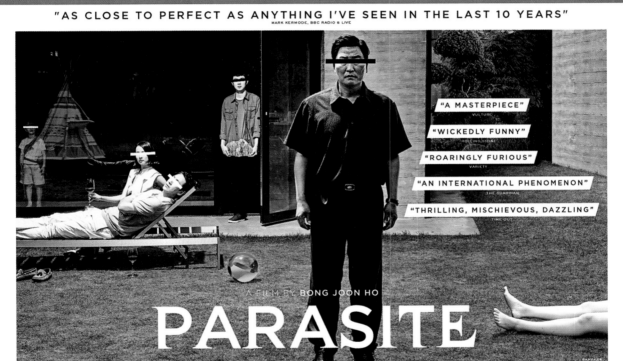

Poster for *Parasite* (2019, dir. Bong Joon-ho), Korean film's most successful export and winner of five Academy Awards.

Sketch for *Parasite* set design, 2018. Production design by Lee Ha-jun

Webtoons: From Scrolling to Streaming

Rosalie Kim

Since the outbreak of the Covid pandemic, a rising number of viewers around the world have been 'binge-watching' K-dramas through various over-the-top (OTT) platforms, such as Viki or Netflix. Their cinematographic quality, heart-warming nature, and unusual array of genres with addictive plots provided comfort and guilt-free pleasure during lengthy lockdowns. In 2019 Netflix launched the first two Netflix Originals series to be made in Korea: *Love Alarm* was a rom-com based on the premise that an app called Joalarm could detect people with romantic feelings for the user when they were within a ten-metre range, while *Kingdom* was a historical thriller, set during the sixteenth-century Joseon dynasty period, and revolving around a mysterious epidemic that turns innocent people into blood-thirsty zombies. These series achieved global success overnight, prompting Netflix to commission second seasons and invest more in Korean content.[1] Another Original series, *Hellbound* (2021), was top of Netflix streaming ratings in 80 countries, including Saudi Arabia and South Africa, just a day after its release.[2]

What is perhaps less well known to a non-initiated audience is that all these series are adapted from popular webtoons: a Korean innovation consisting of a digital cartoon read vertically by scrolling down on a mobile phone. Accessible anywhere and practically free of charge, each episode takes less than five minutes to read, providing an easy pastime while waiting in a queue, on a daily commute or before going to sleep. Webtoons are thus often considered as the embodiment of so-called 'snack culture', culture as consumable commodity in 'conveniently packaged bite-size nuggets made to be munched easily with increased frequency and maximum speed'.[3] This rings particularly true for a society like Korea, which achieved the 'miracle on the Han river' based on the *ppalli-ppalli* (quick-quick) mindset that still pervades all areas of life, from swift, round-the-clock food delivery to fast internet connection and speedy construction works.

In this context, webtoons are perceived as a light and nippy form of entertainment that fills the countless lacklustre gaps in daily life, but this attitude overshadows the genuine skills of creators and the wealth of content that attract the attention of millions of users.[4] And webtoons are economically lucrative too: according to the Korea Creative Content Agency (KOCCA) – a governmental agency affiliated to the Korean Ministry of Culture, Sports and Tourism, which oversees and supports the creative content industry – in 2020, webtoons' combined sales topped 1 trillion won (£684.6 million) for the first time, representing a year-on-year increase of over 64 per cent despite (or rather because of) the pandemic.[5] Furthermore, in the past decade webtoons have noticeably become a steady source of inspiration for other creative industries, including films, TV dramas, musicals and computer and mobile games. This underlines the growing prominence of webtoons as a transmedia storytelling conduit leading the creative content industries of hallyu today.[6]

Birth of a storytelling nation

Webtoons started to appear at the turn of the twenty-first century. The *manhwa* market (Korean printed comics) had begun to weaken in the second half of the 1990s, when the form was blamed as the main cause behind the rise of sex, bullying and violence at schools. In response, in 1997 the government set up the Youth Protection Committee and the Juvenile Protection Act to apply stringent rules to the publication and distribution of manhwa. Comics confiscated at school were burnt en masse once a year, 'in front of the Seoul City Hall, where municipal authorities invited the national media to record the spectacle of thousands of comic books going up in flames.'[7] Bookstores and *manhwabang* (a manhwa library-cum-café) were severely affected by the new measures; many stopped selling comics or closed their business completely. Manhwa magazines, once a popular platform on which a wide range of

K-Drama, Webtoons and Film

Poster for season two of *Kingdom* (2019–), a blockbuster K-drama on Netflix based on the webtoon *Sinui nara: beoninghel* (Kingdom of the Gods, 2014–), written by Kim Eun-Hee and illustrated by Yang Kyung-Il.

comic genres and styles were introduced, disappeared one after the other.[8] In addition, the artists' IP rights were not well protected, with illegal uploading of scanned versions online and *manhwabang* lending the books many times over without monetary benefit for the author. Also, the lifting of a 53-year ban on Japanese culture in 1998 flooded the Korean market with manga.[9] All of these factors contributed heavily to the virtual extinction of manhwa by the new millennium.[10]

This period of turmoil coincided with the Asian Financial Crisis and the birth of the ICT revolution in Korea. Unemployment was high, especially for young graduates. Meanwhile, the country was rolling out the infrastructure for one of the fastest internet broadbands in the world. PC Bangs – a Korean innovation of 1988 that became the blueprint for future internet cafés and gaming centres – were multiplying rapidly across Korea, providing young people and the unemployed with a social space and community in which to play real-time computer games or design their minihomepy on Cyworld, an early social media platform combining the equivalent of today's Spotify, Facebook, Sims and bitcoins.[11] By July 2000, 46.4 per cent of households owned a computer and time spent online had more than doubled in three years.[12]

Webtoons emerged during this hinge period, when many individuals began chronicling anecdotes from their daily life on personal homepages and blog posts. Rather than words, these short diary-type entries often took the form of clumsy yet cheerful drawings, by no means polished.[13] Unlike paper publication – which took time and was expensive to produce, meaning that quality drawings and storylines were essential selection criteria when recruiting artists – webtoons required only a computer and digital pen, and could be uploaded swiftly by the artists on their personal page or webtoon platform.[14] The webtoon boom thus started with myriad enthusiastic amateur artists, many of them aspiring manhwa artists, taking the chance to 'self-publish' their work. These were no dilettantes but 'Pro-Am, amateurs who work to professional standards'.[15]

These creators represented a much broader sample of the population, and came from different educational backgrounds to manhwa artists.[16] Their lack of drawing skills or knowledge of manhwa convention were often subject to criticism, but these were precisely what gave the Pro-Ams the freedom to express their stories in bold and unexpected ways that gradually superseded traditional storytelling practices. Firmly driven by narratives, their work introduced alternative subjects that were in tune with the evolving social and technological fabric of contemporary Korea.

Some enjoyed growing popularity and loyal readership, and went on to careers as paid professionals by migrating to webtoon-dedicated websites or capturing the attention of web portals. Daum and Naver, two such Korean internet service providers, incorporated webtoons on their platforms in 2003 and 2004 respectively, initially as a strategic device to expand traffic on their news pages. This was achieved by organizing open calls for new artists, serializing webtoons and making them available free of charge thanks to the income those portals generated via their online advertisements.[17] Diversification of genres (thriller, horror, romantic fantasy, sci-fi...) and an increasing improvement in quality were matched by the proliferation of omnibus series, helping to swell audiences and boost wages for creators. Soon, webtoons received their own devoted webpages: the autonomous websites Daum Webtoon (now Kakao Webtoon)[18], launched in 2016, and Naver's webtoon site, known internationally as Line Webtoon, which followed in 2017, were fast to reach a worldwide audience.[19]

Webtoons' key asset is undeniably this young, wide and diverse pool of tech-savvy talents. And they are thrown into a fiercely competitive environment. KOCCA estimated that 2,617 new series were published in 2020 alone (despite a reduction from the previous year due to Covid) and that there were 7,407 registered artists in 2021, with 83.9 per cent of artists under 30 and 24.2 per cent debuting since 2019.[20] Naver webtoon currently fosters 140,000 creators working across their platforms. The sheer number of weekly updates and new episodes is phenomenal and pushes artists to develop a spartan discipline and cultivate their creativity relentlessly in order to survive. It is noteworthy that readers can add their reactions at the end of each episode, building an online community that engages directly with the artists and provides them with instant gratification or recognition. Despite anonymity prompting many to post negative criticism that can be harmful and stressful for the artists, this 'interactive' format offers a valuable and swift testing bed for new ideas, without much financial cost involved.

Webtoon experimentation

Initially, webtoons were enjoyed on PCs with dial-up internet access but the arrival of mobile devices, particularly smartphone technology using wireless broadband services, made webtoons ubiquitous, inaugurating the golden age of webtoons. Between 2010 and 2015, the new vernacular of the webtoon became well cemented, with colour-filling and top-down scrolling at its core: a far cry from the left-right page-turning manhwa publication.

Kang Full, a prolific webtoon pioneer and veteran in the field, originated this vertical format for his hugely popular *Love Story* in 2003.[21] Unlike early webtoons, which started as scanned versions

Hallyu! The Korean Wave

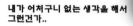

Extract from *Sunjeong manhwa* (Love Story, 2003–4) by Kang Full, which was adapted into a movie, *Hello, Schoolgirl* in 2008. Kang here introduced the vertical layout that broke the conventional 'page' frame of manhwa.

Bokhakwang (King of Returning to School, 2014–21) by Kian84 illustrates how some webtoons reflect current social issues, such as the concerns of the *sampo* or *opo* generations (see K-Drama, Webtoons and Film, note 12).

Detail from a promotional video for *Encountered* (2017–18) by Ha Il-gwon x Naver Webtoon, in which the reader turns into an avatar, becoming part of the webtoon.

of paper drawings or replicated manhwa's traditional conventions, Kang favoured a long vertical strip, replacing the rigid frame surrounding each cut with empty spaces to pace his narrative. His method was a 'breath of fresh air'[22] that revolutionized the design but most importantly the reading of webtoons, providing an uninterrupted, immersive experience for the reader, which could not be achieved with a traditional publication where turning a page, for instance, interrupts momentum.

To illustrate the point, Lee Jong-beom, creator of the *Dr Frost* webtoon, takes the example of the gaze line. In books, two protagonists in conversation are often drawn in profile facing each other, at times even taking advantage of the double-page spread. This layout supports the natural horizontal eye movement reading the scene. The narrow and vertical format of a mobile phone or tablet does not easily accommodate this type of arrangement. Instead, both protagonists are facing the reader one cut at a time, inviting them to be part of the conversation rather than a bystander. This strategy fosters the reader's empathy for the storyline and its characters, an effect amplified by the 'gaps' that provide the mental space for the reader to deep dive into the narrative.

Nowadays, it is not uncommon to see music tracks, moving images and AR/QR technology being used in webtoons to enhance the mood, embed secret messages or provide additional layers of experience for the reader.[23] In 2017 Ha Il-gwon and Naver Webtoon produced *Encountered*, which became an instant hit with a young audience. Using the selfie mode on the Naver Webtoon app, the reader could become an avatar who was then animated and woven into the storyline using programmes including facial recognition.[24] With the catchphrase 'Your love story with the webtoon character begins', *Encountered* literally thrusts the reader into the heart of the webtoon. This followed on from another striking project from the previous year, the popular three-episode horror webtoon *Phone Ghost*. Made available only through the Naver app, the webtoon offered different options according to the phone model. Each episode provided a distinctive chilling experience: the phone's camera sneakily activating at strategic moments to bring the

ghostly figures alive through AR in the reader's real room; the vibration mode triggering when a ghost jolted out of its screen to attack the reader; the phone suddenly ringing to connect the ghost and the reader; or the hunting of the AR ghost by moving the phone around the room. Each episode was uploaded at eleven o'clock at night during the Halloween period for maximum effect. Kim Jun-koo, CEO of Naver Webtoon and Web Novel CIC, declared that artists as well as webtoon platforms were eager to collaborate and experiment with new technology in order to enrich both content and the means of delivery for digital storytelling.[25] Although some technological innovations have been criticized for being clunky or gimmicky, these types of webtoons are still in their infancy and give a taste of what is yet to come as they push the boundaries of the webtoon universe. This broad range of raw to expert talents, who were willing to experiment and take risks, quickly turned webtoons into a lucrative business, an inexhaustible source of inspiration for online advertisement, merchandising, paper book serialization and, particularly in the past decade, for movies and TV dramas.

Transmedia storytelling

Turning successful comic series into films, animations or TV dramas is not a new undertaking, as demonstrated by the popularity of superhero movie franchises based on countless Marvel and DC Comics characters and universes. Webtoons, however, boost that 'one-source-multiple-use' (OSMU) concept much further, faster.

Webtoons are far cheaper and quicker to produce and are consumed on a daily basis by a much younger audience at a more significant scale. The mammoth number of Pro-Am artists generates a continuous stream of successful, thought-provoking and imaginative stories that capture the zeitgeist and draw in global fandoms; online feedback from readers can rapidly and cost-effectively shape story concepts, a process that would be challenging for the movie and broadcasting industries. Popular webtoons therefore present a reliable and financially sound source of inspiration for film and TV producers, particularly at a time of media convergence.

Before the advent of Netflix and other OTT platforms, webtoons were mainly adapted into films.[26] Webtoons' shorter duration and strong, compact plotlines suited the film format well, while their dynamic and cinematographic qualities, reflected in the uninterrupted vertical sequence of scenes, facilitated the visualization and designing of film storyboards too. Nowadays, the serialization of webtoons has spawned complex plotlines and lengthened their running time, making them suitable for reworking into a multi-season TV drama format. The cross-pollination process, however, is not a simple matter of replicating the same content in another medium. Much like a spin-off, the essence and tone of the original webtoons are preserved but movie and drama plotlines may expand the stories with new materials to enhance the viewer's enjoyment and experience across different media.[27] Narratives need to be adjusted for thriller webtoons to avoid spoiling the end and to keep original fans hooked on their screens. At the same time, much-loved webtoon characters from romantic series need to keep their identifiable attributes and key moments to maintain their appeal with their original audience.

It is important to note that all IP rights belong to the Pro-Am creators, which facilitates the selling and buying of webtoon rights for adaption. Webtoon platforms have now set their sights on identifying and nurturing projects with the most potential for transmedia storytelling, with the ultimate purpose of making webtoons the bedrock of all entertainment industries.[28] Labelled 'Super IPs', those webtoons are perceived as a catalyst for the platforms' rapid expansion at a global scale.[29] A good illustration of a Super IP is Cho Gwang-jin's *Itaewon Class* (2016–18). Beyond its overarching narrative of revenge and social injustice, the webtoon is famed for engaging with subjects that are uncomfortable in Korea, such as adoption, racism or

K-Drama, Webtoons and Film

The webtoon source of 2015 drama *Misaeng* (Incomplete Life) is acknowledged in these posters for the series. The original webtoon was by Yoon Tae-ho.

Webtoons with strong messages and huge numbers of followers, such as *Itaewon Class* (2016–18) by Cho Gwang-jin (opposite page), provide a lucrative source of transmedia storytelling: the television adaptation has become a hit across the world (above).

the LGBTQ+ community. Cho foregrounds those issues through his protagonists' backgrounds and struggles, making a case for an inclusive society. With 400 million views and 20 million subscribers, *Itaewon Class* became one of the most popular series on Kakao Webtoon. In 2020 its eponymous K-drama version, also penned by Cho, produced by JTBC and distributed worldwide by Netflix, was received to great critical and public acclaim, garnering multiple awards along the way. Boasting a stellar cast and an original song by V from BTS, *Itaewon Class* became the emblem of cool Korea across the world and one of the highest-rated dramas in Korean cable history. The K-drama's success on Netflix Japan prompted a whopping 454 per cent increase in the sale of *Roppongi Class*, the Japanese version of the original K-webtoon that was made available on Piccoma, the Japanese subsidiary of Kakao Webtoon.[30] TV Asahi is currently preparing the release of the Japanese remake in 2022,[31] while JTBC has hinted at a Hollywood version of the original K-series.[32] Webtoon, the versatile storytelling vehicle that crossed different media, is now crossing borders too, affirming Korea's role as a leading international cultural powerhouse.

Beyond webtoons and Korea

Webtoons' emergence and rise to prominence stem from the early access to ICT and the swift grasping of the economic value of the OSMU strategy. Their development is supported by governmental schemes that encourage content diversity, artists' incubating programmes and creative ecosystems within the domestic market. Since 2014, those schemes have also boosted the IP business via their financial support for webtoons' adaptations in other media and the rooting out of pirate platforms. With the limited market that Korea offers, webtoon providers like Naver and Kakao also export their creative content to sustain their business. These ambitions are again backed by the Korean government, which provides assistance for translation services, the establishment of overseas networks and marketing campaigns.[33] KOCCA reported that webtoon export is on the increase, with 56 per cent of webtoons

exported in 2020, particularly to Japan, China and North America.[34] These platforms encourage the discovery and debut of artists in countries where webtoons are distributed, though this may have more to do with increasing local readership and subscriptions than inclusivity. This localization of the expansion process is a salient point to make, however, as it ensures that – amid the chase for Super IPs in Korea – small, commercially non-viable stories will continue to develop and guarantee webtoons' diversity in the domestic market.

As seen in the global dissemination of *Itaewon Class*, webtoon platforms acquire or build partnerships with local comics providers and video production companies to expand the reach of, and multiply the creative output based on, webtoons. This transmedia-transnational approach steps up to the next level with the involvement of the K-pop industry. In 2021 Naver started a collaboration with Hybe Entertainment to produce a series of webtoons featuring as protagonists BTS and other idols from Hybe's portfolio.[35] The world of webtoons has collided with the K-pop universe, expanding the spectrum of media both for Super IPs and their respective audiences. These so-called 'Super Casting' projects are set to grow, this time starring American superheroes, thanks to Naver's new venture with DC Comics and Kakao's partnership with Marvel.

Finally, another source of transmedia storytelling even more compelling than webtoons comes into sight: webnovels. These serialized narratives share the same biographical trajectory, working pattern and distribution platform as webtoons, minus the illustrations. The pool of talent is wider as they only involve writers, the cost of production is cheaper, and they are easier to export as they require only text translation, rather than the page redesigns that webtoon translations often necessitate. Not only are they slowly overtaking webtoons as the leader in transmedia storytelling in Korea, but they are also becoming a regular source of inspiration for webtoons.

Whether it be webtoons or webnovels, Korea's transmedia storytelling is on a stellar rise and will have global audiences scrolling down their phones in no time.

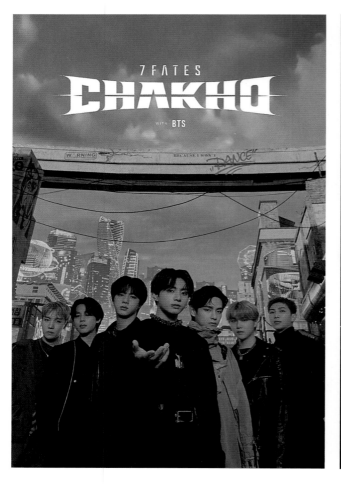

Pre-release marketing poster, 2021, announcing a collaboration between Hybe corporation and Naver Webtoon on a series of webtoons featuring Hybe's artists including BTS (above), TXT and ENHYPEN as lead characters.

The sci-fi/fantasy webnovel *Na honjaman lebeleop* (Solo Levelling, 2016), written by Chugong, was adapted into a hugely popular webtoon in 2018. There are plans for a computer game by Netmarble and a US drama series.

Promotional images for the webtoon and live action versions of *Yumi's Cells* (webtoon, 2015–20; drama series, 2021). Written and illustrated by Lee Dong-geun, it exemplifies a popular strand of cute romantic webtoons.

Film Make-up: In Search of the Right Keyword

Song Jong-hee

(Above)
Actor Kim Min-hee wears an asymmetric chignon inspired by Gustav Klimt in this test image for *The Handmaiden* (2016, dir. Park Chan-wook); the final chignon is seen in a production still of Lady Hideko.

(Below)
Song Jong-hee experimented with smoky green eyeshadow on Lee Young-ae in early tests for *Sympathy for Lady Vengeance* (2005, dir. Park Chan-wook) before settling on the distinctive red eyeshadow look.

I am a pretty slow reader when it comes to printed literature such as books, newspapers and film scripts. For film projects on which I've pledged to work, especially film scripts with a considerable amount of conversational dialogue, I find myself reading the lines over and over again. And as I follow this process, I get to empathize with the characters, which helps create specific images in my head.

When I proceed to research people, photos and objects to realize these specific images, I once again find influences through which I discover the keyword that defines the film project and its thematic colour.

In *My Mother The Mermaid* (2004), Jeon Do-yeon plays two roles, Na-young and her mother Yeon-sun. Na-young appears in the present day, while Yeon-sun's story takes place in the past, when she was young. In order to distinguish these two parts – similar in age, and played by the same actor – I ensured there were differences in the characters' skin tone and hairstyles. My inspiration for Jeon Do-yeon's double role was the Japanese

filmmaker Iwai Shunji's film *Love Letter* (1995), in which actress Nakayama Miho plays both Watanabe Hiroko and Fuji Itsuki. My inspiration comes not only from films, however: when developing the image for Kim Min-hee, who plays Lady Hideko in Park Chan-wook's *The Handmaiden* (2016), I used Gustav Klimt's *Judith* as a reference, which organically led me to create Hideko's femme fatale image and her asymmetric chignon.

The heroine of *Sympathy For Lady Vengeance* (2005), Geum-ja, has been imprisoned for 13 years, accused of kidnap and murder, and lives now only for revenge. On this occasion I became obsessed with the *shade* of revenge she needed, and looked all over to find a colour that represented the sense of violence and independence which I believed suited her. I tried various colours of eye make-up, from a smoky blue to bright blue or purple, but eventually settled on a red eyeshadow to convey Geum-ja's state of mind. Vivid red signifies independence and passion; it also suited actor Lee Young-ae's eye colour. In the film, another character asks, 'Why do you colour your face red?' In

A still from *Oldboy* (2003, dir. Park Chan-wook) shows actor Choi Min-sik sporting the iconic 'wild mane' hairstyle.

her dry, deep voice, Geum-ja replies, 'Otherwise I'll look too kind.' These lines weren't in the original script, but were added to reflect the colour I had chosen for the character.

Every film character I've worked on was born through such numerous hours of intense contemplation. There is always a reason and meaning to the creation of each character and this is also why I have clashed with actors from time to time.

One October day in 2002, I attended the first concept meeting of Park Chan-wook's *Oldboy* (2003). When I described the main idea I had in mind for the character of Oh Dae-su, I immediately faced resistance from the actor, Choi Min-sik: 'I'm no punk, you know. How am I supposed to work a hairdo like that?! Do you even understand what the film's about? You think that style would suit me? That's out of the question!' He adamantly refused to accept the character concept I brought to the table. Nevertheless, I was confident enough to respond, 'The Oh Dae-su I understand is a man who was kidnapped out of the blue to spend 15 years in confinement. He was born with extreme curly hair and to adjust to social norms he had to straight perm it all the time. But during his imprisonment, he no longer has the resources to perm his hair. I believe this forced situation ultimately becomes a time for him to live as his genes define him. Oh Dae-su's confinement becomes the turning point that transforms him into a man with extreme curly hair. I feel the equation of extreme curly hair = wild mane = symbol of rage, and want to express the diverse emotions specific to Oh Dae-su through his hair. It's imperative and it's the definitive Oh Dae-su style. These are the keywords for hair and make-up I've come up with!' When the actor and I failed to come to an agreement,

Park intervened. 'There must be a valid reason for our film's make-up director to insist on a concept like this. Why don't we do the first-look poster and work on the image, and then make a decision?'

The preliminary or 'first-look' poster was a trend in the Korean film world during the 2000s: as part of advance marketing, poster images of a film scheduled to go into production would be created and distributed to visual art-related media and theatres to assess the public response. I immediately went into combat mode to create the 'extreme' curly hair that Oh Dae-su was supposed to have, making Choi Min-sik endure hours of cooking foil-wrapped hair. And that is how Oh Dae-su's mane of hair that existed in my mind became a reality. Oh Dae-su's character look was recognized as 'thinking out of the box' and became an inspiration to other crew members. My make-up team's contribution to the success of *Oldboy* was significant.

During my sabbatical in Canada, I received an email from filmmaker Jung Ji-woo, with whom I had collaborated on *Happy End* (1999). He told me he was planning to direct a film based on writer Park Bum-shin's original story *Eun-gyo*, in which the main character is Lee Juk-yo, a poet in his seventies. He then explained he wanted to cast a young male actor and age him, just as David Fincher had done with Brad Pitt in *The Curious Case of Benjamin Button* (2008). When I asked why he wished to create a character using special make-up, director Jung's response was that by showing a body and face in which youth and old age simultaneously coexist, he hoped to inspire the audience to experience the reality that our body ages. He wanted this character to look more real than the one in

The Curious Case of Benjamin Button, which enjoyed Hollywood's technology at its finest, and asked me to help him make this happen.

I wasn't sure if this would be possible, but nevertheless, I sat down and read through the book in one sitting. To me, *Eun-gyo* came across as a mesmerizing piece that expressed the idea of 'dealing with the non-repudiable reality of growing old, and the emotions which often get disregarded with old age'. It coincided with a time when I was hungry to create a three-dimensional character, making it an easy decision to join this project to develop a character that was convincingly lifelike.

Park Hae-il – aged 34 at the time – was confirmed to play the elderly poet. The actor, who required special make-up for his role, fully understood the challenges and accepted them. The role models used as references for the character concept were Irish novelist and playwright Samuel Beckett and *Eun-gyo* writer Park Bum-shin himself. I worked hard to re-create the intellectual sensibility and colour tones of the character Lee Juk-yo from the original story, as I transformed Park Hae-il into an old man. Numerous trial-and-errors were slowly eating away at me. Ultimately, I was able to use Gel 10 silicon and more theatrical prosthetic deadener to create the 70 year-old's make-up. Gel 10 can be difficult to work with – if it gets too watery, it is hard to apply on set – but it was the best material for making saggy skin and detailed wrinkles. As I slowly moved towards a lifelike image of the poet in his seventies, I was filled with happiness.

In parts of the film Lee Juk-yo recalls his past. For the scenes where he is delivering lectures at university in his fifties, I created facial wrinkles and nasolabial folds with acrylic-based bondo transfer pieces, Cab-O-Sil to prevent sagging and a special adhesive called Pros-Aide. I used the partial application of latex and an old-age stippling technique to create the wrinkles around Lee's eyes, and all colourings were done using skin illustrator liquid and completed with a spattering technique. A shaved hairstyle was suggested by the actor for the scenes in which the character is in his twenties, which saved make-up time as we didn't need a bald cap to create the elderly look.

Work on *Eun-gyo* started in February 2011 and was wrapped up after more than ten test shoots and 60 applications of special old-age make-up. My special make-up team, comprising five members, dedicated thousands of hours to create Lee Juk-yo, a monumental character in the history of Korean cinema.

The challenging example of *Eun-gyo* also helped to expand this type of genre in Korean films. Old-age make-up served significant roles in films such as *My Brilliant Life* (2014), *Ode to My Father* (2014), *My Dictator* (2014) and the TV drama *Mr Back* (2014). Lifelike characters, created by the hands of the make-up team, earned more fans for certain actors and actresses, as well as paving the way to broaden the horizons for film genres.

Film is a total art, and film make-up is a field that cannot work independently. Reinterpreting a sensibility and colour that convey a film's theme and tailoring them to a character can only be done by collaborating with other film teams and fields. It requires a process of understanding and feeling, and diligently working over long hours.

As a film make-up director, it is exclusively my duty to create the concept for a specific film. During the course of breaking down a character to come up with the make-up concept, a character that at first exists only in my mind becomes someone in the real world. And while there are no 'correct answers' in this work, the moment at the first showcase when crew members exchange signs of approval always fills me with tension – but also a strange sense of exhilaration. It makes my heart flutter to imagine how the audience will respond to a character that I have created through my work and how that opens up a realm of imagination.

I do hope the characters that I have participated in realizing hold value and are remembered throughout the years.

November 2021

34-year-old Park Hae-il – seen here in the make-up chair (above) – was cast to play both past and present scenes in Park Bum-shin's *Eun-gyo* (2012). A very short-haired look was used for scenes in which he had to appear younger (middle), which made application of ageing make-up easier for the scenes in which the character is older (below).

K-Drama, Webtoons and Film

The Conundrum of Global Korean Culture: On *Squid Game*

So Hye Kim

Battle Royale (2000, dir. Fukasaku Kinji) set a precedent for the last-person-standing genre.

When we look at the globally enthusiastic reception of Bong Joon-ho's 2019 film *Parasite* and the 2021 Netflix show *Squid Game*, there seems to be no question that Korean culture has smoothly transcended national borders – or the 'one-inch-tall barrier', as Bong called subtitling in his acceptance speech at the 2020 Golden Globes. However, looking closely at both works, we can find a common narrative strategy that requires more in-depth analysis than the mere celebration of the global dissemination of Korean culture. What *Parasite* and *Squid Game* achieve is the delicate balance between universality and specificity – in other words, between globally ubiquitous themes and the verisimilitude of national detail. Both attend to issues of neoliberal capitalism universal enough to make their stories easily relatable for anybody living and surviving in the same system. At the same time, the way in which they present that ubiquitous subject of global capitalism relies on seemingly uniquely Korean descriptions, such as the semi-basement dwellings in *Parasite* and the old-time Korean children's games in *Squid Game*. Irhe Sohn, a Korean film scholar at Smith College in Massachusetts, has analyzed Bong Joon-ho's play with mis/translation as a response to the dilemma of a South Korean spectatorship that wants to see Korean films be part of global cinema while also remaining part of national cinema.[1] Given Bong's earlier two English-language films, *Snowpiercer* (2013) and *Okja* (2017), and their lukewarm reception both in the global and domestic market, his rather daring move in *Parasite*, which leaves a number of details as authentically Korean or 'untranslatable' as possible, looks to have killed two birds with one stone: it is not crucial for the global audience's enjoyment to feel that they have fully understood the narrative, and the Korean audience feels that they have understood more of the complexities than the foreign audience.

Squid Game follows in *Parasite*'s footsteps not only in its criticism of the unlimited power of capitalism but also in its play with translation, or what is designed to be lost in translation. The show opens with a somewhat lengthy explanation of the complicated rules of Squid Game, a children's game popular in Korea decades ago. Both audiences overseas and the younger generations in Korea might initially have difficulty understanding the specific rules of the game, but as the story unfolds, they will recognize that the detail of the game is not that important. The programme's real game is what they are already familiar with: that is, the game of capitalism. However, one might then ask why the show begins with seemingly unnecessary information about somewhat obsolete Korean culture. In other words, what does the show let us know about Korean society and, at the same time, what does it mean to not talk about it further? Thus, our discussion must begin by addressing the side of Korean society gradually being rendered obsolete in the cinema and TV narratives of the global hallyu era.

Inter-East Asian history of popular culture

The narrative and visual style of *Squid Game* refers to various inter-East Asian influences, both in the popular culture industry and history. First of all, the show can be said to draw from the 'survivor game' film genre that has been popular in Japan since the late 1990s. At that time, Japanese society encountered an unprecedented economic recession, and the mass media began to portray young people partaking in life-threatening survivor games, echoing the frustrations of their generation. The most representative work among them must be Fukasaku Kinji's *Battle Royale* (2000). Set in the near future, the film follows a group of students who have to kill each other to survive. This violent dystopian film gained incredible attention both in and outside of

The triangular arrangement of the control room in *Squid Game* (2021, dir. Hwang Dong-hyuk, below)
echoes the configuration in audition show *Produce 101* (2016, above and opposite)

Japan and several similar films followed, cementing these types of survivor or death game films into a *Battle Royale* subgenre. The plot of the survivor game was widely adopted in Japanese manga, which is also extremely influential for Korean people.

Meanwhile, *Squid Game* pertains to a different type of survivor game genre, too: that is, the survivor audition TV shows like the *American Idol* series, a format that has been popular in America since its golden age of television in the 1950s. Soon thereafter, survivor games became a near staple of national television outlets of the US's Cold War allies in East Asia, a reflection of the American hegemony in the region. In Japan, Nippon TV launched *A Star is Born! (Sutā Tanjō!)* in 1971. It went on to gain national popularity and has been a major gateway to idol stardom for young people for decades. This format of a singing competition that solicits viewer participation was refashioned in South Korea with the recent international attention gained by the K-pop star system. While this audition format will be a familiar reference point for *Squid Game*'s global audiences, East Asian viewers will make a more specific connection to the well-known *Produce 101* series, produced by CJ ENM and aired over four seasons on the Mnet channel from 2016 to 2019. In each season, the major entertainment agencies of Korea competed to form their project groups from 101 trainees. Viewers participated in the decision-making process by voting by phone message. The show was so popular that the copyright was sold to production companies in Japan and China, with similar shows subsequently being made throughout East Asia.

The trainees in *Produce 101* wore school uniforms, reminiscent of the students in *Battle Royale*. While the trainees seemed delighted with this opportunity for fame, the competition could be seen as cruel, not unlike the games of survival portrayed in *Battle Royale*. Additionally, the triangular arrangement of the trainees in *Produce 101* reappears almost exactly in the *Squid Game* operations room. In echoing formats such as this, *Squid Game* highlights the fact that its audience may have been implicated in the pleasure of witnessing painful 'elimination' before.[2]

Colonial and capitalist Korea

Another inter-Asian influence can be found in the children's games featured in *Squid Game*. On its release, a few people pointed out that the show has aspects in common with Miike Takashi's 2014 film *As the Gods Will*. As both films are influenced by the *Battle Royale* subgenre, it would be difficult to accuse *Squid Game* of plagiarizing the Japanese film. Yet what fostered doubt surrounding this issue was the similarity between the first games portrayed in the two works, *Daruma-san ga koronda* in the Japanese film and *Mugunghwa kkochi pieotseumnida* in the Korean show (translated as 'Green Light, Red Light'). Even though it is difficult to trace their origins, there are obvious similarities between the Japanese game and the Korean one: the rules of the two games, along with the rhythm of the accompanying song, are almost identical, and the phrases of both consist of ten syllables. Korean ethnomusicologist Hong Yang-ja argues that many Korean children's games that are believed to be traditional were actually imported from Japan during the colonial era (1910–45) and disseminated nationwide through the modern education system under the colonial government.[3] She notes that the mass production of children's toys used in those games, such as glass marbles and rubber bands, began in late nineteenth-century Japan, and the toys, too, were introduced to Korea during Japan's colonial rule. She writes that *Mugunghwa kkochi pieotseumnida* is also transmitted from Japan, but the phrase – which means 'the mugunghwa flower, or Rose of Sharon, has blossomed' – could have been changed to reflect the longing for the nation's independence. Yeongi Folk Museum director Im Yeong-su argues that Namgung Ok, an independence movement activist and educator who disseminated the mugunghwa flower as a symbol of national spirit during the colonial era, is particularly responsible for changing the phrase.[4]

Thus, *Mugunghwa kkochi pieotseumnida* embodies both the colonial legacy and the longing for an independent nation; later, when the South Korean government designated mugunghwa as the national flower, the game also came to symbolize the legitimacy of the South Korean nation-state.

In the sixth episode of *Squid Game*, a flag appears in the background of a set intended to re-create a South Korean neighbourhood of the 1960s or 1970s. The flag features the square and triangle that form the lines of the squid game, but it also looks very similar in colour and shape to the flag of the nationwide New Village movement of the 1970s. The New Village movement, or *Saemaeul Undong*, was a state-led rural modernization project of the Park Chung-hee regime (1963–79), and symbolizes both South Korea's dramatic economic growth and the brutal dictatorship of the era.

With this in mind, and considering that all these games have been designed by the elderly man Number 001, Oh Il-nam, it is possible to argue that Oh is an allegorical character representing South Korean capitalism, which began under Japanese colonial rule and continued to grow under the nation's own military dictatorship. To be specific, what Oh can be seen to symbolize is industrial capitalism in South Korea, sustained in large part by the exploitation of natural and human resources cultivated in newly modernized rural villages throughout the countryside. Therefore, globalized neoliberal capitalism persists even after the demise of industrial capitalism, just as the *Squid Game* system continues to operate even after its creator's death. This allegory of South Korean capitalism combined with patriarchal autocracy might also explain why mostly boys' games were chosen, and why female characters are marginalized in this setting.

Decontextualizing the social trauma of South Korea

Another detail lost in translation that merits further discussion is the backstory of the protagonist. Gi-hun is an unfilial son, an irresponsible father and a gambler with no long-term plans. Nonetheless, he shows solidarity and compassion in his interactions with fellow participants throughout the series. These complexities of character become more fully fleshed out when, in Episode 5, his trauma is finally revealed: he was one of the workers dismissed by the fictitious automobile company Dragon Motors, and witnessed his friend's death during a fierce battle with the police.

Riot police face strikers during protests against dismissals at SsangYong Motors, 2009.

At this moment, many Korean audiences might have thought about the SsangYong Motors sit-in of 2009. SsangYong Motors was one of Korea's major automobile companies until the late 1990s, when the global economic crisis forced the sale of the company's controlling stake to foreign investors. In 2009 SsangYong carried out large-scale restructuring that culminated in the dismissal of 2,500 workers. The workers declared a full sit-in strike, occupying the factory from March 2009; for over two months, the company failed to respond to the union's request for negotiation and instead cut off access to electricity, water and food despite the summer heat. After 77 days, police mobilized antiterrorist manpower and weapons, and the sit-in ended in a brutal crackdown on the terminated workers.

What further exacerbated the injuries incurred by the workers was a lawsuit by the state, which saw their possessions seized for damages. In 2009 police filed a suit against the participants of the sit-in, demanding compensation for a helicopter and crane damaged during the strike. The result of these two trials saw courts ordering workers to pay around 2.5 billion won (US$2.16 million) and, following a series of appeals, the case is still pending a decision in the Supreme Court. During and after the strike, 30 workers and their family members died:

some committed suicide, while others died from the trauma of the crackdown. South Korea witnessed the tragedy of the SsangYong workers over a decade ago, but for civil society at large, the events remain truly traumatic.

The director of *Squid Game*, Hwang Dong-hyuk, mentioned that Gi-hun's character was directly inspired by the laid-off workers of SsangYong Motors. However, it can be seen as problematic that Hwang makes Gi-hun's PTSD-like trauma exclusively personal. Even Gi-hun's family do not fully understand it, but only suffer from his negligence. Given that many former SsangYong workers fell into debt because of the state lawsuit, for Hwang to create a character who is poor because he gambles risks decontextualizing the major social traumas of 2009. For many South Korean people, these traumas are not a game at all, but part of everyday life.

With all these details in mind, I now wonder if a Korean audience can enjoy the show as much as a non-Korean audience did when unaware of this background. Maybe all the details should have been necessarily lost in translation to make the show an entertaining cultural commodity, financed and distributed by a major American media company. Hwang has mentioned in interviews that he had this project in mind for a

A scene from *Squid Game*. Director Hwang Dong-hyuk has said he was directly influenced by the crackdown at SsangYong Motors (see opposite).

decade, but no Korean producers were interested in it. Since Hwang's sole investor Netflix launched its Korean branch in 2016, it has become a means not only for global audiences to view previously unavailable Korean films and TV shows, but also for many Korean directors to realize bold ideas that barely meet the broadcast regulations of national television channels in Korea. In that sense, Netflix looks like the smartest and most generous investor for making Korean directors' challenging projects come to life beyond national, cultural and linguistic boundaries, and then to reach a global audience. However, the Netflix system of investment and distribution of profit leaves open to question who truly profits from this globalization of Korean content. Once Netflix decides to invest in a project, it provides producers with the whole production budget up front with almost no interference about the content, but it does not share profit gained by the projects. On the one hand, it guarantees stable production of quality shows (particularly compared to Korean broadcast TV shows, which must incorporate a number of Pay Per Lead advertisements in order to secure a production budget); on the other, the success of a show is not shared in equal monetary terms with its producers, albeit those producers may gain international fame. In this sense, the phenomenal success of

Squid Game lets us reckon once more with the irony of global capitalism and the tangled relationship between the global and the local aspects of the series.

What the unexpected success of the show engendered is the redirection of the discourses about *Squid Game* in Korea. Since its initial release, it has received contrasting reviews in Korea. Some found it disturbing and problematic, especially regarding violence and what they felt were sexist depictions; others evaluated it as stimulating and refreshing. However, as global attention on the show has surged, most of the discourse within Korea has begun focusing on its international success as a symbol of the power of hallyu. *Squid Game* might have satisfied both the domestic and global audiences with its combination of local details and universal themes, just as *Parasite* did in 2019. But as *Squid Game*'s reach extended far beyond that of *Parasite*, so too did its games turn into memes and its characters to Halloween costumes. Meanwhile, its socio-political implications seem to have faded away. Maybe the truth of the lives of Korean people suffering under the cruelties of capitalism will be lost in spectacle, like the coffins of *Squid Game*'s victims wrapped up in their huge pink ribbons. Perhaps this is the real conundrum of hallyu today.

K-Pop and Fandom

K-팝과 팬덤
부 문

K-pop music has fuelled the recent explosion in Korean popular culture across the globe. Its unbridled dissemination was largely powered online by a young tech-savvy generation of fans at a time when smartphone technology and social media platforms like YouTube, Facebook and Twitter began to emerge in the mid-2000s (see Sun Lee, pp. 126–9). K-pop's success was a major factor when, in 2008, Korean cultural exports exceeded for the first time foreign cultural imports into the country.[1] Today, BTS and BLACKPINK dominate charts worldwide and have broken a number of global records.

Despite the language barrier, K-pop is enjoyed around the world for its immersive experience that blends addictive tunes, relatable lyrics, slick choreography and striking visuals into a polished spectacle. It conveys *heung*, a contagious and overwhelming sense of joy and enthusiasm that builds and brings a community together. Its music often draws inspiration from, and mixes, a wide spectrum of world cultures and musical genres: from folk music, EDM, jazz, hip-hop and rap to melodies rooted in local traditional repertoires like *pansori*, an oral tradition of musical storytelling. Songs and dances are performed by idols, charismatic and accomplished artists, many of whom undergo several years' strict training in a highly competitive environment. K-pop's iconic trademarks are its synchronized choreography and the cinematic quality of its music videos. Choreographers, some still in their teens, conceive complex dance routines in a matter of days, capturing the concept of a new song while reflecting the idols' personalities (see Lia Kim, pp. 114–19). Music videos, important tools for translating a song into a compelling visual narrative, are also peppered at times with hidden clues for fans to discover and unpick over many reruns of the clip. All these ultimately contribute to the building of an artistic universe unique to each K-pop band (see Dasom Sung, pp. 120–5).

In 1992, the debut performance of Seo Taiji and Boys on *Saturday Night Music Show*, a well-known television talent contest programme akin to *X Factor*, marked the seismic moment that shook the Korean soundscape.[2] The hip-hop band stood out amid a sea of soft melodies and melancholic *teuroteu* (or 'trot', a popular Korean music genre originating in the colonial period), and left the jury bewildered with their pumped-up dance moves, baggy street-style fashion and an experimental tune that mixed ballad and metal rock with new jack swing beats and rap – recited in Korean, no less. Black American youth music had only begun trickling into Korea in the late 1980s via the US military base following the lifting of long-standing censorships, so the band's references were unfamiliar, too, to the majority of the audience. The trio scored the lowest rating that night, but enthralled the 'new generation' (*sinsedae* or Generation X) hungry for a fresh and exciting sound,[3] and their first album achieved record sales on its release, collecting prestigious awards along the way. Rebel with a cause, Seo's lyrics provided socio-cultural commentary on academic pressure, the reunification of Korea and the generation gap. They gave voice to teenagers whose anxieties and aspirations were fundamentally different to those of the previous generations who had lived through economic and political unrest. Seo was equally bold in his musical choices and experiments, adjusting and blending the African American music vernacular with local language, interests and a traditional Korean repertoire reimagined for a modern audience. By so doing, Seo Taiji and Boys brought hip-hop, R&B and reggae musical genres into mainstream Korean music, but also generated a distinctive musical genre, now considered the forerunner of K-pop today.[4] The trio disbanded at the peak of their career in 1996, but their legacy in the domestic music industry was deep and long-lasting.

During the same period, music recording studios and broadcasting companies were gradually being replaced by entertainment companies, with financial support from *chaebol* investing in the field in the way they also did for K-drama and cinema. The 1997 Asian Financial Crisis saw this support withdrawn, and the music industry – seeing the successful inroads K-drama and cinema made in China and Japan – likewise pinned its survival hopes on the export market.[5] In this context, the companies SM, YG and JYP gained momentum by producing a flurry of K-pop artists who were soon attracting hordes of fans across East Asia (see Joanna Elfving-Hwang, pp. 130–5). This movement was spearheaded by SM's H.O.T., whose 2001 concert in Beijing cemented K-pop as the foremost Korean cultural export and hallyu as the key term to describe this wave of adulation for K-culture.

With K-pop's success came some criticism. Many condemned the cultural appropriation of Black American music and Black performance in K-pop, seen as

Front cover for Seo Taiji and Boys album *Gyosil Idea*, 1992, which blended various youth music genres with a local Korean repertoire to create a fresh new sound.

a reflection of a vastly monoethnic society still struggling with racism and cultural diversity. Some offered a more nuanced approach to the debate by looking into the cross-cultural dynamics and socio-economic contexts that gave birth to K-pop (see Crystal S. Anderson, pp. 100–7). Entertainment companies were labelled 'idol factories' and heavily denounced for their arduous training programmes, manufactured sound and for favouring commercial outcomes over artistic pursuits. Stories of physical exhaustion, mental health issues and emotional blackmail among trainees and idols appeared regularly in the press, as did so-called 'slave contracts', which bound the K-pop trainee to the company until they paid back the monies invested to train them. Reports of sexual harassment and gender discrimination against female idol groups were also commonplace. These groups tend to have shorter lifespans than their male counterparts, with more focus on their looks; they also have a relatively limited input in the creative process. Female idol groups are expected to embody a hypersexualized image offset by *aegyo*: an infantilized cuteness or behaviour to suit the male gaze both in and outside of Korea. Closely scrutinized for their behaviour, personal lifestyle, diet and fashion, they regularly face misogyny within a still conservative and patriarchal society.[6] These issues are not unique to Korea, or to the music field for that matter,[7] but have certainly been amplified in the K-pop world by its newly acquired status of cultural challenger, and the scale and speed at which such incidents can be reported at a time when the world is socially more engaged. In fact, the concept of the 'idol factory' was initially designed by the talent agency Johnny & Associates in 1980s Japan: idols signed a long-term contract to be trained in singing and acting within a structural frame provided by the company.[8] These J-pop idols were calibrated for the local audience, however (to this day the world's second largest music market), whereas Korean entertainment companies have pushed the Japanese system further to reach a global audience.

Additionally, some have argued that the K-pop idol factory is not that dissimilar to Motown, the music assembly line founded in 1960s Detroit by Berry Gordy, the former car factory worker turned music mogul. Motown's Hitsville was 'a black-owned, black-centred business that gave white America something they just could not get enough of – joyous, sad, romantic, mad, groovin', movin' music'.[9] Gordy's music production line sought collaboration with white practitioners and offered an 'artist development' course including speech and etiquette lessons, with an overall aim of breaking the white dominated music market at a time when racial segregation was rife in America.[10] A notable comparison can be drawn with the hybrid strategy adopted by Korea, a peripheral culture, in its attempt to go global.

Others argued that the K-pop trainee's rigorous discipline and diligence were ingrained Korean characteristics rooted in the Neo-Confucian ideology dominating Korean society, and that the Joseon dynasty's emphasis on academic excellence and self-cultivation had simply been transposed onto the entertainment environment in the twenty-first century.[11] The mixing of styles and the hybrid nature of K-pop songs could further be perceived as a historical continuation of *changga*, a late nineteenth-century music style introduced by British and American missionaries that fused western melodies with the Korean pentatonic scale, lyrics and themes.[12] This trend extended into the colonial period with the introduction of *teuroteu* inspired by the Japanese *enka* genre, and carried on in post-war Korea with localized cover versions of the Euro-American hits that had been introduced by American military personnel stationed on the peninsula. In sum, hybridity historically recurred each time Korea encountered a foreign culture and K-pop turned this model on its head to reverse the cultural flow.

Beyond simply inverting previous models, K-pop's hybrid nature is expressed in multiple forms: from the inclusion of non-Korean Asian members in a band to collaborations with international songwriters and composers, and playful yet meaningful dual-language lyrics. In recent years, the hybridity extended to K-pop's delivery, with the music industry making use of technology found in other fields such as esports to provide new experiences for audiences.

Meanwhile, the global fanbases behind K-pop have grown into cultural phenomena in themselves. More than merely consumers, fans have become overnight translators, content creators, fundraisers, archivists and activists (see Mariam Elba, pp. 108–13). They carry out good deeds on behalf of their idols, propagating a positive image of K-pop that further enhances Korea's soft power. Korean language courses have boomed across the world in the wake of hallyu and many K-drama and K-pop fans now subtitle film dialogue and song lyrics overnight to quickly spread K-cultural content among their local communities. Indeed, it is arguably easy to learn Korean as a phonetic language using the 24-character hangeul alphabet, which can, unlike Chinese or Japanese ideograms, be typed readily on a conventional QWERTY/AZERTY keyboard. Fans are also collectively hosting and managing K-pop's largest repository, which is found online. These prosumers/produsers are constantly generating new digital content on K-pop, thereby amplifying its presence online.[13] This complex, rhizomatic infrastructure developed for disseminating K-pop content can be remobilized swiftly by fans to join forces across the world and actively address various socio-political and environmental issues they hold dear. Culturally diverse and cross-generational, K-pop fans' vocal engagement in these societal discourses further raises the profile and relevance of hallyu.

K-Pop and Fandom

K-pop fans gather for the YG Family flashmob in London's Trafalgar Square, 2011.

These stills from Orange Caramel's 'Catallena' music video of 2014 can be seen as a playful comment on a system in which Idols are presented for consumption and are seen to have a sell-by date.

₩ 1,000
(Mackerel)

₩ 1,000
(Salmon)

₩ 1,000
(Shrimp)

₩ 8,000
(Octopus)

₩ 8,000

Beyond Appropriation and Appreciation: The Cross-Cultural Dynamics of K-pop

Crystal S. Anderson

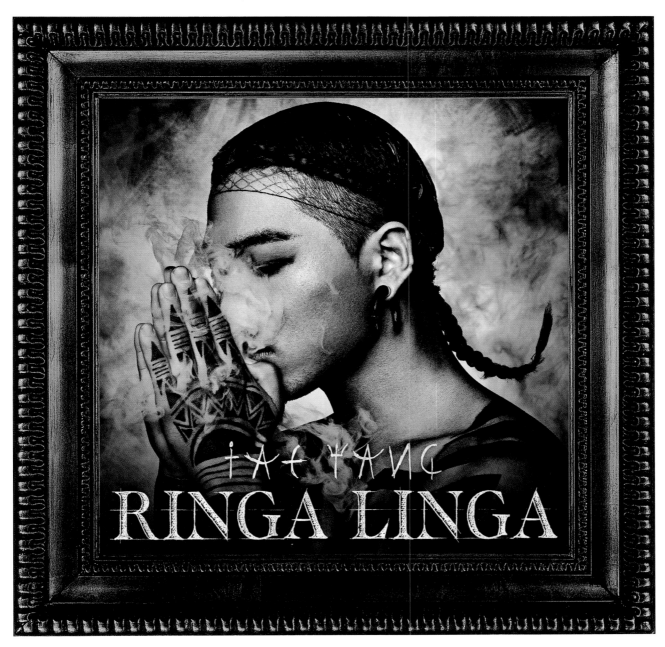

The styling for the cover of K-pop artist Taeyang's album *Ringa Linga*, 2013, shows the influence of African-American popular music.

With the recent explosion in awareness of K-pop globally, music outlets like *Billboard* and platforms like Spotify frequently herald the success of K-pop music through metrics such as streams and views. The increased visibility of K-pop has also sparked commentary about the way it incorporates foreign musical styles and cultures, including those that originate and are largely associated with Black popular culture. Such commentary tends to characterize K-pop's cultural interaction with Black popular culture in two distinctly different ways: as either cultural appropriation or cultural appreciation. While commentators ranging from music journalists to podcasters have used these concepts as a lens through which to view K-pop, neither label fully recognizes the complexities and nuances of the kind of cultural exchange that K-pop embodies. Focusing on K-pop's cross-cultural dynamics, this essay shows how K-pop – like other musical traditions such as jazz, rock and hip-hop – has blended music traditions in a way that ensures Black expressive culture remains visible. Specifically, K-pop not only authentically and intentionally engages Black expressive culture, but also benefits from the direct musical contributions of Black creative personnel.

Appropriation vs. appreciation

When commentators level charges of *cultural appropriation* against K-pop, they incorporate a variety of behaviours and incidents. Cultural appropriation can range from a failure to acknowledge the origins and innovators of Black expressive

Music-video still from ONEUS's 'Lit' ('taekwondo version', 2021), which features traditional Korean buildings, clothing, instruments, dancing and martial arts, an example of K-pop sharing Korean culture with the wider world.

culture from which K-pop artists draw, to the promulgation of negative stereotypes. *Dazed Digital*'s 2020 article 'How K-pop is responding to its longstanding appropriation problem' cites instances of blackface by K-pop artists, as well as the incorporation of styles associated with people of African descent, as examples that prove K-pop's cultural appropriation.[1] The practice of blackface is clearly a form of negative racial performance that mocks or demeans, but the use of styles associated with African Americans is a bit different. Some criticize K-pop artists for taking on Black hairstyles, fashion styling and performance. While this is not a negative racial performance with the intent to demean, critics complain that such artists fail to recognize the cultural origins of their actions, accusing artists instead of using these styles as a costume. Such criticisms are extended to artists' incorporation of Black music – which many see as integral to their global success – in ways that erase Black people.

These are the latest episodes in a long-running narrative around the musical exploitation of Black popular music by those outside of Black communities. Critiques of the appropriation of Black music by white artists go as far back as jazz, when white artists were credited with the work of Black pioneers unknown to the mainstream, and to the early rock and roll stars who covered songs by Black artists, thus becoming the face and voice of groundbreaking musical movements. More recently, white performers like Justin Timberlake have been accused of using Black popular music to gain popularity but then failing to participate politically in the culture. Writing for *Cosmopolitan*, Kendra James chastises Timberlake: 'Justin Timberlake has never done or said anything to prove he's in any way connected to or concerned with Black Americans – at least not Black Americans who exist outside of the recording studio.'[2] Even performers of colour have faced similar charges of appropriation: Bruno Mars has been described as an originator

who does not cite his sources, despite acknowledging the Black artists that have inspired his work. For some, K-pop artists appear to fall into the same category, 'taking' from Black popular culture and benefiting in terms of attention and profits.

On the other hand, some commentators call for viewing K-pop artists as engaging in a form of *cultural appreciation* that boosts the impact of Black popular culture. Cultural appreciation represents an earnest exploration of different cultures in an effort to further understanding, and this argument therefore suggests that K-pop acts function as a conduit for foreign fans to learn about Korean language, history and culture, and for Koreans to appreciate the vast contributions of African American culture. While cultural appropriation can often be promulgated by mainstream media outlets, the cultural appreciation argument is often promoted by fans. For example, speaking to the news site of a high school in Coppell, Texas, Nhan Pham, an attendee at a Korean festival in the Dallas County city, said: 'The importance of [cultural festivals] especially in America, and all over the world, [is that] everybody should learn about anybody's culture so you can appreciate it ... Without cultural appreciation, we disregard other people's beliefs and traditions.'[3] Moreover, cultural appreciation helps to support soft power, whereby cultural capital can be gained not through formal diplomacy or military coercion but through persuasion and exchange.

However, cultural appropriation and appreciation are binary approaches that fail to consider the complexities embodied in K-pop. Sometimes, claims of appropriation fail to acknowledge the fact that cultural exchange results from the travel of cultures and in some ways is inevitable; at others, such critiques reveal a lack of knowledge about the hybridity of musical cultures that K-pop replicates. On the other hand, cultural appreciation tends to focus on the celebration of a culture, leaving out historical contextualization and the recognition of intertextuality. While cultural appreciation may lead audiences to source material and cultures, it tends to uncritically focus on positive qualities while acting to rebuff arguments for cultural appropriation.

Cross-cultural dynamics

If we focus on the cross-cultural dynamics of K-pop music and its development and history beyond its recent global popularity, we can see how it shares characteristics with other hybrid music traditions. K-pop is the result of the incorporation of Korean production and promotion strategies into foreign music traditions; it has always had global aspirations and sought to appeal to a global audience to spread its own culture. Political and economic factors historically helped propel K-pop globally: the Korean government had a vested interest in supporting this effort through agencies and companies, while creative and business personnel saw an opportunity to redirect their music to the larger, global audience outside Korea. However, this would not have been be possible without prior political and economic shifts within Korea that set the stage for the kind of cross-cultural dynamics that form the heart of K-pop.

In the late 1980s South Korea experienced a growing democratic environment, but by the late 1990s the country was experiencing economic setbacks as a result of the International Monetary Fund crisis. The country therefore invested in culture industries, including the music industry, and looked to rehabilitate its global reputation. In addition to modernization strategies in the area of technology and media, this saw South Korea open up to an influx of foreign cultures. Furthermore, due to the American military presence since the 1940s, Korea had long been exposed to a wide variety of American culture, particularly an American music culture saturated by Black popular music. By the 1990s, South Korea was well positioned to draw from not only R&B genres like soul, disco and funk, but also the newest genre, hip-hop.

Initially, K-pop's reach was primarily to East Asian countries such as China and Japan. Over time, K-pop has spread not just to places like the United Kingdom and the United States, but also other global locations, including Latin America and the Middle East. Yet even as K-pop sought a global market, it made use of expanded access to foreign cultures to incorporate elements from those other cultures, and while K-pop was open to a variety of influences from China and Japan, it was the incorporation of elements of black popular music – including the genres, performance and visuals of African American culture – that contributed to the foundation of the sound upon which K-pop is built. K-pop has since engaged in collaborations that span the globe, working with musical personnel from across national boundaries and following in the footsteps of other hybrid music like Black popular music.

The signature sounds of Black popular music have often been the product of collaborations between Black and white musicians and producers. For example, Motown developed its in-house talent to produce music, but so did the Brill Building, which housed creatives including Carole King and Burt Bacharach, who wrote songs that would go on to become R&B staples such as King's '(You Make Me Feel Like) A Natural Woman', popularized by Aretha Franklin, and Bacharach's 'Walk on By', perhaps best known from Dionne Warwick's version. White musicians were often session musicians involved in the creation of tracks at the Fame Studio in Muscle Shoals, providing instrumentation on dozens of classics of R&B. Hip-hop, meanwhile, owes part of its origins to Puerto Rican pioneers in the Bronx in the 1970s.

Similarly, K-pop participates in a collaborative tradition, one that sees not only a cross-pollination of musical elements, but also collaborations between creatives that go beyond copying or imitating music production and diluting its essence. As well as drawing on historical black popular music and performance (thereby incorporating context), it collaborates with black creative personnel (thereby avoiding the erasure of Black practitioners).

Members of PRISTIN winning Best New Female Group at the Mnet Asian Music Awards (MAMA) at Yokohama Arena in 2017, an indicator of the enormous popularity of K-pop in Japan.

An examination of one of K-pop's creative personnel, veteran music producer Yoo Young-jin of SM Entertainment, reveals K-pop's cross-cultural dynamics. It is not an exaggeration to call Yoo a primary architect of the sound of K-pop. Yoo was initially signed to SM Entertainment as an artist, and has released several solo albums, including *Blues in Rhythm* (1993), *Blue Rhythm* (1996) and *Agape* (2001). His track 'Unconditional Kismet' would not be out of place in a quiet storm rotation on a Black radio station. Opening with a cappella vocals, the track has a rhythm so often heard on slow jams, the slow-tempo R&B tracks of the 1990s. The instrumentation allows the vocals to shine. In 2011 Yoo surprised K-pop fans with a vocal appearance on a teaser for the music video for SUPER JUNIOR's 'Mr. Simple'. While 'Mr. Simple' reflects SUPER JUNIOR''s penchant for upbeat, electronic-infused dance music, the vocal interlude features Yoo's improvisation over sparse jazz instrumentation; open and syncopated drums contribute to its swing feel. His albums often feature guest vocalists, including African American rapper Coolio, thus paralleling the collaborations we see in 1960s soul music production rather than the exploitation by white music producers of the 1950s. Yoo's own creation of music would inform his style of production, in that he authentically draws from the music tradition of Black popular music by working with Black creatives and not watering down the resulting music to obscure its origins.

Yoo has had a hand in shaping the sound of many of the artists on the label with his signature, R&B-based music production. His use of R&B illustrates the impact of globalization on the cross-cultural dynamics of K-pop; it also meant that K-pop would come to be defined by the R&B vocals and rhythms that would serve as a solid foundation for the genre's performance aspect, particularly the 'idol' groups that led

K-pop group EXO in front of the Burj Khalifa, Dubai, 2018. Their popularity in the country earned them a star on Dubai's 'walk of fame'.

Aretha Franklin collaborating with Black and white musicians at Fame Studios in Muscle Shoals, Alabama, 1968: a precedent for the cross-cultural dynamics that are seen in the production of K-pop.

its initial wave, those Korean artists and groups who sing and dance as well as participate in extra-musical activities. S.E.S.'s 'I'm Your Girl' (1997) is an early track produced by Yoo that has the earmarks of popular R&B girl groups of the early 1990s. The track blends an intro by male rappers and rap bridges with the sweeter R&B-inspired vocals of the members, Eugene, Bada and Shoo. The mid-tempo song includes poppy, syncopated beats and sound effects such as chimes that lend themselves to the choreography of the group's accompanying performances, not least because the song was written with the choreography in mind. Anyone familiar with 1990s R&B would find echoes here of such tracks as 'What About Your Friends' (1992) by R&B group TLC, which has a similarly upbeat tempo, syncopated dance beat and combination of rap and female vocals. And unlike covers by white performers of Black songs in the 1950s, Yoo's incorporation of musical elements into K-pop does not result in distortion. It is, in fact, 1990s-era R&B/hip-hop that does not try to obfuscate what it is. Yoo has cited popular African American artists of the time as a huge influence on his music production, including drawing on rhythm-driven artists like Janet Jackson to create music that supports performance.[4] Moreover, the Black popular music of the 1990s that inspired Yoo was itself widely diverse and continued the hybridity of previous genres such as jazz, soul and funk.

As Yoo's production style developed, he continued to draw on elements of Black popular music. At the same time, he also became known for combining various genres within one song

to support eclectic performances, resulting in what came to be known as the SM Music Performance (SMP), 'a type of song that is created together as a complete song and performance, which cannot be separated'.[5] Even when the shifts in genres are not pronounced, SMP is linked to songs that 'play with structure in strange ways and swap genre without any notice. Pop songs were designed to lull you into security, make you feel at ease so you won't go against the system. SM does the opposite'.[6] While media coverage of K-pop tends to use a contemporary lens to level charges of appropriation, it often misses how K-pop acknowledges older genres that are not as popular as current music trends. Yoo often achieves this sense of dissonance by drawing on older Black popular music genres. For example, 'Spellbound' (2014) by male group TVXQ! combines jazz-inflected harmony and horns with a more contemporary rhythm. The jazz influence is underscored by a music video that makes use of jazz dance movements as well as visuals that hark back to the height of the American jazz age.

Like the hybridized Black popular music that preceded it, K-pop has been driven by collaborations with Black creatives. Sometimes such collaborations are at the business level. Quincy Jones entered into a partnership with Korean agency CJ E&M in 2013 to promote K-pop globally. On other occasions, collaborations are at the artistic level: long before Park Jin-young produced artists and groups under his own label JYP Entertainment, he wrote songs for the R&B singer Omarion. The media has often focused on SM Entertainment's

The cover of S.E.S. album *Remember*, 2017. The band's sound was heavily influenced by R&B.

TVXQ!'s music video 'Spellbound', 2014, features jazz dance and jazz-age styling.

use of Swedish and British music producers to collaborate on making music, citing music camps in Europe, while scholars have also noted the use of global music producers: 'Like the famous Korean electronics and automobile industries, K-pop companies must outsource original music scores to western (notably Swedish, American, and British) composers'.[7] These constructions, however, focus on the use of western music producers, overlooking how consistently K-pop has sought out Black creators, and thereby actually obscure the influence of practitioners of Black popular music. These creators may be from the west, but their racial identity and participation in a distinct ethnic music culture distinguishes them from their (white) European counterparts. Indeed, K-pop has been a place where music producers such as The Underdogs (Harvey Mason Jr. and Damon Thomas), Teddy Riley and Rodnae 'Chikka' Bell have found the opportunity to make music in a very different way: as Bell notes, 'American pop artists want repetition in their music while K-pop artists want more complex melodies and changes within their music'.[8] Such producers also make collaborations visible by adding K-pop artists to their musical résumés.

In turn, K-pop has developed strategies to make creative personnel more visible. In addition to a continued reliance on physical copies of musical releases that contain liner notes, K-pop agencies release highlight medleys as part of music promotions. Initially, these highlight videos provided snippets of songs from the upcoming album, but eventually also included song credit information for listeners. Such teasers function as promotion, but also use the popularity of social media to promote the creatives who work behind the scenes – creatives who are often Black.

Cultural appropriation and appreciation become the poles between which K-pop is positioned. However, like any binary construction this fails to get at the complexities and nuances of the kind of cultural exchange the genre represents. Neither cultural appropriation nor appreciation leaves much room for the hybridity that informs K-pop or for the various music traditions that influence it. While it is true that American popular music has often drawn from Black genres and erased Black artists, it is also the beneficiary of Black and white artists working together to create signature popular music sounds. K-pop likewise draws on the music of other cultures, but it does so in a way that points the listener to the original sources. It maintains the quality of the traditions it draws from, rather than watering them down to make them palatable for a largely white mainstream audience. K-pop artists have been working with Black artists since the early days and continue to do so, raising the profile of this cross-cultural dynamic.

Quincy Jones, American music producer, and An Seok-jun, former managing director at CJ E&M, joining forces in 2013 to promote K-pop internationally.

R&B singer Omarion, Korean music producer Park Jin-young and Korean singer Rain (Bi), 2006. Park has produced tracks for both artists.

Music producer duo The Underdogs (Damon Thomas and Harvey Mason, Jr.), seen here in 2007, have produced tracks for bands such as EXO and Girls' Generation.

'Into The New World': K-pop Fandom, Civic Engagement and Citizenship in the Global South

Mariam Elba

BLACKPINK fans in the Philippines arrange to send food and supplies to those affected by Typhoon Ulysses in November 2020.

What can fans do as a collective? When K-pop fans come together en masse, they can break streaming records, bring a group to the top of the *Billboard* Hot 100 and garner billions of views on YouTube. In other words, they can force the music industry in the west to re-evaluate its entrenched beliefs about the popularity of music from outside the English-speaking world. But while these fans have shown their power over the music charts, perhaps what is even more interesting is how fans have used these same networks for purposes seemingly unrelated to their favourite artists: serving and taking action for their local communities.

Fans taking collective action, whether political or civic in nature, is not a new phenomenon. But the summer of 2020, in the thick of the Covid-19 pandemic and in the aftermath of George Floyd's murder by Minneapolis police, K-pop fans drew worldwide attention for organizing several high-profile activities. As protests supporting the Black Lives Matter movement were sweeping the United States, the Dallas Police Department solicited videos of 'illegal activity' from the protests through an app called iWatch.[1] Instead, fans flooded the app with fancams: short clips of their favourite K-pop singers. Just a couple of weeks later, K-pop fans were among those who took part in mass-reserving tickets for former US President Donald Trump's campaign rally in Tulsa, Oklahoma, with no intention of showing up, resulting in a thinly attended event.[2] For several weeks afterwards, fans hijacked hashtags started by far-right netizens in an effort to drown out their messages.

Little of the coverage of these online political actions organized by and including K-pop fans explores how collective action of varying degrees, of a political or civic nature, has long been a part of the fandom experience. For many years before this most recent upsurge of Black Lives Matter protests in the USA, fans of all kinds, from 'deadheads' (aficionados of The Grateful Dead) to Harry Potter devotees, have participated in collective civic action.[3] Fan communities outside the west are even more underexplored, even though they have long been mobilizing for their communities, often using symbolism and messages from their favourite music and artists. Nor has there been a significant attempt to add nuance to the conversation about collective action and its potential pitfalls, including how limiting and toxic online fandom spaces can be.[4]

In today's world, actions like civic and political engagement and charitable organizing are increasingly becoming part and parcel of being in a fan community, especially in K-pop fandom. As Ashley Hinck, professor of communication at Xavier University, Cincinnati, states in her book *Politics for the Love of Fandom*, 'understanding fan practices, identities, and communities is becoming increasingly important as fandom has become more popular, visible, and accessible than ever before.'[5]

This essay explores how K-pop fan communities in the Global South have mobilized to give back to and help their local communities in a material sense. This is not meant to be an all-encompassing look at fan activism in the Global South; rather,

KPOP 4 Planet
@kpop4planet

Congratulations on the latest release, @Stray_Kids! 😊

Carla, one of the #STAY from Portugal shared her thoughts on how Stray Kids encouraged her to join a climate-related campaigns 🙌

She and other STAYs will fully support #JYP if they are taking more advanced climate action.

10:21 AM · Aug 23, 2021 · Twitter for iPhone

Bangtan Egypt 🇪🇬 🐱
@BTS_EGYPT_ARMY

[✨]

JK is known for his pure personality that heal and help us overcome many difficult in our lives ❄️

So.. we tried to reflect his effect on other people The Egyptian ARMY donated with medical supplies for oncology patients to celebrate his birthday ✨

#HAPPYJKDAY
@bts_twt
+

5:28 PM · Aug 31, 2021 · Twitter for Android

7 Borahae ⁷ EGO 🖤
@BtsFazkook

#TwitterBestFandom #TeamBTS #SoompiAwards
@BTS_twt
Of the protests in Algeria 🖤 ⭐
Algerian army love BTS forever 🖤 ✨

5:20 PM · Mar 18, 2019 · Twitter for Android

SHINeeWorld_Kenya
@KenyaShinee

Its 2 years of #SHININ
@realjonghyun90
@shinetter
@shiny90408
@SHINee_Africa
++

7:18 PM · Jan 30, 2020 · Twitter for Android

(Bottom Left): Tweet: BTS fans in Egypt fund medical supplies for cancer patients in honour of member Jungkook's birthday, 2021;
(Top Left): Tweet: A Portuguese fan of Stray Kids expresses concern about climate change and advocates for K-pop companies to embrace sustainability, 2021; (Top Right): Tweet: Algerian BTS fans attend the 2019 protests holding signs with BTS references and lyrics; (Botttom Right): Tweet: Kenyan fans of SHINee participate in a tree-planting campaign in honour of late member Jonghyun, 2020.

I highlight representative examples that have emerged in the past couple of years, including how fans across the world have used K-pop as political symbolism, as a mobilizer for charitable functions and to rally fans and local community members to protect and sustain them during the Covid-19 pandemic and the incoming threat of climate change. Through these examples, I hope to show that K-pop fandom communities are an influential force outside of the online, western spaces that garner international media attention.

K-pop as political symbolism

> *I love you, just like this. The longed end of wandering.*
> *I leave behind this world's unending sadness.*
> *Walking the many and unknowable paths,*
> *I follow a dim light.*
> *It's something we'll do together to the end,*
> *into the new world.*

In 2016 students at Ehwa Women's University in Seoul crowded together in the hallways of the campus, protesting the decision to create a new degree programme that would enable cronyism among the school's leading administrators.[6] With linked arms, they sang 'Into the New World', a popular song by one of the leading K-pop girl groups at the time, Girls' Generation.[7] The protests contributed to exposing corruption not just at Ehwa but also within the presidential administration: they were the seeds for the Candlelight Revolution that eventually led to Park Geun-hye's impeachment.[8] Along with 'Into the New World',[9] girl band TWICE's 'Cheer Up' was also used as a protest song,[10] while lyrics from their song 'TT' were employed for satirical protest signs.[11]

The use of K-pop in grassroots movements goes far beyond Korea. During the 2020 protests in Thailand – which called for democratic reforms and changes to the country's monarchy, among other things – and in the midst of internet censorship and mass arrests, Thai K-pop fans used their fan community networks to actively participate in protests and form a kind of mutual aid network. The same online fan groups that regularly raise money to buy advertisement space to display their favourite artists this time raised money for protective gear for protesters, and to engage Thai Lawyers for Human Rights (TLHR) to provide pro bono legal help to the dozens of arrested protesters. Even in Thailand, 'Into the New World' was sung as a rallying cry.[12] Natchapol Chaloeykul, a Thai fan who took part in the protests, saw the song as a reflection of the protesters' hopes. 'Like in the song, we want new things for our country too,' she told Reuters in 2020.[13]

Even in a country as far from Korea as Algeria, in 2019 K-pop fans brought signs that bore lyrics from BTS's song 'Not Today' to protests calling for the resignation of then President Abdelaziz Bouteflika. Another BTS fan carried a sign stating 'BTS is coming back in April and I have no time for ya!'[14] In the 2019 uprising against the neoliberalization of public institutions in Chile, authorities directly cited K-pop fandom as a 'foreign' influence responsible for the so-called 'social rupturing' sparking the protests. This framing by the conservative government of K-pop fandom was ridiculed, but the report inspired K-pop themed protests after the government report was made public. In one example, protesters organized a 'K-pop for dignity' protest, in which they planned to dance to PSY's 'Gangnam Style'.[15] As Camilo Diaz Pino, professor of communication and media at West Chester University in Pennsylvania, wrote in his 2021 paper 'K-Pop is Rupturing Chilean Society', '[President Sebastián] Piñera's administration had effectively transformed K-pop into the same tool of dissent they had framed it as.'[16] In December 2021 K-pop fans in the country were among those who strongly mobilized to elect Gabriel Boric as President; Boric posed with photo cards of TWICE's Jeongyeon and Stray Kids' Han.[17] In another notable recent example, K-pop fans in the Philippines actively campaigned for Vice President and current presidential

candidate Leni Robredo. Elsewhere, the group KPOP STANS 4 LENI organizes voter education forums, and a 'Mass Power Hour' in which fans report election disinformation that they see online.[18]

K-pop did not emerge with political intent; nor do the vast majority of K-pop songs and content have explicit, or even implicit, political messaging. But fans and general admirers of the songs have injected meaning through causes and values that matter to them.[19] As Ashley Hinck notes, such fan activities spur affective relationships and solidarity among fan communities. The above examples, all from very different geographical locales, illustrate how fandom communities use their common interest 'to develop new public values, envision a different status quo, and find passion, enthusiasm, and commitment for public issues'.[20]

We also see this clearly with fandom organizing that is not as politically overt. Across the world, K-pop fandom is adopting idols' birthdays as markers for what Hinck terms 'fan-based citizenship' and a conception of fandom rooted in public service and civic engagement.

Idols' birthdays and charitable giving

In K-pop fan culture, idols' birthdays are not only occasions for celebration, but also increasingly opportunities to start fundraising drives for charitable causes and take part in charitable action. Among the most visible fanpages to do this is One In An ARMY, a group of BTS fans that organizes charity projects in honour of the BTS members year round, including on their birthdays. One In An ARMY is among the more prominent organizations engaging in such work, but it is a common practice across fandoms.

These birthday projects can be shaped by cultural practices in a given locality. Bangtan Egypt is a fanbase that exemplifies this well. As one of the BTS fan communities in the country, Bangtan Egypt organizes charitable events and fundraisers for each of the BTS members' birthdays. In 2019, for V's (Kim Tae-hyung) birthday, fan organizers across the country visited local orphanages, donated toys and spent time with the children.[21] This specific birthday project mirrors an Egyptian national holiday called Orphans' Day, in which citizens donate not only money but also their time in going to visit orphanages, and hosting activities like face painting and games for the children.

In another example, for Jin's birthday in 2020, Bangtan Egypt organized a project called 'Eat Jin', named after the singer's 'mukbang' broadcasts on the V Live streaming service. Bangtan Egypt members pooled their funds, put mealboxes together and distributed them to homeless people in their immediate locales. While this is a common charitable practice worldwide, it also recalls the practice in Egypt in which citizens donate meals, fund *mawa'ed al-rahman* (large meal gatherings) for those who cannot afford a full meal, and donate food essentials like flour, rice and beans, activities that take on a unique, Islamically influenced character during Ramadan, the month in which those who are able fast from dawn to sunset.[22] In other examples, fans have contributed to bail funds for women in debtors' prisons,[23] and donated funds for medical treatment for burn patients,[24] as well as medical supplies for hospitals.[25]

Fatima, one of the organizers with the Bangtan Egypt birthday projects, told me: 'We started doing these because we wanted to spread [BTS'] message': a message Bangtan Egypt sees as one of self-love and love for others regardless of nationality, religion or language. Motivation also comes from their pride as a fan community, and as concerned citizens in their material communities in Egypt. 'We are not just obsessed teenagers', Fatima commented in response to the stereotypical portrayal of K-pop fans. 'We want to give back to society', she said of their fan group, many of them in their teens and twenties.

Birthday projects like these, which involve deliberation, organizing and actions like pooling funds together, are powered by affect – or, as Hinck puts it, 'the close connection fans often feel towards their object of fandom.' In *Politics for the Love of Fandom* she defines this kind of engagement as 'fan-based

Image from a tweet: Indonesians watch a BTS performance while waiting at a Covid-19 vaccination drive sponsored by Indonesian BTS fan community Senyum Army, August 2021.

A street food vendor in Thailand hoists a birthday advertisement for actor Song Kang, part of a larger effort from Thai fans to sustain the country's small businesses in the midst of the Covid-19 pandemic, July 2021.

citizenship', or 'public engagement that emerges from a commitment to a fan-object.'[26] The congruence of love for the idol group and concern for issues in their local, material communities gives ways for 'fan citizen' communities to flourish. And even beyond their local communities, fans are engaging in transnational citizenship on issues like climate change.

Climate change and K-pop

At the end of 2020, BLACKPINK came out with a brief address on their YouTube channel, speaking on the importance of climate change ahead of COP26, the UN Climate Change Conference that took place in Glasgow in November 2021. As designated goodwill ambassadors of COP26, the members of BLACKPINK spoke about the erosion of natural habitats, the urgency of learning about climate change and the action needed to stop global warming. A month prior to the conference, they spoke again on the quickly deteriorating condition of the planet and the need to take action.

It is clear that their message ahead of COP26 resonated. In October 2021 a group of BLACKPINK fans in Indonesia gathered to plant mangroves in Jakarta over a period of several days, in an effort to help restore natural landscapes.[27] Other fans around the world were sharing their tree-planting initiatives via the hashtag #ClimateActionInYourArea.

In addition to BLACKPINK fans, other groups of K-pop fans are making global climate change their focus. Groups like KPOP 4 Planet and Kpop 4 Climate emerged, and are sharing educational materials about climate change, even material directly related to K-pop. Nurul Sarifah, an EXO fan and organizer with KPOP 4 Planet, says that K-pop fans' motivation for climate

change advocacy comes from the congruence of their love for K-pop and their growing concerns over the climate crisis. In 2021 she and her fellow fans from Indonesia and internationally 'decided to combine both of the things we love, K-pop and our planet'. Seeing fans across the world come together for the Black Lives Matter movement and engage in tree planting campaigns in honour of their favourite artists motivated Sarifah and fellow fans to start KPOP 4 Planet.

Recently, they began a petition to stop the construction of a coal power plant near Maengbang Beach in Korea (one of the settings for BTS's photoshoot for their 'Butter' single). Sarifah says, 'as K-pop fans are mostly made up of Gen Zs and Millennials, we are the ones facing the immediate impact of the climate crisis.'

Fans have also been advocating for the big production companies – namely HYBE, JYP, YG and SM Entertainment – to minimize their use of plastic and non-recyclable material in the manufacturing of merchandise and physical albums.[28] 'The solidarity all across borders is desperately needed for the climate crisis', Sarifah says.

Collective action in the age of Covid-19

The worldwide onset of the Covid-19 pandemic in early 2020 brought forth significant challenges in the Global South from a public health as well as a socio-economic standpoint. Fan groups continued to use their networks to aid their communities.

Thailand's K-pop fan communities modified a long-existing fan practice in an effort to support rickshaw drivers and street stalls that were facing economic hardship as a result of tourists not visiting the country due to the pandemic. Paying for and preparing billboard birthday ads in public spaces is common

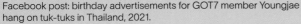

Facebook post: birthday advertisements for GOT7 member Youngjae hang on tuk-tuks in Thailand, 2021.

Tweet: Indonesian BTS fan community Senyum Army advertises in support of a Covid-19 vaccination drive in Jakarta, 2021.

fan practice around the world. In Thailand, these billboards are frequently found in the Bangkok subway system, but in the aftermath of the 2020 protests, in which the subway was shut down, fans started to make and fund ads to hang up at street stalls and on the back of rickshaws, instead of using subway billboards. In collaboration with Tuk-Up, an initiative started by university students, fans made the funding of K-pop ads on rickshaws a common fan practice overnight.[29]

A significant factor in facilitating such organizing is the elaborate social infrastructure that exists within fan communities. The same networks that fans reach out to in order to disseminate news about their favourite groups or streaming goals are being used to direct economic support to their fellow Thai citizens. One Thai K-pop fan believes this action is a rejection of existing systems. 'It's a political expression that we don't support capitalists', Pichaya Prachathomrong told Mashable.[30] Thai fan communities are creating a kind of 'fan citizenship' that is unique to the lived experience in Thailand.

This essay only scratches the surface of how entrenched K-pop fan civic engagement and activism are in K-pop fandoms in the Global South, particularly with regard to how fans organize and mobilize in material ways outside of online fan spaces. The above examples show not just an array of causes that fans care about, but also how civic engagement and 'fan citizenship' are becoming integral to the experience of being a K-pop fan. Lori Morimoto, professor of media studies at the University of Virginia, says that the way that fandom is 'very much wrapped up in your self-identity' is part of what makes the forming of social infrastructures so effective. Fandom is personal, but when working with fellow fans who identify and relate to what it means

to be a fan, it is possible to form a collective and achieve your goals, whether that involves supporting your favourite idol group or standing up to injustice.

Many fans will say that one of the most rewarding aspects of being a fan is the sense of community. Even in my own experience as a fan, witnessing this kind of collective action is a joyous and enthralling part of being in a fan community. In the autumn of 2018, when I was going to my first K-pop concert – to see BTS perform their first US stadium show at New York's Citi Field[31] – I saw One In An ARMY hold a canned-food drive. Fans showed up with canned soups, beans and other non-perishable food to donate to their fellow New Yorkers living without food security.

Looking at the way in which these community networks are established and what they are capable of perhaps explains the appeal of K-pop fandom. Beyond catchy music and elaborate music videos, affect is perhaps the strongest glue that bonds fan communities. Because of that affect, fans seamlessly work together to form a demographic that holds influence in their communities, and use that influence and social infrastructure to support their fellow citizens both within fandom and in their local areas.

Because of these factors, and because K-pop fans are growing in number internationally, we are likely to see more and more fans around the world mobilizing for political causes, charitable causes and everything in between. As Lori Morimoto told me, the way that 'fandom and activism intersect is through that one very common denominator that motivates us all as humans': love, for the artists and for our communities.

K-pop Choreography –
An Interview with Lia Kim

Lee Sol

From flash mobs to fans' cover-dance challenges, dance has been a major gateway to K-pop alongside music videos and idols who star as spectacular performers. The choreographer, a hitherto under-acknowledged industry creative, is now coming to the forefront with more K-pop acts tapping into the dancing fanbase and choreographers emerging themselves as original content creators. Lia Kim is one of the most prolific and successful K-pop choreographers, and has created mega-hit dance routines for BoA, Lee Hyo-ri, TWICE and Mamamoo, among many others. She is also the co-founder of 1MILLION Dance Studio, which has been offering dance classes to K-pop lovers and producing mesmerizing dance videos since 2014.

Lia went from training street dance every day after school at a local youth centre in Anyang, Korea, to teaching trainees at the biggest K-pop agencies and choreographing performances and music videos. Dance was an incredible outlet for the lonely teenager, who ended up choosing to follow her passion rather than go to college. She recalls: 'When I finished high school, my sole desire was to be the world best in street dancing. Nothing fascinated me more than the street dance did. Determined not to go to university like others, I geared my life towards honing my dance skill and winning the battle. Whenever I went to the competitions in the USA, Hongkong or Korea, I attended dance workshops, as many as possible, which were held by original dancers in hip-hop, popping, locking, waacking and other styles, such as Boogaloo Sam or The Original Lockers.'

Lia's relentless practice eventually won her the world dance competition 4 Da Next Level twice, in 2006 and 2007. However, the trophy did not drastically change her career or guarantee her life as a dancer. She felt stuck at that moment, but little did she know a new path was about to open for her as a choreographer. Entertainment companies including SM, JYP and YG were looking for a female dance teacher, and they reached out to Lia, who was then a member of a dance crew called Winners. At that time, Korean choreographers behind the scenes were given even less recognition than their western counterparts, but Lia's background in street dance and her voracious appetite for learning new dance genres would bring freshness to the industry. 'It was the early 2000s, even before Girls' Generation, Wonder Girls or 2NE1 debuted. The companies asked me to teach dance to trainees, especially popping, and I took the job to make a living. I was lucky enough to be one of the few who had had a fair amount of experience in the genre. The girls I met at the companies were just as young as I was, and we were all as ardent in what we were doing', says Lia. The companies assessed their trainees' progress at monthly evaluations, and Lia had to develop a new choreography each time so that the trainees could perform in front of the executives. 'That was a start. That was my first experience in K-pop choreography. The trainees inspired me a lot and I started to realize the joy of creating dance and sharing with others.'

In 2013 Lia had the chance to create a dance for Sunmi, a former Wonder Girls member whom Lia had known since she was a trainee at JYP and who was releasing her first single '24 Hours' through JYP's label. Heavily influenced by the modern dance that Lia was obsessed with at the time, Sunmi's sassy and seductive barefoot performance immediately received a vigorous response from fans and critics alike, which led to an array of remakes and covers by other celebrities and fan dancers. The dance borrowed expressive elements from modern dance while experimenting with asymmetric formation, which was rather unusual in K-pop performance. It was as successful a debut for Lia as a K-pop choreographer as it was for Sunmi's solo career.

No routine better illustrates Lia's versatility than 'TT' (2016) by TWICE. For this playful love song with its saccharine vocals and bubblegum visuals, Lia came up with a witty and adorable hand gesture that is as catchy as the song itself. She describes this piece as a quintessential K-pop dance: 'Compared to other dance routines, K-pop dance consists of meticulously

Lia Kim body-popping to 'Take Ü There (feat Kiesza)' by Jack Ü, outside the LA Philharmonic, 2016.

Stills from Sunmi's 2013 music video '24 Hours' show Lia Kim's use of modern dance to create a seductive and sassy effect.

divided small moves that closely support the lyrics. 'TT' is a good example. Among all the ideas for expressing the letter 'T', the chosen move worked the best. One can easily recognize it as the universal crying emoticon on which the song is based. It's very eye-catching, easy to remember, and effectively highlights the lyrics and the emotion as well.' The easily followed, memorable 'hook dance' – like the hand motion Lia describes developing for 'TT' – is the most iconic part of K-pop choreography. Often accompanying the chorus, these movements gained greater importance as short-form video platforms like TikTok became a major playground for viral cover dancers. Here, fitting core choreography into a 15–30 second time-frame is vital for captivating the viewer's attention.

For some acts, especially boy bands, Lia is renowned for some of K-pop's most intense choreographies. With these boy bands' highly choreographed, in-sync performances loaded with jumps, drops and stunts, the intensity of the performance and how the members pull it off frequently act as criteria for gauging how good they are. The dance for 'Cactus' (2017) by Ace, which Lia developed in collaboration with emerging choreographer Jung Koosung, consisted of a series of powerful rotational arm movements with fragmented steps, which the singers practised twice as fast as the original tempo to perfect the performance. 'When people come to me for a commission, I believe they aren't expecting a "mild" routine', Lia says. 'I enjoy creating the most complex and sumptuous pieces.' For her, it is easier to make a complicated routine than a simple, easily copiable one. Compromising is not her thing. 'The fact that the performers sing and dance simultaneously is not a valid excuse for easier choreography. Nobody asks for that nowadays, anyway', she adds.

When asked about recent changes in K-pop dance, Lia happily pointed out how diversified K-pop girl bands have become. Before 2010, 'The K-pop girl group dance moves came across as mostly cute and shy – and not just the dance. More fundamentally, the groups' concepts were largely homogenous. The way they presented was also similar because many groups had the same make-up artists, stylists and choreographers. But it has changed over time. 2NE1 played a pioneering role and we now have Jessi, Hyuna and Mamamoo all representing unique female figures. I'm happy to see different styles, music and dance being explored, along with different professionals playing a role in the industry.'

1MILLION Dance Studio, co-founded by Lia, and where she works as lead choreographer, employs around 25 individual choreographers of different styles, many of whom Lia met when creating guide videos for commissions. Upon receiving a project request, Lia assesses which of the studio's choreographers would best suit the song. Once she has decided whether or not to undertake the project and with whom she would collaborate, the actual choreographing process is carried out in an astonishingly short period of time: it takes only three days to create a routine for a three- or four-minute track. A draft video with dancers is then sent to the agencies to assess. Once the studio has given its approval, Lia or other dancers in her team teach the routine to band members. Due to the quick turnaround, the dancers who draft and teach choreography are not necessarily those who perform onstage or in music videos: depending on their particular skills, some show more strength in performing while others are better suited to directing. In general, it takes between two and four weeks for a K-pop act to master a routine and shoot the music video.

When Lia choreographs, she starts by finding the right character for the singer. Listening to the song repeatedly, she seeks to understand the concept or the 'worldview': an extensive background narrative that some K-pop bands eagerly embrace. Then she creates moves for the most significant part of the song, which varies from track to track. Often it is the hook – the catchiest part of the song – but not always. In the case of Hwasa's 'Maria' (2020), for example, Lia started with the intro,

Lia Kim at 1MILLION Dance Studio, Seoul, in 2020, sharing her choreography for Earth, Wind & Fire's 'September' (1978).

K-Pop and Fandom

Stills from the music video 'Until We Rise Again', 2020, choreographed by Lia Kim, a collaboration between 1MILLION Dance Studio and the Ministry of Culture, Sports and Tourism Republic of Korea.

developing a premise in which Hwasa breaks the fetters that have been holding her back and arises as her powerful true self. Without the need for fancy props or splendid costumes, Lia's choreography ensured the performance convincingly encapsulated the essence of the song.

Before the Covid-19 pandemic hit, dance classes at 1MILLION Dance Studio were full of K-pop enthusiasts from all around the world. Since Lia began uploading videos of the classes to YouTube, their global popularity had skyrocketed. Lia's original purpose for the channel was to document the choreographies and the dance classes whose ephemerality she always felt sorry for. 'The choreographers, and the dancers in general, have been suffering from so little regard in K-pop', she laments. 'When you watch music programmes on TV, the credits list the songwriter, the lyricst, but never the choreographer. People easily forget how much time and creativity is put into a work of dance. And there's no sense of copyright or protection whatsoever regarding choreography.' Uploading to YouTube was a way of archiving the studio's works and making their presence known to a broader public. 'We don't upload a dance that we didn't produce ourselves', says Lia. 'I didn't expect the channel to be so popular, though. People stumbled upon us when listening to music and ended up appreciating the performance and enjoying the pure energy of the dance classes.' Sometimes, the channel's playlist acts as a portfolio that the agencies browse to find the right choreographer for a new project. 'We're a whole creative bunch. We plan our content together and create videos to promote ourselves.'

Commissioned by the Ministry of Culture, Sports and Tourism Republic of Korea, in summer 2020 the studio made a performance video titled 'Until We Rise Again'. With Lia featured as lead dancer, the crew performs in protective suits with masks on, while their detached formation suggests social distancing. The performance expresses a shared frustration and collective longing for normality; it ends with the dancers throwing off their protection and cuddling up, which provides a sort of catharsis to viewers. The video ranked as one of the most-watched policy-promotion videos of the year.

The stage for Lia's imagination is not limited to the video platform. In 2021 Zepeto, a Korean avatar simulation app with over 200 million global users, incorporated her dance moves as an item. No matter how poor dancers the players are in real life, in this metaverse they can easily pull off the dance moves exactly like Lia within a few clicks. Technology has always been a source of inspiration to Lia: for her photo book *Reality, No Reality* (2020), a collaboration with photographer Cho Gi-Seok, she appeared as a cyborg. 'I've always wanted to create something that involves robots and AI because I've always been intrigued by future-related things. I'm eager to know what kind of world we're going to live in. That's a theme I want to explore in my future work.'

November 2021

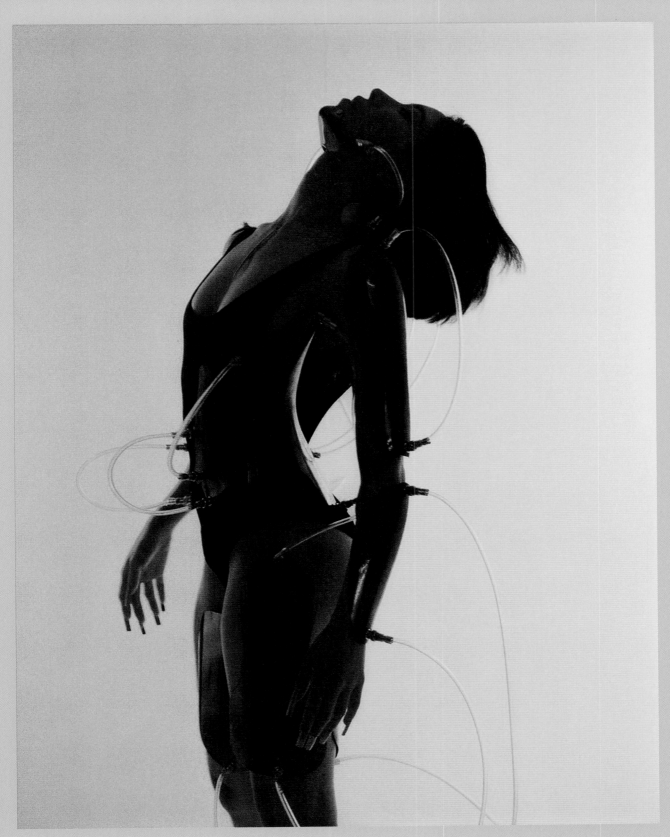

Photograph of Lia Kim by Cho Gi-Seok for Kim's 2020 book *Reality, No Reality*.

K-pop's Fictional Universe: Symbols and Hidden Clues in K-pop Music Videos

Dasom Sung

Still from EXO's 'Mama', 2012, showing Suho controlling water. Each EXO member's superpower is portrayed in this music video.

Ever since Buggles's aptly titled 'Video Killed the Radio Star' launched MTV, the first 24-hour music video channel, music's visual aspect has often been regarded as equally important as its sound. With the advent of the internet, online platforms like YouTube and Vimeo further facilitated the distribution of music videos, enabling wide access to material from all over the world. Nowadays, the music video is one of the most significant mediums in the global music business.

There are many types of music video: from straightforward footage of the musicians' performance[1] to clips from existing movies; from narrative-led film[2] to experimentally fragmented montages;[3] from backstage footage[4] to animation.[5] After 2010, a new genre arrived courtesy of K-pop: the Fictional Universe.

The Fictional Universe is not an unfamiliar idea. Simply put, it is a fictional narrative that develops via an internally consistent setting. It has been widely applied in pop culture: in fantasy novels, Japanese animations and the Marvel Cinematic Universe, among others. We can find precedents in music as well. One of the most notable is David Bowie's concept album *The Rise and Fall of Ziggy Stardust and the Spiders from Mars* (1972), in which Bowie's alter ego, the fictional rock star Ziggy Stardust, is sent to Earth as a messenger from Mars to save the world from the apocalypse. Other examples might be the Spice Girls, who presented themselves as distinctive characters – Ginger, Sporty, Posh, Scary and Baby – or Gorillaz, who introduced a new form of band, with virtual cartoon characters standing onstage representing real performers.

In K-pop, this strategy has been powerfully developed, and helped to propel K-pop culture in a whole new direction. K-pop idols have embodied and expanded distinctive virtual identities, placing K-pop culture in a unique and original position. Some of the most popular K-pop groups, such as EXO, Red Velvet, Seventeen, BTS and aespa, are equipped from their debut with their own creative and unique narratives.

The first group to present such a total and impressive narrative was EXO, who struck the K-pop world like a comet in 2012. According to their Fictional Universe, EXO hailed from an unknown exoplanet and each member possessed a supernatural power, from being able to control water, light, fire or wind to having extraordinary strength. EXO's Fictional Universe was meticulously designed, boasting so many details that 23 teaser trailers appeared even before the release of their first EP, 'Mama'. The 'Mama' music video describes the essence of EXO's narrative as well as each member's supernatural power; numerous subsequent music videos revealed that the individual members' superpowers could be used collectively to construct an expanded universe, with many hidden clues scattered through different music videos shaping the consistent elements and mythology of this Fictional Universe, in which pairs of members live parallel existences and are only able to make contact with their counterparts on days of the sun's total eclipse.[6] EXO took the lead in the K-pop Fictional Universe craze by giving fans the pleasure of not only listening to songs and watching performances, but also actively finding and interpreting symbols, a practice that became known as 'EXO-logy' among fans. This helped EXO to become one of the representative idol groups of the 2010s, and they were the first band in 12 years to achieve a million album sales in the Korean music industry.

The Fictional Universe concept may seem unnecessarily complicated, but as the idol industry in Korea boomed and the market became overcrowded with talented groups, Fictional Universes allowed each idol group to differentiate itself with a specific narrative. Shining a spotlight on each member to make them distinctive and attractive 'idols' with mystical but compelling backstories expands and deepens groups' appeal. Over time, people began to focus on the narratives, growing into communities of loyal fans as they exchanged their interpretations of the Fictional Universe. The more scattered the clues of a Fictional

A still from the extended version of BTS's 2018 music video 'Fake Love' (above) shows the band masked and hooded. This contrasts with the confident colours of 'Idol', released later the same year (below).

Universe and the more complicated the narrative, the more eager fans are to explore the universe and find the threads within.

The fragmented nature of K-pop's Fictional Universes, with its multiple metaphors and cues, draws on the visual language of music videos: audiences are comfortable with the fact that music videos can lack causal sequences, narrative connections and coherence in characters' emotions, with editing determined by the beat and rhythm of the music rather than a single storyline, and with characters' frequent costume changes (and sometimes their refusal to play a single identity). Often, the lyrics are not even aligned with the images. This makes the music video a suitable medium to convey a Fictional Universe, avoiding an integrated story to instead promote the song and the musician's originality, preferably through disrupted, distracted, divorced montages that can encompass secret narratives. Music videos from one K-pop group usually refer to each other to construct greater meaning. We can discern meaning through the fractured images in a single video, but with further variations and repetitions of symbols, images from one video can be connected to similar images from other videos to establish a wider meaning and stronger narrative.

These characteristics are most evident in BTS's music videos. Following EXO, BTS was the group that firmly rooted Fictional Universe culture in the idol market. In their videos and the 'BTS Universe', BTS depict the process of growing up, little by little. Important symbols recur throughout BTS's videos.[7] In 'Fake Love' (2018), BTS pretend to love themselves for self-defence but suffer inside; the members wear black robes and hide their faces with masks to cover their true feelings. In 'Blood Sweat & Tears' (2016) they share a secret banquet at a large table, in a similarly sequestered mood. However, in 'Idol' (2018) they move on to growth, with vivid, explosive colours conveying a message of solidarity and positivity.[8] The table from 'Blood Sweat & Tears' reappears here, but instead of holding an isolated banquet BTS joyfully invite the audience to share in it, gazing straight at the screen. The members, who have gained self-confidence by expanding their affection for each other, now show their love for

Stills from aespa's music video 'Savage', 2021, showing aespa members' arch-enemy Black Mamba, symbolized by a venomous snake.

everyone. The core theme of BTS's music – having compassion, healing through music in solidarity with others – is emphasized through their music videos. BTS's worldwide popularity is the result of a combination of factors, including performance talent and active communication with fans via social media, but the power of the Fictional Universe cannot be ignored. When the fictional narrative of BTS reached its peak and the boys achieved full growth (in 'Dynamite', 2020), BTS accomplished massive success in reality as well.[9]

Aespa debuted in 2020. Their name means 'face another self and experience a new world through an avatar' and, using avatars alongside their 'real life' band members, aespa have expanded their universe to the virtual world of unlimited space. For aespa, the Fictional Universe is not just an advertising tool to promote the group; instead, it is a core identity, and announces the birth of the 'next level' K-pop idol.

In aespa's Fictional Universe, everyone has their own avatar – 'ae' – created from personal information shared online.

The short film aespa, *ep1. Black Mamba*, released before the band's debut, tells the story of how the villainous Black Mamba prevents the connection between people and ae, bringing chaos and diffusing her evil through ae. Aespa first recognize Black Mamba's powers ('Black Mamba', 2020),[10] then travel to KWANGYA[11] to find her ('Next Level', 2021) and defeat her using their special superpowers ('Savage', 2021). With its compelling narrative, 'Black Mamba' became the fastest debut music video by a K-pop act to reach 100 million views on YouTube.

The Fictional Universe is clearly an appealing and effective ploy. Indeed, videos uploaded to YouTube in which fans share their interpretations of hidden elements and clues in each idol group's music videos are more numerous and popular than YouTube videos analyzing the groups' lyrics. This shows that today's K-pop fans value the visual experience as much as, or possibly more than, the auditory experience. The Fictional Universe is like a special lens that makes things visible to those in the know; and the more you know, the more apparent it becomes.

In aespa's 'Black Mamba' music video, 2021, Ning Ning is shown as a hacker who fights against the cyber-attacks by Black Mamba.

K-pop and YouTube

Sun Lee

Promtional poster for *BLACKPINK: THE SHOW*, 2021. This online concert was a collaboration between YG Entertainment and YouTube, and allowed audiences to connect with the artists during the restrictions of the Covid-19 pandemic.

Music has always been an integral part of YouTube. A lot of our users come to YouTube to enjoy their favourite music. In fact, each month more than two billion logged-in viewers watch a music video on YouTube. We understand and appreciate how music enriches the content on our platform, and are doing our best to provide a better experience for our users as well as to support music labels, aggregators and distributors around the world.

For our users, we strive to provide them with the best possible music experience. On YouTube, users can access official music videos, live performances, cover songs and much more. We have enhanced the experience with YouTube Music, our dedicated music streaming service, offering exclusive live events, access to official songs and albums, as well as deep cuts, live performances and remixes. We also offer personalized playlists, as well as thousands of playlists across different moods, genres and moments.

I would also like to highlight the healthy partnership we have with the music industry. Across just 12 months, from June 2020 to June 2021, we paid over US$4 billion to the music industry. Over 30 percent of this came from user-generated content, which proves that fan-powered videos help artists grow their audiences and revenue. To help the industry find new sources of revenue, YouTube launched direct-to-fan products such as merch, ticketing, memberships and virtual ticketed events.

In January 2021 YouTube partnered with BLACKPINK for a paid virtual concert titled *THE SHOW*. Nearly 280,000 channel memberships across 81 countries were sold for this event, and BLACKPINK's channel gained 2.7 million new subscribers. The pandemic was the biggest challenge to carrying out *THE SHOW*. It had originally been scheduled to take place at the end of 2020, but we had to postpone the concert to late January 2021 as the government placed stricter restrictions on using the concert venue due to the worsening Covid-19 situation. As we return to normal, we once again see live concerts where artists can interact with their fans offline. However, I do not think this will completely offset the demand for online concerts: K-pop labels, who have been, and will be, agile in adopting new technologies to scale up their businesses, will leverage the technology to supplement offline concerts by diversifying content, expanding the audience and maximizing their revenue. K-pop labels will be able to re-create live concerts online with augmented visual effects, and artists will be able to meet their fans in more regions via new online components such as multi-camera streaming and real-time chat.

Building the best music experience for fans and empowering all artists to grow their careers are mission-critical for us. This is why YouTube has been supporting artists and helping them amplify and spread their music while expanding their fanbases. We have been running diverse programmes including Foundry, our annual global artist development programme, to assist independent artists, help them find and engage fans and build careers on their own terms. As part of the programme, artists receive dedicated partner support from YouTube, and seed funding invested into the development of their content. The combination of access to resources and brilliant teams enables artists to create and launch their music with greater impact and global reach. SE SO NEON were one of Foundry's acts in 2021 and we will continue to collaborate with K-pop artists in 2022 and beyond.

We also run Artist on the Rise, a programme dedicated to supporting up-and-coming artists, creating special videos.[1] In addition, we've been assisting artists in promoting their new albums through the RELEASED scheme, enhancing their discoverability on YouTube.

Promotional image for YouTube's behind-the-scenes series *TWICE: Seize the Light*, 2020.

As the Director of Music Partnerships for Korea and Greater China & Artist Relations for APAC, my job is to help music partners in the Asia-Pacific (APAC) region grow their businesses and fanbases on YouTube. It includes building partnerships with new music labels and aggregators, supporting existing partners by identifying opportunities for them to maximize their businesses and creating new initiatives for partners. I also work with music partnerships managers within YouTube APAC to promote local artists in and out of the markets.

More specifically, I identify key artists and their major activities, discuss how to amplify their activities with local and global teams, and coordinate internal and external communications. We partnered with BTS before they became big and released the YouTube Originals show *Burn the Stage* in 2018, showing behind-the-scenes footage of their 2017 world tour. I work both on localizing global campaigns for the APAC markets and on bringing local ideas to our global teams to amplify scale and coverage. As many K-pop artists are expanding their global presence, I am spending more time these days on transnational promotions.

I am often asked why K-pop has become so popular across the globe. As a partnerships manager who has worked very closely with a lot of K-pop labels, I think what makes K-pop truly special is these labels' strategy and their investment in globalization. Major labels carry out global talent scouts and train talented individuals for years before their debut; in addition, they work with local and international producers to develop tailored success formulas for their artists. This is not limited to music and performances: K-pop artists have stage names that are easy for foreigners to pronounce, and many of them learn foreign languages to be able to communicate with their fans around the world. And, of course, they are dedicated to being the best they can be on the musical side as well, from perfecting their vocals to state-of-the-art stage performances. YouTube

Originals shows such as *BTS: Burn The Stage* and *TWICE: Seize the Light* (2020) offer an exclusive behind-the-scenes sneak peek at this incredible process.

Another noteworthy factor is that K-pop artists are very savvy at using YouTube and other social media platforms to connect with their fans. Jennie from BLACKPINK runs a personal YouTube channel that gained 7.7 million subscribers in just one year. Artists like this have built communities and robust fan cultures all over the globe, making sure to connect with their fans as much as possible despite their hectic schedules. Nowadays, K-pop audition programmes include global fan votes in the judging process, so fans feel part of their favourite artists' journey from their debut, and K-pop artists appreciate their fans for supporting them throughout their career, creating a very special bond between them.

K-pop will continue to evolve and create new trends; K-pop labels will leverage technologies to reach and engage more broadly with fans, beyond borders and generations. For example, YouTube recently kicked off a remastering project with SM Entertainment. By upgrading the quality of K-pop music videos from the 1990s and 2000s, we aim to diversify K-pop music catalogues on YouTube and contribute to the growth of the Korean music business.

Many people think that the K-pop phenomenon began with PSY and 'Gangnam Style'. However, it started even earlier. YouTube has been working closely with Korean music partners for over 15 years, helping them strengthen their global presence. In 2012 YouTube, in association with a Korean broadcaster, co-hosted the *Korean Music Wave in Google* concert at the Shoreline Amphitheatre near Google's headquarters in Mountain View, California. More than 25,000 fans and casual listeners gathered to see K-pop artists perform. It was also livestreamed on YouTube to an audience of fans around the world.

MBC x Google K-pop concert in Mountain View, California, 2012.

The year 2012 was incredible for K-pop: people became curious about PSY and started discovering more Korean artists and tracks on YouTube. Seeing this rise in demand, Korean labels worked hard to perfect their artist training programmes and invested further in music production. And this led the K-pop trend to evolve into the enormous global cultural phenomenon that we see today.

Through the power of fan engagement and global exposure on YouTube, K-pop has broken many records, starting with PSY's 'Gangnam Style' reaching two billion views. On our All-Time Top 24 Hour Music Debuts chart, nine out of ten music videos are from K-pop artists (as of June 2022). K-pop labels choose YouTube as the primary channel on which to release a new music video, using YouTube Premiere to drive fans to the release. In 2020 BTS reached more than 100 million views 24 hours after the release of 'Dynamite', then promptly broke their record a year later with 'Butter' reaching 108 million views. Meanwhile, BLACKPINK's YouTube channel is now the most subscribed official artist channel on YouTube. Both as a Korean and as a music partnership manager at YouTube, it is truly amazing for me to see K-pop thrive on YouTube.

This phenomenon could be replicated elsewhere, but only if the level of effort and investment that the Korean music industry has put in over the past few decades is matched. K-pop labels have developed entirely new success formulae on YouTube and many other online platforms, and they will definitely be of help to non-Korean labels in their quest for the global market.

YouTube's mission is to support artists and music industries around the world in amplifying their music and expanding their fanbases, and we hope to be part of many more global music trends to come.

From left, Lee Sung-su, co-CEO of SM Entertainment, aespa's Karina and Giselle, and Sun Lee at an online event to mark the launch of the SM/YouTube remastering project, 2021.

Pretty Tough: The Aesthetics of K-pop Masculinities

Joanna Elfving-Hwang

To those unfamiliar with K-pop, the physical aesthetics of male idols may seem at first glance 'soft' or perhaps even effeminate. For K-pop fans, however, the idols simply represent another masculine aesthetic.

Another frequent misinterpretation of male idols' onstage and even offstage aesthetics is that they represent an alternative – or possibly a threat – to normative Korean masculinity. In fact, onstage performances of K-pop masculinity should be understood primarily as part of the K-pop genre's wider visual aesthetic, which may or may not be emulated by young men, but which are certainly not intended to redefine normative masculinity in Korea. Closer inspection of how aesthetics are utilized in K-pop music videos soon reveals that what initially may appear as 'soft masculinity' signifies what could be more accurately termed 'soft-hard', designed to appeal to multiple potential audiences. K-pop is, after all, produced for the consumption of fans and, as such, it aims to reach the broadest possible audience.

Therefore, the key to understanding the visual appeal of K-pop masculinities is to recognize that fans consume images of their idols not simply as objects of desire, but also as familiar 'semiotic signs' integral to the K-pop package. While there tends to be a focus on emphasizing the eye, clean features with flawless skin, muscular bodies and athleticism, the interpretation of these signifiers can be as diverse as the global K-pop fan-base itself. In other words, there is no one way of 'reading' K-pop male beauty because, increasingly, consumers of K-pop are invited to attach their own meanings to the aesthetic as each fan sees fit.

In this essay, I illustrate how the male idols' appearances, fashions and dance choreographies have evolved from earlier 'soft' boy-group aesthetics – which focused on a cute image designed to appeal exclusively to primarily Korean teenage girl audiences and their desiring gaze – to a globally consumable style that remains 'soft' yet emphasizes the hypermasculinity and athleticism of the idols, as well as positioning them as examples of successful living in an increasingly confusing social world. This ensures that although the idols are undoubtedly style icons, they are not simply stylized celebrities to be adored from afar; their appearance is not designed to threaten or to create distance by being impossibly perfect, but to encourage fans to form a strong emotional attachment to their chosen idol. In many ways, then, K-pop fandoms are key to understanding how idols as gendered semiotic signs are intended to be consumed and interpreted.

So how did the story of Korean male idols and fandoms begin? Following the phenomenal success of the first Korean hip-hop band Seo Taiji and Boys in the early 1990s, some Korean music producers identified a lucrative market in boy bands created to appeal specifically to teenage girl consumers. These did not, however, simply take their cue from popular boy bands in the west such as Take That, Backstreet Boys and *NSYNC. The incorporation of the Japanese *aidoru* (idol) system in the Korean entertainment industry means that fandoms have become an important part of the idol industry, with the mostly female fans' responses to promotional teasers or idol appearances helping to shape bands, even before a first single is released.

Soo-Man Lee (pp. 48–53) was the first producer to introduce a complete idol band production system incorporating the full cycle of auditioning, styling, training, producing and managing an idol group with distinct assigned stage 'personalities' or roles in the group. In 1996 Hi-five of Teenagers (H.O.T.) released their single 'Candy'. The song was an instant hit, selling 800,000 copies in the first 100 days of release.[1] H.O.T. brought an entirely new stage aesthetic and representation of stage masculinity to Korean music; unlike the moody or detached attitude of previous popular male singers, the group's music video and stage performances were meant to attract high school students, and indeed the image of five bright, happy, non-threatening teenage boys turned out to be highly appealing. The music video itself was an explosion of bright colours: amid footage of the band members frolicking

A promotional shot for H.O.T.'s 1996 single 'Candy' (above) showcases a friendly, accessible image for the band, while the cover of the album from which it comes, *We Hate All Kinds of Violence* (below), conveys a more introspective mood.

Rain performs at his world tour premiere in Seoul, October 2006, at a time when muscular torsos were becoming a common sight in K-pop performances.

in a popular amusement park, extreme close-ups show the band members' boyish friendly faces as they profess eternal devotion to the girl of their dreams. This representation of K-pop masculinity made H.O.T. the first band in Korea to intentionally seek to reduce the distance between fans and idol, offering fans the tantalizing fantasy of an accessible and idealized boyfriend.

H.O.T.'s success demonstrated to the emerging industry that a well-designed idol concept that was non-threatening and created a sense of imagined intimacy could attract loyal fandoms, and bands such as S.E.S. (1997), SHINWA (1998), FLY TO THE SKY (1999) and g.o.d. (an acronym for 'Groove Overdose', 1999) followed in quick succession. With the help of professional composers, lyricists, choreographers and stylists, the aesthetics of these early bands focused less on sex appeal and more on approachability and a friendly teenage look. Cultivating closeness-at-a-distance between fans and idols continued to be a ticket to success.

Initially, the focus of the aesthetic appeal was on generating short-term profits and creating a consumable item appealing to specific Korean audiences. The preferred stage aesthetic changed, however, as K-pop began to garner international recognition and fandoms, particularly from the mid-2000s. While the facial aesthetic remained youthful and approachable, the bodies of K-pop male idols became increasingly muscular, a shift highlighted by powerful dance moves and the use of low-angle view shots and zoom-ins to amplify the dynamic nature of the choreography. Their facial features might have been soft

and their body hair minimal, but onstage and in music video close-ups, their chiselled midriffs left the viewers and fans in no doubt about their idols' strength and athleticism.

However, it was the emergence of new social media platforms in the first decade of the 2000s that truly revolutionized fan–idol relationships, effectively putting fandoms at the centre of the idol industry ecosystem. In relation to K-pop aesthetics, fandoms have emerged as communities within which stage performances and their implied meanings are collectively interpreted and generated. K-pop fandoms do not simply consume images of their idols, but play a role in creating a web of implied knowledge about the idols as imagined 'significant others', allowing their members to feel that they have real and meaningful interactions with their idols online. This relationship, in which the emotional investment is real but one-sided, is known as a 'parasocial relationship'.[2]

With online social media and streaming websites meaning that idols are now expected to be available 24/7, fans can also gain access to heavily curated behind-the-scenes moments with the idol. These live, intimate performances, often filmed on a mobile phone or webcam, allow individual fans to post comments for the idol to read and respond to in real time while livestreaming. Of course, this too is a performance of intimacy aimed at reducing the distance between the fan and the idol, who is now both an object of desire and a friendly, approachable significant other. Yet because of this performance of both onstage (often openly sexy and hypermasculine yet emotionally available and vulnerable) and offstage (still staged but appearing

An image for ATEEZ's music video 'Eternal Sunshine' contrasts with those taken for 'Deja Vu' (both 2021; see overleaf).
The band switches between a colourful and approachable stage image, and a darker, strong and hypermasculine one.

ATEEZ in a promotional image for 'Deja Vu', 2021.

authentic) masculinity, the aesthetics of K-pop masculinity have become more diverse in recent years, with fans coming to feel that they *know* the 'real' idol behind the stage persona. This has allowed artists, stylists and choreographers to experiment with an ever-increasing repertoire of aesthetic choices without alienating the fans.

For example, ATEEZ (an acronym for 'A TEEnager Z'), an idol band that debuted in 2018 and soon won a significant international following, began building a fanbase even before launching their first single. Their management company, KQ Entertainment, introduced the boy band to fans through a series of YouTube videos, followed by a reality TV show in the run-up to their actual debut six months later. By then, the ATEEZ fandom was already in place and keenly following the band's next steps.

ATEEZ's physical aesthetics are highly diverse and make heavy use of make-up, fashion and colour, as well as choreography that emphasizes strong hip-hop movements and stylized references to traditional Korean culture in videos with a darker urban colour scheme. As such, ATEEZ follows what has come to define the visual aesthetic of K-pop music videos, which are designed to be visually arresting while reducing the emotional distance between the idol and the viewer. The cinematography typically alternates between wide shots that emphasize impossibly muscular and athletic bodies skilfully executing powerful dance moves in unison, and close-ups of the idols' perfectly made-up faces that highlight moments of vulnerability and emotional availability – demonstrating, respectively, the idol as an object of desire onstage and simultaneously approachable and relatable offstage.

BTS, arguably the most famous idol band in the world today,

are another example of how implied knowledge informs viewers' readings of gendered visual signifiers in the group's stage and music video appearances. The fans understand, through studying the band members' views and values as espoused in reality TV shows, Instagram messages and livestreaming on the band's dedicated VLive channel, that the powerful hypermasculine image of BTS's music video performances is intended to entertain but not to intimidate. 'Kinetic Manifesto' (2020) is an example of a 'soft-hard' choreography and cinematography that borrows from both hip-hop and commercial jazz dance styles, and whose narrative relies on fans' familiarity with the backstory to the piece. While the moving camera cuts frequently from wide-angle shots showing powerful synchronized group choreographies to travelling shots that highlight the strong moves of the individual band members, the semiotics of the video reveal it to be a call to conquer one's fears and find self-acceptance. When violence arises in a storyline, it is used to achieve not submission but justice for others. In many ways, then, K-pop masculinity and the narrative arcs of these videos are more traditional than many might initially think; they can even be seen to borrow from the superhero genre, combining dispays of athleticism with a message of social justice.

The visual aesthetics of K-pop masculinities are therefore less about the loss of hard masculinity and more about expanding the possibilities for how masculinities are performed onstage and imagined offstage. As such, they represent a fantasy, rather than an imitation or redefining of normative Korean masculinity. What is more, as the bold aesthetics of K-pop increasingly influence the global pop scene, they are also broadening global definitions of attractive and appealing stage masculinity.

For BTS's music video '"ON" – Kinetic Manifesto: Come Prima', 2020, a combination of wide-angle and close-up shots highlights powerful dance choreography that is designed to project both strength and self-belief.

K-Beauty and Fashion
K-뷰티와 패션

In 2014 headlines were made when the K-drama *My Love from the Star* sparked a craze for the Jimmy Choo Anthracite pumps worn by its main character. The shoes swiftly sold out across Asia, Europe and America, soon followed by a worldwide shortage of the coral lipstick from YSL wrongly rumoured to be worn by the actress.[1] This collateral success took the fashion houses, and everyone, by surprise. Recognizing the lucrative potential offered by K-dramas and K-pop, K-beauty and fashion soon expanded their presence in these sectors. Products were woven into plot narratives, shaping the protagonist's career and enhancing their charisma, ultimately strengthening K-dramas and K-pop's beauty and fashion credentials, which in turn drew in a wider audience for all sectors involved.

K-beauty industries have steadily grown in the past decade, bolstered by campaigns fronted by K-celebrities with flawless skin and sustained by a plethora of step-by-step tutorials and rave reviews by online beauty enthusiasts on YouTube. Despite a small decline in sales during the pandemic, Korea ranked third in the cosmetics export market in 2020:[2] as K-beauty mainly targets a healthy skincare regimen with well-being in mind, these products remained in demand for tackling skin outbreaks caused by wearing masks, or to indulge in self-pampering during lengthy lockdowns. The same year, Korea launched the world's first customized cosmetic service, which saw shops selling fluid foundations, serums and 3D-printed hydrogel masks tailor-made for the consumer's skin colour, condition and face shape using state-of-the-art technology. This reinforces the reputation of K-beauty products being ahead of their time, a consequence of heavy investments in cosmetics R&D aimed at constantly pushing boundaries and innovating in the field.

These new developments nonetheless remain anchored in historical precedents and traditions, building on centuries-old formulas and ingredients to provide new ranges fit for modern living conditions (see Yoojin Choi, pp. 158–67). In particular, men's cosmetics have bloomed thanks to the concept of new masculinity brought in by hallyu; figures like G-Dragon, Kang Daniel and Lee Dong-wook have epitomized and propagated the image of *kkonminam* 'flower-boy' soft masculinity around the world, helping normalize men's cosmetics in the beauty industry.

Korean culture has long been concerned with public image. In Joseon Korea maintaining a proper appearance was a moral obligation that expressed one's social status and virtue, rather than merely a sign of vanity.[3] This was in addition to the ancient belief that facial features were intimately connected to one's fate (*gwansang*),[4] which continues to have a strong influence in today's saturated and ageist job and wedding markets in Korea: a face without inauspicious features and which conveys youth and vitality is considered an advantage in getting ahead of the competition.[5] Beyond feminist or postcolonial discourses, it is in this context that cosmetic surgery – an umbrella term covering services provided by dermatological clinics, beauty salons and plastic surgery clinics, and popular with both men and women – has been assimilated into Korean society.[6] Highly prominent K-pop idols have become new beacons of beauty and success that drastically diverge from traditional models: the moon face, interpreted as a fertility symbol during the Joseon dynasty, has been replaced by an idol's smaller face with a sharp V chin line, while the double eyelid that is seen to emphasize youth and alertness is preferred over the mono-eyelid.[7] The prestige once attributed to professions like medicine, law or architecture, which required prolonged study and the moral fortitude advocated by Joseon Neo-Confucianism, is now associated with K-pop idols and celebrities, thanks to their enviable social standing and international recognition. These glitterati of the entertainment world, however, have intensified the pressure to look a certain way,[8] while also positioning Korea as a destination of choice for medical tourism.

Hanbok imagined through hallyu

With the growing popularity of the Korean Wave, hanbok, the national costume, has enjoyed a resurgence aided by colourful K-dramas and flamboyant K-pop performances that have expanded hanbok's aesthetic appeal while underscoring its Korean origin. Hanbok design and style have constantly evolved with the fashion of the time (see Yunah Lee, pp. 168–75), and present-day hanbok takes its shape from the late Joseon dynasty (1392–1910). It consists primarily of a jacket with lightly curved sleeves tied with sashes (*jeogori*), worn by men over a pair of roomy trousers (*baji*) and by women with a voluminous floor-length wrapping skirt (*chima*). By the 1970s, Euro-American clothing had become the most prevalent daily wear in Korea, leaving hanbok reserved for formal occasions and celebrations. Various attempts since then to make it suitable for daily life met with a lukewarm reception.

G-Dragon wearing Chanel on the cover of the August 2016 editon of *Vogue Korea*, photographed by Karl Lagerfeld.

Attributed to Chae Yong-shin, an early twentieth-century eight-panel folding screen shows 'Eight Beauties of the Joseon dynasty' with their fashionable hairstyles and voluminous wrapping skirts (*chima*).

A new appreciation for hanbok in Korea gained ground in the mid-2000s, when the *manhwa* series *Goong* and the historical TV drama *Hwang Jini* began to take creative licence with factual accuracy regarding hanbok's traditional design.[9] *Goong*, Park So-hee's romantic comedy set in the royal palace of an imaginary Korean Kingdom, enthralled teenage girls with its portrayal of a spirited high-school heroine, and especially her memorable wardrobe of modern 'fusion' hanbok and accessories (see p. 169). Park rejuvenated the hanbok's grown-up elegance and solemn decorum by blending casual western garments and hanbok formal components, a fresh and playful styling that resonated with the young audience. In 2006 *Goong* was adapted for an equally successful TV drama, *Princess Hours*, which brought to life this modernized hanbok.

The same year, another TV drama offered a spectacular parade of lavish modern hanbok. The historical drama *Hwang Jini* told the story of the most eminent *gisaeng* (female court entertainer) of the Joseon dynasty, who lived during the sixteenth century. Despite originating from the lowest class of slaves and servants, *gisaeng* were highly educated and trained performing artists who entertained royalty and *yangban*, the ruling upper classes. In a hierarchical and gender-segregated society where women were relegated to the back of house and where upward social mobility was virtually non-existent, *gisaeng* held a unique position: considered the beauty and fashion influencers of the time, they enjoyed a level of freedom unfathomable to other women. It was precisely this audacious spirit and freedom that hanbok designer Kim Hye-soon endeavoured to capture for the TV drama by introducing contemporary fabric, bold decorative patterns and unusual colour combinations into the silhouette of eighteenth-century hanbok.[10] The clothes became an overnight sensation: the TV series spawned an exhibition and book on its hanbok (as well as a feature-film adaptation the following year), while Kim noted an increase in student applications to the Korean costume departments at universities where she taught.[11] Despite a conservative backlash claiming that these anachronistic features undermined hanbok's original subtle beauty and national identity, this modernizing trend continued to gain traction in the entertainment and fashion worlds under the name of 'new hanbok' (*sin hanbok*).

Coinciding with the release of the *Hwang Jini* movie in 2007, the cover of *Vogue Korea* featured for the first time in its history not only a Korean celebrity – the movie's star, Song Hye-kyo – but also one wearing new hanbok. The final look was styled in Paris by a team of high-profile international experts, then photographed by Paolo Roversi. The cover drew criticism for perpetuating a nineteenth-century orientalist gaze that exoticized the *gisaeng*. Nevertheless, hanbok was visibly making forays into the world of high-end fashion magazines, stepping up out of its ethnic dress category. In this context, Suh Younghee, a former stylist and contributing editor to *Vogue Korea*, has been a key figure in challenging the common perception of hanbok as outmoded, entrenched in tradition and nationalism. Since 2006, stunning *Vogue* editorial photos have normalized her thought-provoking new hanbok styling, demonstrating its relevance to contemporary lifestyle, as well as its artistic potential. Mixing hanbok with both low- and high-end Euro-American fashion to emphasize its versatility and Korean essence, and rejecting conventions of dressing order by exposing undergarments, Suh advocates for a hanbok that develops with society's changing tastes and needs. For her, this is more than a stylistic matter: a thriving hanbok industry will ensure the livelihood and skill transmission of craftspeople, including traditional weavers, hanbok seamstresses and embroiderers.[12]

In 2021 the Oxford English Dictionary formally incorporated the Korean word 'hanbok' into the English language, putting it on a par with 'kimono' and 'qipao'. This was a result of the growing awareness of hanbok overseas since the mid-2010s thanks to historical K-dramas and an increasing number of K-pop idols donning (and even collaborating in the design of) contemporary hanbok worn on- and offstage, marking their cultural identity while promoting the Korean costume worldwide. Boy bands in particular seem to prefer a deconstructed, layered hanbok in diaphanous fabric with sashes and straps that flap and twirl dynamically as the idols dance onstage. The hanbok amplifies their movements and emphasizes the nimble, energetic quality of their performance, as illustrated by designer C-Zann E's garments for the band ATEEZ.

In recent years, wearing new hanbok has become a fashion statement among a young generation of trendsetters taking pride in their Korean identity, and an affirmation in the Korean diaspora of its cultural heritage.[13] Similar reasons motivate a new generation of fashion designers drawing inspiration from hanbok and its

For *Beyond Underwear* (2021) Suh Younghee explored the use of undergarments for shaping outer garments in Korea and in Europe. She combined multiple layers of summer hanbok underskirts, underpants and underjacket with an eighteenth-century European hoop skirt to create a unique look. Preparatory sketch by Suh Younghee; hanbok by Kim Hye-soon.

Hanbok ensemble by Kim Hye-soon, designed for the KBS series *Hwang Jini* (2006), mixing bold contemporary patterns and fabrics with a traditional silhouette.

ATEEZ's Kim Hong-joong wears C-Zann E's hanbok-influenced ensemble for the performance at online K-pop festival KCON:TACT Season 2, 2020.

Saekdong stripes in signature designs by Darcygom, photographed by Jihoon Jung for *Kaltblut Magazine*, March 2020.

K-Beauty and Fashion

(Above)
Photograph by Hasan Kurbanbaev for *Vogue Korea* showing Jenia Kim's *jeogori*-style jackets made from vintage Uzbek bekasam textile, 2019.

(Right)
Hanbok school uniforms designed by Dolsilnai in 2019. These were rolled out in Korean schools in 2020, as part of the Hanbok School Uniform Design Development & Supply Project initiated by the Korean Ministry of Culture, Sports and Tourism, organized by the Korea Craft and Design Foundation (KCDF).

(Overleaf)
Ji Won Choi's collaboration with Adidas Original in 2019 resulted in hanbok-inflected leisurewear.

traditional patterns: from Darcygom's celebratory *saekdong* stripes to a hanbok-emulating tracksuit by Korean-American Ji Won Choi and Korean-Uzbekistani designer Jenia Kim's *jeogori*-like blouses using vintage Uzbek bekasam fabric. In 2019 the Korean government banked on this global interest and enthusiasm with a pilot project promoting the wearing of hanbok in daily life in the form of hanbok-style school uniforms. The initial response among students was mixed, but the following year, 16 out of 22 schools permanently adopted the scheme.

Emerging fashion designers

The launch of each K-drama episode and K-pop music video is awaited with great anticipation at the prospect of a line-up of impeccable fashion styles. According to Jeong Yun-kee, the renowned stylist and publicist who worked on blockbuster series *My Love from the Star* and *Crash Landing on You*, this international appeal is partly down to the growing scale of these productions: while a character's overall look used to be defined by one costume designer, it now hinges on a team of experts, each responsible for a specific area covering make-up, hair, nails and fashion. It can take up to 20 attempts to produce one complete look, and that look can no longer be reused multiple times due to a growing cohort of savvy viewers analyzing and unpicking each one. This pushes Korean stylists to keep up with seasonal trends and to test unconventional silhouettes by boldly mixing-and-matching and embracing genderless styling.[14] In Jeong's view, K-drama channels contemporary fashion trends layered on timeless basics, while K-pop leans towards avant-garde and quirky styles (see InHae Yeo, pp. 182–7).

This fashion-forward nature of hallyu brought the Korean fashion scene into the global spotlight. Seoul Fashion Week (SFW) was established by the Seoul Metropolitan government back in 2000 with the ambition of placing the capital firmly on the world Fashion Week circuit. This aspiration was cemented by the inauguration of Zaha Hadid's Dongdaemun Design Plaza in 2014 at the heart of the garment district, which provided an eye-catching neo-futuristic backdrop to the SFW in the era of Instagram (see InHae Yeo, pp. 176–81). SFW shows are mainly divided between the Seoul Collection, presenting established designers, and Generation Next, which showcases exciting creative talents with fewer than five years of practice. Fashion designers from Korea have thereby increased their profile on the international scene.

Initially trained as a painter, Kim Seo-ryong started making clothes as a hobby before gaining a name for the striking tailor-made suits that have become one of K-pop's trademarks. Korean-American Kathleen Kye has reached 'pop icon' status herself, while her label KYE, launched in 2011, presents cool, cheeky streetwear whose combination of bold graphics and colours with couture details has won over the K-pop world. Minju Kim, winner of the first season of the Netflix show *Next in Fashion* (2020), anchors each collection in a strong narrative of imaginary world and quirky characters, ranging from gothic to fairytale, producing clean-cut garments with a strong colourful palette and bold graphic design that are now recognized as her signature look. Freshly graduated from Central Saint Martins, Sohee Park of Miss Sohee has been heralded as a 'New-Gen Couturier' by *British Vogue*; her glamorous sculptural silhouettes, carefully crafted and embroidered by hand, are made with sustainability in mind, using deadstock and recycled fabric, and have gained popularity in the fashion and music worlds in Korea and beyond. By contrast, Park Hwan-sung's D-Antidote occupies the niche market between high-end luxury and street fashion, making it accessible to young Gen Z customers. His chilled urban athleticwear branded under the slogan SEOULONDON draws inspiration from the youth cultures of the two cities that shaped his career. Design duo Shin Kyu-yong and Park Ji-sun are behind Blindness's unapologetic gender-fluid take on fashion. They mix a conceptual approach with rebellious attitude to create a neo-romantic spectacular of organza tulle, pearls and layered transparencies that defy Korean patriarchal society. Han Hyun-min, founder of the Münn label, excels in unusual silhouettes using detailed sewing techniques that blend hanbok-making tradition and western tailoring. He experiments with new approaches to pattern-making and to sewing orders and methods in order to produce a sense of 'defamiliarization'.

The rise of hallyu has had an economic impact beyond the simple export of K-cultural content. It has provided a prism for generating a vibrant spectrum of creativity and entrepreneurial verve, bringing to light designers, makers and practitioners across disciplines. These creative industries have benefited from powerful branding at a scale never before seen, regalvanizing the image of contemporary Korea as a global creative leader.

Catwalk image showing a coat from Kim Seo-ryong's 2019 Autumn/Winter collection, worn later that year by Jin from BTS in 'Summer Package in Korea'.

Evening dress from the 2016 Baemin x KYE Spring/Summer collection. It features images of street signs and celebrates hangeul, the Korean alphabet. This collection was a collaboration between KYE and Baedalui Minjok (shortened as Baemin), a nationwide delivery service.

Dress for Minju Kim's 2021 Autumn/Winter collection, which imagines Edward Scissorhands's first Christmas, filled with joy and happiness. The dress combines a bold icy blue silhouette with a playful pattern showing a paper cut-out garland made of tiny Korean moon jars.

The Peony dress by Miss Sohee, highlight of her 2020 graduation collection 'The Girl in Full Bloom', dazzled the fashion world with its flamboyance, beautifully crafted details and sustainability. Photograph by Daniel Sachon.

Neon streetwear from D-Antidote's 2019 Spring/Summer collection, which was inspired by the movie *Beat* (1997), renowned for its portrayal of the angst and rage of Korean youth in the 1990s.

Ensemble from Blindness's 2019 Spring/Summer collection in London, showcasing the opulence and romantic sensibilities of design duo Shin Kyu-yong and Park Ji-sun, whose garments defy the gender norm.

Ensemble from Münn's 2020 Spring/Summer collection. This unisex translucent bomber jacket is filled with petals of fake flowers to create a texture evocative of traditional Korean ink painting.

Formulating K-beauty: A Century of Modern Korean Cosmetics

Yoojin Choi

Nature Republic collaborated with EXO to advertise their sheet facemasks, 2018.

With the global rise of hallyu, K-beauty is one of the most prominent visual manifestations of the Korean Wave. Among worldwide beauty industry professionals, the Korean beauty industry has been known since the early 2010s for its advanced technology in ingredients and formulation, focus on skincare and eye-catching packaging. This has been further expanded in recent years by the soaring popularity of K-pop stars and K-drama or film actors whose beauty looks have instigated make-up trends. It has been boosted still more by a cohort of 'beauty influencers' across social media platforms, who have pushed Korean cosmetics products and beauty standards to the fore. Beauty editors have stated Korea to be around 10 to 12 years ahead in Research and Development in the beauty industry, and Korea has now grown to be the third biggest exporter of cosmetics in the world after the USA and France, meaning that K-beauty forms a major part of Korea's exports.[1] By 2026 K-beauty is predicted to grow by an average of 11.3 per cent per year to become a market worth US$21.8 billion.[2] To set this global twenty-first-century fashion for K-beauty style in context, this essay explores the major developments in Korean cosmetics during the twentieth century, and the social impact of these innovations, together with the impetus behind cosmetic trends that led to the current prominence of K-beauty.

In fact, beauty and cosmetics have an enduring history in Korea. Evidence of cosmetic usage stretches back to the Three Kingdoms period (57 BC–AD 668). Male *hwarang* warriors of the Silla kingdom (57 BC–AD 935) were famed for their stylized look of white jade-like skin and red eyeshadow, while ladies of the Goryeo dynasty (918–1392) were noted as wearing face powder and drawn eyebrows.[3] Even with the Confucian values that upheld modest taste during the Joseon dynasty (1392–1910), cosmetic trends were set by trained female court entertainers (*gisaeng*). Female pedlars (*maebungu*) would travel from home to home between women's quarters (*gyubang*) selling cosmetics, then known as *bundae*, which consisted of three elements: white powder made of ground rice grain for the skin, a type of safflower rouge (*yeonji*) for the lips, and black charcoal for the eyebrows. Worn by aristocratic ladies and female members of the royal household, *bundae* reveals a culture in which beauty was deeply ingrained. Emphasis was given to the skin: unblemished fair skin was seen as a sign of social status or wealth – of not having to work outside in the fields – and skincare has therefore long been at the forefront of K-beauty. This preoccupation with facial appearance also derives from the Confucian value of *yeongyugilcheseol*, meaning a oneness of outer body and inner mind, with the outer considered a reflection of the inner state.

Occupation and the New Woman: 1910–45

The importance of flawless skin continued into the era of Japanese-occupied Korea (1910–45), when mass-produced cosmetics were first imported from Japan, France and the USA. During this period the modern-day Korean term for cosmetics, *hwajangpum*, first entered the Korean vocabulary, the word expanding the definition of a consumable commodity beyond

Korea's first mass-produced modern cosmetic Bakgabun, launched in 1915.

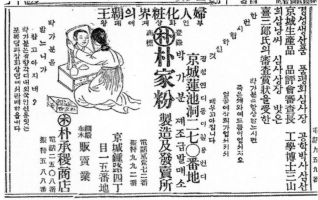

The first advert for Bakgabun was printed in the newspaper *Dong-A Ilbo*, 24 February 1922.

the traditional *bundae*. Korea's first mass-produced make-up, Bakgabun – the name translating to 'Park's Powder' – was created in 1915 by Jeong Jeong-suk, wife of the founder of the eponymous Park Seung-jik store. After seeing an old female pedlar selling cosmetic powder, it struck Jeong Jeong-suk that this could be an additional small enterprise within her husband's store. Initially given out as a complimentary gift when a customer bought textiles, Bakgabun was produced by a dozen women employees in what amounted to a cottage industry. However, the product was an instant hit among women: it flew off the shelves, and distribution expanded with merchants from across the country flocking to Park Seung-jik to purchase stock. At its height, the product sold 10,000 boxes per day, prompting Mr Park to focus on Bakgabun as his main enterprise.

The popularity of Bakgabun was due to its simplicity of use: the block of powder could be applied easily to the skin, and it dissolved well with water or oil to give a flawless finish. It incorporated some of the ingredients of the traditional face powder, including rice, barley, arrowroot and burnt ground shell-powder. The secret of the absorbent formulation was, however, the introduction of lead, which was mixed with vinegar and subjected to an air-tight heat process that caused it to bloom into a white powder called *nab-kkot* or 'lead flower'. Over time, the high lead content of Bakgabun had an adverse effect on the skin, mottling it with long-term use; the product fell out of fashion and was discontinued by 1937. Despite its demise, Bakgabun marked the beginning of the K-beauty industry.

The early success of Bakgabun was in part due to its affordable price point in comparison with extremely expensive foreign products.[4] The other factor was its eye-catching packaging. In contrast to traditional cosmetic powders, which were sold wrapped inside thin white paper to be decanted to a reusable ceramic container, it was sold in luxurious decorative boxes that sported a colourful printed label of pink peonies against a yellow background, and a diagonal blue banner emblazoned with the Bakgabun brand name. This pioneering way of marketing a cosmetic product attracted copy-cat versions such as Suhgabun (Suh's Powder), Janggabun (Jang's Powder) and Cheongabun (Cheon's Powder), whose unmistakable similarity to Bakgabun's decorative floral boxes may have prompted Mr Park to register Bakgabun as Korea's first officially trademarked cosmetic product in 1920.[5]

Bakgabun was also the first K-beauty product to have an advertising campaign. First published in the Korean newspaper *Dong-A Ilbo* in 1922, Bakgabun's advert was printed in both phonetic hangeul script and the scholarly Chinese character-based Hanja, as more women could read the former than the latter. The accompanying illustration, depicting a Korean woman dressed in traditional hanbok contentedly examining her face in the mirror of her vanity, besides which sits a box of Bakgabun, would have stood out at a time when cosmetic adverts in Korean newspapers and magazine were predominantly for Japanese imports.[6]

The introduction of modern cosmetics in Korea coincided with the increasing public prominence of the *sinyeoseong* ('New Woman'), a new class of educated Korean women under Japanese colonial rule. Bob-cut hairstyles (*tuiraemeori*), a shorter hanbok hemline, heeled shoes and a red scarf were the identifiers of a New Woman, as seen in the eponymously titled magazine *Sinyeoseong*. Emerging as a feminist ideal for women seeking independence and radical change in the late nineteenth century in Europe and America, the New Woman movement reached China, Japa, and Korea by the early twentieth century.[7] In the Korean context the fashions worn by the New Woman marked a deeper shift, as the preceding 500 years of patriarchal rule by the Joseon dynasty forbade upper-class women from being seen in public spaces and maintained the long-held Confucian belief that hair, as a gift from one's ancestors, should not be cut. The movement was initially critical of cosmetic use as frivolous and indecent, however by the 1930s the painted face had become another key marker of the New Woman, and *Sinyeoseong* was full of cosmetic advertisements and featured articles such as 'How to achieve the make-up look of a female student in 3 minutes' and 'New Woman Beauty Technique Lecture'.[8] While the traditional male viewpoint continued to decry her as an immoral rebel, the New Woman's performative act of wearing cosmetics delivered, to an extent, a new agency in femininity, with the use of cosmetics to highlight facial features making them stand out against the backdrop of masculine hegemony.

One influential *sinyeseong* who set the modern beauty look ablaze was Oh Yeop-ju, one of the first Korean women to have formally studied 'beauty'. In an interview, she stated: 'People think that beauty techniques are only for prettifying the face, however that is not the case. Beauty makes the body healthy'.[9] Whether wearing red lipstick only on her lower lip or drawing eyebrows in half-moons, Oh launched many beauty trends, and with her signature sunglasses and high heels cultivated a personal brand. Her fame even led to a cameo appearance as a beautician in the Korean film *Mimong* (1936). In 1933 she opened the country's first 'beauty salon', inside the Hwashin department store in Seoul.[10] As the only Korean-run department store during Japanese occupation, Hwashin was a rare site for Koreans to experience modernity, and Oh's beauty parlour became a destination where cosmetic techniques could also be learned and developed. For Oh, the potency of beauty and its new educative role presented an empowering tool within the complex framework of Korea's nation-state as colonial subject.

Investing in beauty: 1945–61

The influence of the silver screen is evident in the landmark Korean cosmetic product called Lucky Cream. Launched in 1947, Lucky Cream's packaging included a photo of the Canadian actress Deanna Durbin, whose movie *One Hundred Men and a Girl* (1937) had been a hit in Korea. The use of Durbin's likeness on the bottle indicates a desire to compete with foreign brands. Lucky Cream was the invention of Lucky Chemicals, founded soon after the liberation of Korea from the Japanese occupation in 1945; its co-founders were Koo In-hwoi and cosmetics manufacturer Kim Jun-hwan, who had installed cosmetics manufacturing machines in his home to start producing Lucky Cream.

Lucky Cream was an instant success. It was sold not just through shops but also by street pedlars, who would bang their drums twice – 'dong dong' – while shouting out 'gurumu!', a performative sales pitch based on the term *dongdonggurumu*, meaning 'face cream'. Purchasers would bring their own pots, and the pedlars would decant an amount of Lucky Cream. Despite the lack of pre-made packaging, this was still a small luxury, with one portion of *dongdonggurumu* costing 15 jeon, around the price of five bowls of noodles.[11] The packaged Lucky Cream was originally sold in a brittle synthetic container that often broke; seeking a solution to this problem, Koo started investing in the early 1950s in a little-known material called plastic. However, Lucky Chemicals discontinued Lucky Cream in 1953 to focus on manufacturing household detergents and electronic goods that helped form the basis of the huge conglomerate that would become LG (first Lucky GoldStar, then Life's Good).

In 1948 Korean cosmetics company Taepyungyang (known from 2002 as Amorepacific) debuted its first mass-produced product, Melody Cream, with a pink rose motif. A men's hair product, ABC Pomade, followed in 1951. Both products featured English text on the packaging, an indication of Korea's desire to compete with existing foreign brands.

By the beginning of the Korean War in June 1950, there were 100 different registered cosmetics companies in Korea, largely producing hair pomades for men, and creams and perfumes for women. With the increase in product range and adverts, in August 1958 Taepyungyang released the first issue of a monthly magazine to boost product promotion. *Hwajanggye* ('World of Cosmetics') included fashion and beauty news as well as articles on make-up application. Though a free magazine, it was so popular that back issues were sold in bookstores, and the magazine continues to this day as *Hyangjang*, its covers often featuring K-pop idols such as Jennie from BLACKPINK. Taepyungyang introduced other innovations in Korean make-up: it was successful in the strategy of releasing 'seasonal' cosmetic products with matching extensive marketing campaigns, and invested in employing women to introduce the idea that it was acceptable to wear colour make-up daily.

'When women put on make-up to go outside, it is not only their face that they make up but also their minds with the cosmetics called freedom,' wrote Jeong Bi-seok in his hit 1954 novel *Jayubuin* (Madame Freedom), originally published

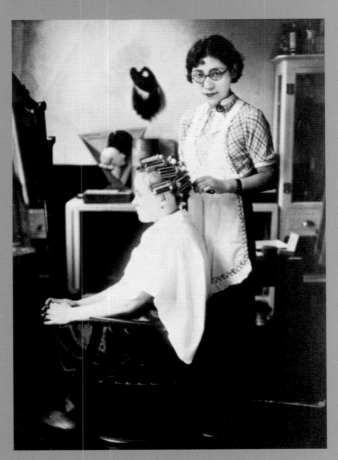

Beautician Madam Oh Yeop-ju at her salon c.1933.

Lucky Chemicals' first commercial product was the hugely popular Lucky Cream, produced between 1947 and 1953.

One of the 'Amore Ladies', selling cosmetics door to door, c.1964.

as a serial in the *Seoul Daily News*, and two years later turned into a successful film, directed by Han Hyeong-mo. *Madame Freedom* tells the cautionary story of a professor's wife who starts working in a shop called Paris, which sells western cosmetics and accessories. She has adulterous affairs, with lasting consequences, reflecting a pervading narrative in which cosmetics, especially foreign imports, were associated with moral failings among women.

Manufacturing Korean cosmetics: 1960s–90s
The sale of foreign cosmetics in Korea came to a sudden halt in 1961 with the Prohibition of the Sale of Specific Foreign Goods Act. Established by the then de facto leader and later President Park Chung-hee, the Act was a part of an aggressive nationwide campaign to boost domestic industries, and remained in place until 1982. Foreign cosmetics were confiscated and sometimes destroyed in public burnings of foreign goods. In one notorious case two Korean actresses were caught trading foreign cosmetics and arrested by the police.[12]

Severe as it was, the Act had a lasting impact on Korea's cosmetics industry, and the 1960s and 1970s saw a boom in domestic cosmetic companies such as Seongmi Juria Cosmetics (founded 1960) and Hankook Cosmetics (founded 1962). Hankook Cosmetics became Taepyongyang's fiercest competitor, launching Danhak Pomade to rival the ABC Pomade, followed by a make-up line, Jutanhak.

By the early 1960s there were 130 registered cosmetic companies in Korea, employing around 370,000 women as door-to-door saleswomen. Many of these women had lost male family members – and thus their livelihoods – in the Korean War, and provided a new workforce for cosmetic companies. Much like the 'Avon Ladies' in the UK and USA, Taepyongyang's *Amore Ajumma* ('Amore Ladies') and the rival Hankook 'Jutanhak Ladies' were trained and then sent out equipped with branded uniform, bags, maps, guidebooks and costumer profile logs. Their maps were so accurate and their costumer profiles so detailed that these saleswomen were sometimes mistaken for spies.

The new distribution model allowed for detailed explanations of products, consultations, free trial periods and flexible instalment payment options. A younger generation was targeted, helping to shift people away from the negative connotations of cosmetics as an indulgent foreign commodity. In addition, this proved to be a successful turning point for Korean cosmetics, bolstering consumer confidence in the quality of domestic cosmetics, which had previously been considered of lower quality than their foreign counterparts. At the beginning of 1962, the domestic market for cosmetics constituted only 100 million won (approximately £62,000), but with the firm establishment of door-to-door sales, by 1973 it had grown tenfold, to 10 billion won (approximately £6.2 million).

In the 1970s, propelled by new television adverts, and posters featuring the latest Korean actors, Amorepacific's cosmetic empire reached new heights of popularity. Counterfeits were so numerous that an exhibition was held in 1974 advising consumers on how to distinguish between a fake and the genuine product. Though Amorepacific had made

Hankook Cosmetics counter at Midopa Department Store, Myeongdong, Seoul, 1975.

K-Beauty and Fashion

Advertisement (1977) and packaging (c.1973) for Sammi Cosmetics, a line produced by Amorepacific especially for export.

forays into exporting Korean cosmetics from as early as 1964 with the Oscar line exported to Ethiopia, at this time it began producing a line specifically for export, Sammi. The packaging drew inspiration from the great canon of Korean art and culture, using the curved silhouette of Goryeo dynasty's *maebyeong* celadon pottery for its bottles and printing Joseon dynasty artist Shin Yunbok's famed genre paintings on the box, so aligning itself with the best of Korea's cultural exports. The brand was sold in the USA, France, Germany, South America and Southeast Asia, and was even stocked in London's Harvey Nichols department store. The brand later evolved into Sulwha, then, in the early 1990s, Sulwhasoo. Sulwhasoo is particularly popular in China: it accounts for 70 per cent of Amorepacific's export sales in Asia, and in 2018 became the first Korean cosmetic brand to reach sales over 2 trillion won (US$1.7 billion).[13] In 2021, Amorepacific reported net profits of 180.9 billion won (US$151.2 million), a year-on-year rise of 727.7 per cent.[14] As of 2022, Amorepacific is the world's seventh largest cosmetics conglomerate, with over 30 product lines, including Innisfree, Mamonde, IOPE and Laneige.

Colour TV was introduced in 1980, and the ensuing decade saw an explosion in the sale of colour make-up, marketed through provocative and eye-catching cosmetic advertisements that presented multiple ideals of strong women, now worn by rising Korean female actors and models: from classical musicians to action heroines, from career women to 'Miss Korea' beauty

pageant winners. Jutanhak's autumn 1975 advert for its High-Best Tone line, omnipresent behind department store cosmetic counters in Korea, featured actress Yu Ji-in with green-tinted eyelids, pink cheeks and a burgundy plum shade for the lips, and the slogan 'Come to the beautiful winter wonderland'. This provides a sharp contrast with a work by artist Oh Yoon, *Marketing II – Bal-la-la* (1980), which parodies the cosmetic advertising posters of the 1970s and 1980s. The colourful upper half shows a woman with a pale face and heavily made-up eyes and lips, red manicured nails and long flowing hair. To her left is an array of cosmetic products, to her right the mock logo with the product's name 'Ballala' – which in Korean can be heard as 'apply' – and the copy line 'From Cradle to the Grave'. This and the central slogan, 'Take care of yourself, you are already a woman at 12 years old', highlight the societal pressures on women to wear make-up to be deemed presentable. Further contrast comes in the lower half of the image, a woodblock print of a cluster of working women: farmers, market sellers and students, their faces obscured in shadow through the weight of work. Part of the 1980s Minjung or 'People's' art movement, Oh Yoon belonged to a group of artists critical of capitalist attitudes, imperialism and authoritarian government. Though the Korean cosmetic industry was booming, its use of heavy marketing strategies to sell consumer goods was still viewed with suspicion.

It was not just women who were targeted by cosmetics companies. In 1974 Amorepacific launched their Vister men's

A satirical take on the beauty industry by Minjung artist Oh Yoon, *Marketing II – Bal-la-la*, 1980.

Poster for Vister Skincare for men modelled by actor Namkoong Won, 1974.

skincare line. It was modelled by Namkoong Won, the foremost actor of the day, and accompanied with the strapline 'The masculine style of a man who takes up the challenge to reach the peak.' Vister projected a male standard of beauty: an active, tough masculinity that chimed with the both the military regime of the time and images of the macho male in Hollywood films. This was followed by the Miraepa men's skincare line in 1993, whose adverts featured sharp-suited career men. This shift towards skincare for men was partly prompted by a drop in sales of hair pomade, as the trend in men's hair turned to long, hippy styles.

Not long after, in 1997, Somang Cosmetics launched the men's skincare brand Kkhotdeuleun Namja, translating roughly to 'Man with Flowers'. Somang took the brand name from a 1997 Korean romantic comedy of the same title, and the cosmetics range became known for its advertising campaigns, which featured the most in-demand male celebrities of the time – from football legend Ahn Jung-hwan to K-drama star Hyun Bin – together with provocative straplines like 'Now even my boyfriend can become a Flower Boy beauty (*kkhonminam*) like them'. This groomed, softer masculine beauty became the epitome of the Korean Wave after the success of K-drama *Boys Over Flowers* (2009) with its flamboyant metrosexual fashions, while the growing number of first-generation K-pop idols often adopted a softer, more androgynous look that became the hallmark of K-beauty first across East and Southeast Asia, and eventually further afield. In recent years, brands such as Laka Cosmetics

have emerged with a 'genderless' or 'make-up for all' approach in their campaigns.

Exporting beauty: 1990s to the present

The International Monetary Fund (IMF) crisis of 1997 led to a stream of Korean cosmetics companies collapsing, as well as the reintroduction of foreign cosmetics products into Korea following the abolishment of the Prohibition of the Sale of Specific Foreign Goods Act in December 1982. Individual Korean brands that were not under the umbrella of a large conglomerate reinvented themselves as Original Equipment Manufacturing (OEM) companies, selling their technology and manufacturing services to the conglomerates and allowing smaller independent businesses to start cosmetic brands as they were able to easily manufacture cosmetic lines through the OEM companies. But it was the launch of Korean brand Missha (Able C&C) in 2000 that created an entirely new model for Korean cosmetics. Initially selling cosmetic products online at an incredibly low price of 3,300 won (£2), Missha would eventually become a specialist beauty store, providing the model for 'Road Shops': outlets at subway station malls or university campuses in Seoul, selling inexpensive Korean cosmetics that did not compromise on quality or R&D. Over the following five years, brands such as Etude House, Innisfree (Amorepacific) and The Faceshop (LG Healthcare) opened up similarly scaled Road Shop-style branches, which now line

Cosmetic stores line the streets of the Myeongdong shopping district in Seoul, 2015.

The Air Cushion Compact, created by cosmetic brand IOPE in 2008, can retain liquid foundation in compact form.

the streets of Seoul's 'beauty Mecca', Myeongdong. Since the late 2010s, another wave of new brands has appeared: Skin Food, Tony Moly and It's Skin all retail at the upper-lower end (£6-12) of the Road Shop market, with a continued emphasis on skincare. This not only brought in many tourists from Asia, drawn in by the first wave of hallyu, but also attracted international beauty industry experts and professional make-up artists wanting to research the latest trends in Korean beauty. Among them was Lisa Eldridge, who created 'Korean "Beauty Trend" Inspired Make-up Tutorial' (2015) and 'Korean Make-up, Skincare and Beauty Haul!' (2015) for her YouTube platform. Several of these brands also went on to launch in other Asian countries, with Tony Moly opening in Hong Kong and Etude House in Singapore, Hong Kong, Japan, Brunei, Myanmar, Dubai and Kuwait.

During the 2000s K-beauty grew in tandem with the spread of hallyu. LG had returned to the cosmetics industry in 1984 with the launch of soap brand DeBon, subsequently releasing cosmetic brands O Hui (1997) and SU:UM37 (2007), once again becoming a prominent producer of K-beauty goods. Its brand The History of Whoo launched in 2003, when the Korean government commissioned LG to create a luxury skincare brand that embodied the country's history. This was reflected in packaging design drawn from heritage objects and the use of Korean traditional herb-based medicinal practice, *hanbang*. The popularity of historical K-dramas during the early to mid-2000s had led to a resurgence in appreciation for Korea's cultural heritage, which filtered into K-beauty, and actor Lee Young-ae from the renowned period K-drama *Daejanggeum* (2003) was chosen as The History of Whoo's brand ambassador.

The Covid-19 pandemic, combined with the arrival of 'drugstore' beauty multi-shops such as Olive Young (CG Group) and the boom in online retail, has seen the closure of many of the Road Shop stores of the 2000s. Cosmetic brands now focus

on 'offline' pop-ups and experiential moments to grow their brand. Social media influencers have also become increasingly prominent. Particularly noteworthy was the arrival of beauty content creators on YouTube; like the Amore Ladies of the 1960s, they promoted not only Korean cosmetic products, but also Korean beauty standards, such as 'glass skin' and the 'ten-step beauty routine', across the world, embedding K-beauty as part of the Korean Wave.

The worldwide impact of K-beauty is perhaps best exemplified by the 2008 invention of the Air Cushion Compact. Developed by the R&D department of IOPE (Amorepacific), the Cushion Compact made liquid foundations portable and easy to apply through its packaging design, in which a layer of sponge holds the liquid product intact and moist (the designer is said to have taken inspiration from the traditional Korean seal and stamp pad), and is reported to have sold at a rate of one every second. The Cushion Compact's innovative packaging design has since been licensed to international cosmetic companies, as well as spawning copy-cat versions from international cosmetics conglomerates.[15]

Korean cosmetics have come to the forefront of the global beauty industry, and continue to seek to set themselves apart from international competition, through such means as 'traditional Korea' branding, eye-catching packaging design and illustration collaborations, innovative formulations from traditional *hanbang* to snail mucin, and by drawing in domestic hallyu actors or idols as models and brand ambassadors.

Cosmetics are an inextricable part of popular culture and self-expression. The Korean word for putting on make-up is *hwa-jang*, 'hwa' meaning to transform or change, and 'jang', to decorate. The potency of cosmetics is not only in their ability to transform one's facial appearance, but also in what they can reveal about cultural shifts and attitudes towards beauty, gender and modernity.

Peripera Cosmetics collaborated with artist Mari Kim on the packaging for their lip tint, 2012–17

Hanbok: Korean Traditional, Contemporary and Fashionable Dress

Yunah Lee

For their 2021 music video 'How You Like That', BLACKPINK wore hanbok-inspired ensembles by Danha Kim of Danha.

In this image for manhwa series *Goong* (The Royal Palace), 2002–12, author/illustrator Park So-hee depicts his protagonist wearing *jeogori* and a short bell-sleeved blouse.

K-Beauty and Fashion

When K-pop girl group BLACKPINK released the music video of their new song 'How You Like That', and appeared on NBC's *Tonight Show Starring Jimmy Fallon* in the summer of 2020, what caught the attention of the media and fans alike was the band's stage costumes. The outfits gave traditional hanbok a modern twist, a bold and spectacular style that fitted the band's song and dance movements.

The designer of the costumes, Danha Kim of Danha, also received much media attention for her hanbok design, and her collection on the internet was visited by many K-pop fans,[1] while the *New York Times* ran a story about the innovative designers whose updates on traditional Korean dress were being embraced by K-pop stars including BTS.[2] This new twenty-first-century generation of hanbok designers bringing fresh eyes to shapes, colours and materials, and unconventional approaches to the styling of hanbok, has been thrust onto the national and world stage through various collaborations in fashion and lifestyle magazines, dramas, cartoons (manhwa), films and K-pop. One could say that hanbok finally arrived at the scene of hallyu as a symbol of the popular contemporary imagination of Korean heritage and tradition.

The roots of the phenomenon of contemporary hanbok can be traced to the late nineteenth century, and various twentieth-century experiments to create a cloth that would be suitable for the lifestyles and aesthetic sensibilities of the time while still retaining the characteristics of hanbok. Hanbok has long straddled the contemporary and the traditional.

Hanbok: Korean (traditional) clothes

Hanbok literally means Korean clothes worn by Korean people. Until the early twentieth century, the basic elements of hanbok remained relatively unchanged, although the types and shapes of hanbok have evolved with the social, economic and cultural conditions and aesthetic consciousness of the times. The hanbok with which we are familiar dates to the Joseon dynasty (1392–1910). For women, it is composed of an inner shirt (*sokjeoksam*), a short jacket (*jeogori*), a pair of inner trousers (*sokbaji*), an inner skirt (*sokchima*), a long and voluminous skirt (*chima*) and an outer coat (*po; jangot*). Men's outfits comprise a jacket (*jeogori*), a pair of trousers (*baji*), a vest (*jokki*) and various types of outer coat (*po, cheollik, durumagi*). Although its forms and shapes underwent alteration and modernization in the twentieth century, the basic composition of men's and women's hanbok remained unaltered.

Since encountering foreign cultures in the late nineteenth century, the sartorial practices of Korean people have undergone significant changes. The Gabsin Dress Reformation of 1884 saw the first modernizations of the uniforms of government officials and the adoption of the European style of military uniforms,[3] while in the twentieth century, Koreans

Stills from *Jayubuin* (Madame Freedom, 1956, dir. Han Hyeong-mo) illustrate how clothing is used in the film to explore ideas about traditional and modern values.

began to adopt Euro-American clothes and fashion: a style of dress known as *yangjang*, encouraged and adopted by the upper class at the end of the nineteenth century and established as a new and modern mode of fashion in the 1920s and 1930s. At that time, the foundation of schools for girls and the emergence of the New Woman movement led to changes to the forms and customs of women's dress: the *jeogori* was simplified, lengthened and given a more generous shape for comfort and practicality. A new type of *chima* was introduced, with shoulder strips added to the top of the skirt for ease and comfort; initially designed for schoolgirls, this style of *chima* was quickly adopted by the rest of the female population. Another change to *chima* was that the seam was closed (compared to the overlapped open seam of the traditional *chima*) and the length was shortened to above the ankle. The length and the silhouette of the jacket and skirt varied according to the trends, as well as to the wearer's social status and personal taste, while the dress was often worn with western-style shoes instead of the traditional rubber or leather shoes, and accessorized with umbrellas (which veiled women's faces from strangers' eyes).[4]

The changes created a dual sartorial system, with hanbok existing alongside *yangjang*. Throughout the Korean War (1950–3), clothing provided through foreign aid and the US military camp provision was funnelled onto market, helping to spread western fashion styles to the wider Korean population. By the end of the 1970s, the Euro-American style of clothing prevailed as everyday clothes for most Koreans and hanbok had become repositioned as a traditional form of dress for important occasions such as national holidays (*Seol* and *Chuseok*), weddings and special birthdays.

Velvet hanbok in *Jayubuin* (Madame Freedom)

The costumes in the infamous film *Madame Freedom* (Han Hyeong-mo, 1956) reflect the dichotomy of the Korean sartorial system at the time. Based on the novel by Jeong Bi-seok serialized in the *Seoul Daily News* in 1954, the film portrays the changing behaviours of married women of the middle and upper classes, and how following their desires brings about their tragic demise. It reflects women's newly emerging consciousness about their roles and identities, and how this was resisted and oppressed by the prevalent patriarchal and moral values of Korean society.[5] The film's heroine Oh Seon-yeong, a housewife married to a university professor, is introduced to dance parties –

a new popular upper-class women's leisure activity – and other pastimes then considered liberal and provocative. She gets a part-time job, and begins extramarital affairs with a younger university student and her manager's husband. In the end, she is punished for the affairs and brought back to her supposed place at home with her husband. Seon-yeong wears hanbok in her role of dutiful wife and mother, the traditional style and materials indicating the traditional values and morals of the good Korean wife. By contrast, at work or when meeting her lover she often adorns herself in western-style garments such as tailored dress suits and cardigans. The dance party scenes fuse these styles, with Seon-yeong and the other female attendees wearing hanbok made with velvet skirts and satin jackets, a fashionable hanbok combination from the 1950s to the 1970s. Newly imported textiles from Japan and Hong Kong such as velvet, rayons and satin were expensive but still sought-after for their luxurious texture and lustrous colours, despite the government's control over luxury consumption.[6] The velvet hanbok featured in *Madame Freedom* not only reflected a fashionable trend in hanbok but also made it even more popular.

Hanbok reform

Following the demise of hanbok as everyday wear, the late 1950s to the end of the twentieth century saw several attempts to modernize hanbok to make it more convenient and less expensive for daily activities. These included shortening the skirt to knee-length, adding more shoulder straps and closing the seams in skirts, enhancing the comfort and practicality of jackets, modifying the designs and silhouettes, using different textiles that are easier to wash and care for. Perhaps the most well-known was the production of readymade hanbok, known as everyday (*saenghwal*) hanbok or reformed (*gaeryang*) hanbok.[7] These efforts bore some fruit during the late 1980s and 1990s, with the adoption of reformed hanbok as a uniform in the tourism industries, and the Jilkyungee brand, established in 1984, has flourished in this hanbok market sector ever since.[8]

Nevertheless, modernized hanbok was embraced only by a small number of people, and by the end of the twentieth century hanbok was firmly established as the Korean traditional dress, with a long and voluminous skirt and a short jacket, made of various silks and linens, and decorated with embroidery or gold stencils. It had become the symbol of traditional Korean beauty and luxury in fashion and textiles.

A lay-flat version of the type of hanbok worn in *Jayubuin* (Madame Freedom) shows the popular use of velvet in hanbok from the 1950s to the 1970s.

Replica of the brocaded Arirang dress designed by Nora Noh and worn by the winner of the 3rd Miss Universe Competition, Oh Hyeon-ju. Nora Noh transformed the traditional skirt and jacket of hanbok into a western-style dress.

Jin Teok's denim and lace ensemble (2007) uses the vest (*baeja*) and embroidery elements of hanbok for a contemporary look.

Fashion inspired by hanbok

Korean fashion and the fashion industry started to develop in the mid-1950s with the introduction of new materials and fashion trends from Europe and the USA. Among the first generation of Korean designers were Nora Noh and Choi Kyeong-ja, who studied fashion design in the USA and Japan respectively, and established their own boutiques and fashion businesses. At that time Korean fashion was dominated by western clothing styles, and hanbok was not considered fashionable. Nonetheless, hanbok has provided fashion designers with inspiration, especially for Korean aesthetics and characteristics. The Arirang dress – designed by Nora Noh and famously worn by Miss Korea, Oh Hyeon-ju, in the 1959 Miss Universe Competition – showcases how the elements of hanbok were adapted in the creation of a new dress representing Korean beauty. Made in lustrous satin silk (a traditional hanbok textile), the deep V neckline, higher empire-line waist, long voluminous skirt and ribbon decoration all pay homage to hanbok. Choi Kyeong-ja also designed an evening dress, Celadon, presented at the first international fashion show in Korea in 1962, and a minidress in satin brocade with a hanbok-inspired neckline, shown in the Korea-Japan Fashion show in 1964.

Since the 1990s, top Korean fashion designers – including André Kim, Jin Teok, Lee Jin-u, Seol Yun-hyeong and Lie Sang-bong – have continued to adapt and appropriate different aspects of hanbok (lines and silhouettes, motifs, colours, embroidery, decorative techniques, textiles) to create a contemporary interpretation of Korean tradition and aesthetics in fashion. This has been particularly noticeable in collections presented in international fashion shows in Paris and New York, reflecting a worldwide promotion of Korean fashion partly propelled by the Korean government's globalization drive of the late twentieth century. Combining the uniqueness of a local identity in fashion – by utilizing the elements of traditional or folk craft and dress – with global forms and visual repertoire is a well-established strategy of glocalism in the global fashion industry.[9]

Hanbok on the global fashion stage

Presenting hanbok on the global stage is one of the strategies for promoting Korean fashion around the world. Hanbok designer Lee Young-hee played a vital role in raising the profile of hanbok as Korean dress and fashion internationally, showing her collections at Paris and New York fashion shows and establishing her business in both cities. Lee started her hanbok design and making in the 1980s, and by the early 1990s had become one of the top hanbok practitioners. Through her participation in Paris fashion collections between 1993 and 2016, Lee explored a variety of fashion possibilities of hanbok, by adapting, appropriating and challenging the rules of hanbok making and wearing. The Wind Dress, which featured in her Paris Prêt-à-Porter Autumn/Winter 1994 collection show, is her signature garment. In her autobiography, Lee revealed how the idea of this dress was formed: 'In Paris Collection shows, evening dress is the last one … I wanted to show something new and modern, something innovative and more impressive than any western designers … We were searching for a dress

Examples of Lee Young-hee's signature 'Wind Dress', first created in 1994, are seen in this 2008 photograph by Kim Jungman, with barefoot models showcasing the beautiful colours and movement of *nobang* silk.

which would excite western fashion specialists and appeal to the taste of the clients ... We came to think, rather playfully, why not take the jacket off.'[10] The dress was made with *nobang*, a traditional Korean silk known for its smooth finish and beautiful colours. Barefooted models in a range of beautifully coloured dresses walked the runway, with air blowing to create billowing movements, hence the name Wind Dress (*costume de vent*). Rather than hanbok dress as Korean ethnic clothing, Lee presented contemporary fashionable dress with a Korean flavour. Her Wind Dress is rooted in the Korean concept of dressing: flat patterned and adaptable to the wearer's body shape, changeable depending on the ways in which the dress is folded and held up. Lee explained, 'it is not hanbok although it looks like one ... It can be worn in endless variations but it can go back to the simple flat square cloth. It has the vitality that I love'.[11] Although the initial response from Korean audiences was lukewarm, and critical of her innovative interpretation of Korean tradition, the dress was well received in Paris. Lee went on to expand her creative interpretation of hanbok, experimenting with Korean textiles and decorative techniques on the global fashion stage.

Lee's growing international profile contributed to the rising recognition of hanbok in global fashion. It was also assisted by hallyu – the increasing global interest in Korean culture, especially Korean popular culture – which started in Asia in the 2000s and expanded internationally in the following decade. Riding this wave, the Korean government's promotion of Korean culture through international exhibitions of Korean traditional and contemporary art and culture provided fertile ground for hanbok to become known more widely. Hanbok's influence on global fashion and high-end fashion designers, however, has been slow and rather limited compared to the long historical presence of the Japanese kimono or Chinese qipao in western fashion history. Carolina Herrera stands out for her appropriation of Korean culture and hanbok: in her New York Spring/Summer 2011 collection, Herrera utilized and appropriated several hanbok elements, including the shape and line of *jeogori*, *chima* and *goreum* (a sash that can be tied into a bow to close the jacket), for the design and decoration of jackets and dresses. She also adapted the men's tall and wide-brimmed hat (*got*) into a women's style.[12] In 2017 Herrera collaborated with the Hanbok Advancement Centre (supported by the Ministry of Culture, Sports and Tourism) for a private show of hanbok at the Museum of Arts and Design in New York and a display in Seoul.[13] She created three pieces reflecting her design aesthetics: a wedding dress, an evening dress and a two-piece skirt suit, all adapting elements of hanbok. Besides Herrera's engagement with hanbok, Chanel's 2016 Cruise Collection, shown in Seoul, was notable for being inspired by Korean traditional culture more broadly, and used various traditional colours, decorative techniques and effects.

Fashioning hanbok

What does hanbok mean for Korean people and their ideas of fashion in the twenty-first century? Many Korean hanbok designers – among them Kim Youngjin for Tchai Kim, Danha

Caroline Herrera's 2011 Spring/Summer collection drew on features of hanbok such as the *goreum* (a long sash that can be tied into a bow).

Kim Youngjin designed this *cheollik* for her brand Tchai Kim in 2014, adapting the form of the traditional Korean men's coat to create a woman's ensemble.

Kim for Danha, Cho Yeong-gi for CheonUiMubong and Leesle Hwang for Leesle – have been exploring this question, and creating their own interpretation of hanbok and its contemporary forms, uses and meanings. These creations are called fusion hanbok or modern hanbok, and some still carry the notion of *saeghwal* (everyday) hanbok. What distinguishes them from previous hanbok-inspired dress and styles is that their designers are conscious of their position not simply as hanbok designers but as fashion designers more broadly. Their designs are tethered to, but not limited by, tradition. Knowledge of hanbok and its history may be the starting point for these designers, but their deconstruction and assemblage of hanbok and its elements according to their personal creative imagination makes their designs equally contemporary. The *cheollik* dress and waistline skirt (*heori chima*) designed by Kim Youngjin for the launch of her second brand Tchai Kim in 2013 is now the prime example of this new trend in fashioning hanbok; Kim reimagined the use of the *cheollik* – a men's coat in the Joseon period – as a woman's dress, feminizing the design with subtle changes to its lines and silhouette and the use of new fabrics and colours. By layering different elements of hanbok in interesting new ways, Kim created a 'beautiful contemporary and global' style, which still resonated with the look and feel of traditional hanbok.[14]

Contemporary trends in hanbok are also hugely indebted to Suh Younghee's fashion styling as featured in many Korean magazines, including *Vogue Korea*. Her images in *Vogue Korea* reflect a process of self-orientalizing by Korean designers, stylists, photographers and fashion editors alike, blending Korean and oriental influences to create a hybrid aesthetic that is deliberately ambiguous about its origin. While this could be seen as problematic, a rehashing of the orientalism that established the idea of 'Orient' through a western imagination and treated all Asian cultures as interchangeable 'others', self-orientalization can be an empowering move to reclaim the meaning of aesthetic elements and affirm that those who employ such a strategy are familiar with the global discourse around fashion.[15]

With their creative reimagining of Korean tradition and sartorial culture, and with a confident grasp of the designs, styles and images relevant to contemporary domestic and international audiences, Korean designers are striving to establish their vision of Korean dress and their own brands in the Korean fashion world and beyond. The international public and media interest in hanbok-inspired costumes seen in BLACKPINK and BTS's music videos and performances proves that hanbok is still relevant in contemporary culture, as does its domestic consumption, and indeed the debates around various contemporary hanbok. Whether in an ever-changing fashion culture hanbok will continue to be contemporary as well as traditional is something only the future will tell.

Suh Younghee styled this shoot, photographed by Kim Kyung Soo, for *Vogue Korea* in October 2007, an example of her deliberately hybrid aesthetic.

Korean Street Style

InHae Yeo with Dasom Sung

Haberdashery outlets in Dongdaemun Market in 2022, part of a system that concentrates the process from fabrication to final fashion in one small area.

The evolution of street style (DS)

Given its well-established fashion and textile infrastructure, and the speed and breadth of its internet supply, it is hardly surprising that Korea has one of the world's most dynamic street style scenes, and boasts some of its fastest changing trends.

In the 1960s and 1970s, the Korean government promoted and supported a national export policy for economic growth. During this period, numerous international brands commissioned OEM (Original Equipment Manufacturer) products from Korea, allowing it to nurture its needle trades and acquire manufacturing expertise that would become a great asset to the Korean fashion industry.

During the second half of the twentieth century, Korean street fashion was hugely influenced by western style, especially American street fashion. From the 1960s to 1990s, there were western-style dress shops in every neighbourhood, and tailors created their patterns by looking at the clothes from American magazines. Young people wanted to have trendy items from Polo, Tommy Hilfiger, Kangol and Dickies, but these were rarely imported at the time. Instead, the shops of Dongdaemun, in the heart of Seoul and previously concerned with selling hanbok, became the biggest manufacturers, vendors and distributors of Korean street fashion, much of it copied from or inspired by international brands. In its heyday during the 1990s and 2000s Dongdaemun had 30,000 retail shops in 31 buildings, and was equipped with an original, efficient system. Finished products were sold by retailers on the ground floor; wholesalers sold on the first and second floors; on the third floor, there was the factory; and textiles and accessories could be bought from the fourth floor. This meant that every process – from first designs to product distribution – could be completed within a maximum of three days. Therefore, if you saw a new trendy item in a magazine, you would be able to find something similar at Dongdaemun the very next day. This killer system brought many young people to the area, where they could enjoy food, shop and attend live gigs at outdoor stages.

In the late 2000s, internet shopping began to gain popularity. Rather than visit the retail shops of the offline Dongdaemun market, people started to buy fashionable Dongdaemun-made items from young online retailers like Liphop and Aboki, where people could find selected stylish items without having to navigate the countless products on offer on the streets of Dongdaemun. This new explosion in the street fashion market brought about a further change: instead of nameless Dongdaemun designers borrowing from overseas brands, Korean designers established their own unique brands, bringing a new wave into K-fashion.

Fashion platforms like Aland, Musinsa and W Concept encouraged young designers, helping with distribution, marketing and sometimes manufacturing as well. They now showcase all the young Korean brands on their websites and in concept stores, and collaborate with famous stylists, fashionable celebrities and social network influencers.

Street style today (IY)

The Zaha Hadid-designed futuristic Dongdaemun Design Plaza (DDP) in Seoul forms the perfect backdrop for looks meticulously styled by young South Koreans. The crowd that flocks to be photographed during Seoul Fashion Week has become the face of Korean street style. Their confidence echoes the country's reputation as the world's most technologically advanced and digitally connected country with some looks reminiscent of the

Street style seen at Dongdaemun Design Plaza during Seoul Fashion Week, Autumn/Winter 2019.

trendy fashion seen in music videos by K-pop bands. But the colourful pop images should only be considered an introduction to Korean street style fashion.

So what is Korean street style, and where is the best place to get a glimpse of the scene? As a latecomer to international trends, Korea now mixes American and European fashions with Korean brands. High-end luxury is often combined with high street styles, genderless fashion leads the trend, and trainers and t-shirts are staples in the wardrobe. Seoul is divided by the River Han: to the north is the old city where traditional palaces remain; in the south, high-rise apartment complexes form the modernized city. Two neighbourhoods in the south and north each stand out for their street style scenes, as well as for the flagship multi-label boutiques that have become destinations for the young fashion crowds. South of the river, the newly wealthy rich settled in Apgujeong-dong and Cheongdam-dong, two wards of the Gangnam District (as immortalized in 'Gangnam Style' by PSY). In the north, the vast Hongdae area, which includes the art college campus, has a lively underground music scene, including clubs, representing the energy of the youth in Korea.

Boon the Shop and Worksout are two multi-label boutiques with a strong presence in these neighbourhoods. Each stocks numerous street style fashion brands targeted at young people. Boon the Shop, Korea's first multi-label boutique, was opened

in 2000 in Cheongdam-dong by Shinsegae Department Store, a retail conglomerate, and has a street style buying team called Case Study. With its energetic sourcing and knack for finding unique and unconventional items that appeal to young people, Case Study supplies multiple branches of Boon the Shop. As Case Study's Senior Buyer Aaron Seong explains, 'The scenes at the DDP are not the energy that represents the Korean fashion entirely but rather one of the tools young people use to express their personal styles. Consider it a good window for opening up your curiosity about Seoul.' Trainers are the main driving force for distribution: they sell well commercially and become the focus point that brings customers to the store. Seong recalls the first time the flagship boutique in Cheongdam-dong announced the sale of the Yeezy Boost collection by Kanye West with Adidas in 2014: 'The young trainer maniacs who had been camping outside since the night before stormed in running, falling and breaking things. The young energy and excitement were amazing! We knew then that this was going to become mainstream.' That was the start of Case Study as the main channel to distribute trainers – edited to include rare items – to designer collections.

Worksout, a multi-label boutique started by Kang Seunghyuk, has two flagship stores, one in Apgujeong-dong and the other in Hongdae. Noticing how Europeans were attracted by flagship stores, Kang was keen to make Seoul a destination for international brands. In 2005 he opened the first Worksout boutique in Apgujeong-dong, selling street style brands, including Stüssy. The store now stocks collections from multiple brands including Carhartt, Obey and Brixton, and focuses on curating styles with a street style vibe. Worksout also hosts special events, parties and launches, mainly with streetwear labels. 'Brands come to us for the synergy effect they get by working with us and we like to work with brands that have fun energy within the street style scene', Kang says. Having started his business with friends while still a high-school student, reselling Nike and Adidas trainers online, he notes, 'The trainers market has become massive now. Collections drop more than three times a week and we still see people camping outside and queuing before the store opens.' Worksout is also investing in supporting Korean designers: 'MSCHF – pronounced "Mischief" – and Thisisneverthat are brands that we collaborate with and which have a genuine and authentic following. We also like to work with newbies so they can be discovered through us.'

'There is a clone culture in Korea', Kang adds. 'Trends spread fast because information is shared quickly. That way, an enormous variety of looks can become one genre!' In Gangnam, people pay attention to brand names and influencers but are keen to express fashion in their own way, to make their style personal and different from others, while still following the trends: 'Exclusive, rare and unique items are very popular in our shops, but the key point is to pull off a style that looks natural and becomes your own. Our customers are bold and not shy about expressing themselves through fashion.' Aaron Seong agrees: 'Koreans enjoy experimenting with their own styles and they really own it. They absorb trends very quickly and can learn how to make them fit their shape and lifestyle.' Kang stresses that because Koreans enjoy discovering new trends, multi-label stores like Boon the Shop and Worksout are important for introducing them to innovative and unusual labels and designers. But these boutiques are also competing with international stores, and have to move fast to make sure they stock these collections right away.

Trainer brands have been actively collaborating with luxury brands, established designers and emerging designers, and this trend attracts a diverse crowd to the multi-label boutiques. For Seong, trainer collaborations feed into Case Study's fashion buying, and are a way to introduce new customers to the fashion collections as well. 'We are lucky because we can introduce the designer's original collection via the collaboration trainers range at Boon the Shop. Asics x Kiko Kostadinov and Kanghyuk x Reebok as well as JW Anderson x Converse have all attracted great interest, not only for the trainer collaborations but also their fashion collections.' Boon the Shop often presents all items in one visual-merchandised space, instead of limiting footwear to the trainers lounge only; this ensures that trainers collaborations become a source of inspiration and an object of desire for the young trendy Koreans.

A growing number of customers no longer simply follow the collaboration fad but focus instead on finding what matches their own style. At the same time, the phenomenon Seong first saw with the Yeezy Boost drop in 2014 continues today, and it is not unusual to see a long queue forming in front of these flagship boutiques in time for the drop of a certain collaboration.

North of the Han River lies a region that includes Hongdae, Dongdaemun Market, university campuses, the quirky cafés and hip restaurants of Yeonnam-dong, and Itaewon, former site of the US military base. Kang spends most of his time in Hongdae, either at the office or Worksout's second boutique, which is larger than the one in Apgujeong. 'Hongdae has more than ten times the transient population of Gangnam. It's exciting and has a unique energy. The area is vibrant, with a fully developed club scene and street busking happening all the time.' This is reflected in a greater diversity of styles and more experimental fashion than seen in Gangnam, with colourful and bold styles mixed and

Interior view of the YK Jeong x Levi's pop-up, at multi-label boutique Boon the Shop in 2021. Buying team Case Study selects and curates items that will appeal to a fashion-conscious audience.

matched. The different demographic and livelier environment means the merchandising at Worksout in Hongdae is unlike that in its smaller sister store, as Kang explains: 'The customers are much younger and they demand a diverse mix of merchandising. They like to explore and discover new items, brands and styles.' Hip-hop artists, for whom fashion plays an important part in how they express themselves, are vital to the street style scene. Many hip-hop musicians are endorsed by fashion and lifestyle brands, and their style attracts a niche audience who admire these artists' cool and edgy image. 'If G-Dragon and Jennie [from BLACKPINK] lead the mainstream trend, hip-hop artists Mino, BewhY, Simon Dominic (aka Ssam D), Beenzino, Oh Hyuk and singer-songwriter Lee Chan-hyuk of AKMU lead the street style with their fashion sense and a philosophy that is more diverse and unique', says Aaron. Hip-hop artists are in a good position: they become iconic for their music, and their fashion consequently attracts a big following too. Some of these artists have started their own brands – Case Study recently opened a pop-up with Chan-hyuk's brand Say Touché at the Boon the Shop's flagship boutique – while others are affiliated with more niche local labels such as Dadaism Club, Darkr8m and IAB Studio. Meanwhile, the hugely popular music survival programmes *Show me the Money* and *High School Rapper* have also given young hip-hop musicians an opportunity to show off their fashion style.

Seong and his team have been monitoring how the influence of hip-hop musicians generally has become a strong trend in street style, as have the individual styles of several artists: BewhY, a big fan of the ALYX label, wears skinny jeans and fitted styles and buys many of his looks from the Boon the Shop flagship in Cheongdam-dong, while Ssam D likes to mix and match his looks with Bottega Veneta and Prada. 'We call this crossover look "High-end Street" and are noticing how it appeals in different ways to 30- or 40-somethings and the MZ generation [Millennials and Generation Z]', he says. 'The younger

Winner of Nike's On Air competition in 2021, Shin Gwang's trainer design 'Neon Seoul 97' was based on Nike's Air Max 97 and inspired by the neon signs found everywhere in his home town.

Korean brand Kanghyuk used recycled airbags from cars for this ensemble in its first collection in 2017.

generation will not hesitate to invest in the brand value of those who they like and follow. Basically, the pie is getting bigger.' The classic 1990s hip-hop styles and boxy t-shirts are no longer in style; today, the fashion is to make your own look fashionable by mixing in trendy designer looks, then spicing it up with your unique mood and style.

Trends often start with celebrities from the entertainment industry, move on to influencers with a large following on social media, then spread massively. Rapper and producer Jay Park was seen showing off a pair of yellow Air Jordan 5 Retro 'Fab Five' trainers in a video for Dingo Freestyle, a popular YouTube hip-hop channel, in which he performed a medley of nine songs. Jay mentions in the video that it is his most expensive pair, and that he is wearing them for the first time. (It is presumed that this is the same pair that is reported to have been sold earlier for US$20,000.) He was also seen performing in 'Neon Seoul' Nikes in 2019, a collaboration between the fashion brand and Korean designer Shin Gwang.

Korean designers are definitely on the rise. Formerly niche Korean brands like Kanghyuk – now sold through multi-label boutiques Ssense and H.Lorenzo in Los Angeles, as well as Boon the Shop, Space Mue and 10 Corso Como in Seoul – are growing in size. Kanghyuk's co-founder, Korean designer Kanghyuk Choi, graduated from the Royal College of Art in London, and has an interesting brand story based on upcycling: he creates menswear using recycled airbags from cars. This unique material, with its red and blue tape, has become the label's signature look, and has been developed into a new pyramid-patterned fabric for shirts, coats and rider jackets. Kanghyuk has presented its creations at installations in Korea, and has told the story behind them in exhibitions at a gallery space. Boon the Shop has been selling the label from day one, attracting a loyal niche following including artists from the music scene. Once more, however, it was a trainers collaboration – with Reebok, soon after Kanghyuk's debut – that helped to spread the brand's name.

So what is the classic fashion look on the Seoul street scene? Basically, anything black. 'Koreans insanely adore black', Kang explains. 'We always start with an edit of looks in black when buying. It has been like that for 20 years. Not all black items are the same – it's about the details, and black gives you the freedom to tweak and style differently.' Hence the popularity of avant-garde fashion by brands like Yohji Yamamoto, Comme des Garçons, Rick Owens and Ann Demeulemeester, which all have flagship boutiques in Seoul, some the largest such stores in the world. Seong agrees: '[Koreans are] good at styling in black in a refined way. Of course, some like to dress in maximalist style. They know how to style according to different

Virgil Abloh in his hoodie bearing the Korean flag sits with Kanye West at the 'Hood By Air' show at the Mercedes-Benz fashion week, Berlin, 2013.

occasions and have a great sense of colour coordination.' Personal style and character are paramount.

Information on new trends spreads widely, and the speed at which the Korean market can learn of a new trend, absorb it and change direction is unbelievable. The current rising trend is the South Korean flag, Taegukgi, an instantly recognizable design with its central red and blue 'Taeguk' (symbol for duality) surrounded by four black trigrams. Virgil Abloh described it as his favourite flag when he presented an installation as part of his Off-White display at Boon the Shop, and the flag recurred in a number of the looks for his Autumn/Winter 2019–20 Louis Vuitton collection. Others are also making use of the icon: 'Nike launched a Dunk with the Korean flag design which sold out instantly. It's a rare item only distributed in South Korea so the resale value will be high', Aaron explains. Seeing the success of this drop, Case Study decided to release an edit of an exclusive collaboration range featuring Taegukgi, due to launch on 1 March 2022 (the date is a national holiday in Korea, celebrating the March First independence movement).

With the MZ generation becoming increasingly tech savvy and better informed, the new trend is now about reforming fashion by crafting your own style, such as painting graffiti or graphics on your jeans. Surely street style in Korea, expanding at speed and with great energy, has only just begun its journey!

K-pop Style

InHae Yeo
interviews Gee Eun

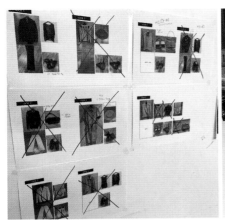

Studio images showing Gee Eun's working process, 2021.

It has been more than 20 years since Gee Eun, currently Visual Director at THEBLACKLABEL, began working with artists on their styling at YG Entertainment, where she formerly held the same title. No one at the time realized the importance of recording the journey of K-pop, let alone its fashion. It was only a few years ago that YG created an archive for its clothes, now known as the YG Wardrobe. As she showed me some of its choicest garments, Gee Eun told me how the archive has evolved: 'The list of items at YG Wardrobe is massive. The collection is made up of looks worn by artists and backing dancers for all projects, and although some of the looks are no longer in circulation, photographs remain as a record. I took back some clothes including these Comme des Garçons x Rolling Stones items which took me more than five years to collect. I wanted all five members of Big Bang to wear the collection together for the music video 'We Like 2 Party' (2015) and we had so much fun! There are only a few seconds in the video where they appear wearing the skinny pants, t-shirts, flannel shirts and jackets with the CDG x Rolling Stones logo and design pattern, but it was a big moment for us. My heart fluttered with excitement to see those clothes again.'

Gee Eun held up a few pieces, including the jacket and the shirt featuring the famous tongue and lips logo. She had requested the looks from the YG Wardrobe and just received them. The artists and the company pay half each for the collection, so if the artist pays for the other half, they can claim items back as their own. 'I also took back the rider jackets I bought from vintage stores in London and painted for Big Bang's "Bang Bang Bang" music video. I heard that G-Dragon also requested some looks from the past and has taken them into his own private collection. We have agreed to meet later and look through the collections. It's a nostalgic moment for us.'

'Many looks from the wardrobe have only been worn once', Gee Eun explains, 'but the company acknowledges their value, and it's willing to invest because these clothes are what form the image of the artists. The relationship with brands is solely based on "fashion" and this is what excites me the most because it's all about being sensitive to current trends and what's to come next, whether it's feminine, boyish, eccentric or humorous styles. My role is to be the matchmaker and persuade the brands, the artists and the company. I'm constantly taking notes of small details that only I can capture.'

Gee Eun's career at YG Entertainment started with the boy band 1TYM. The band's four members included Teddy Park, now CEO of THEBLACKLABEL and Executive Producer at YG Entertainment, responsible for the albums of BLACKPINK among others. 'I was a fashion design student at university at the time', Gee Eun recalls, 'and helped style the group for the hip-hop magazine *Bounce*, then published by YG and distributed free to the public. I stayed on to work on 1TYM's first album *One Way* (2005), and was introduced to international brands like Chrome Hearts that were not yet distributed in South Korea. The members of 1TYM dressed in full looks by Chrome Hearts for their debut music video! For the first time, I had access to international fashion trends and brands. We all loved fashion and could not stop talking about it. The experience opened my eyes, and I started discovering what I like about different designers' collections. That's when I started collecting.'

For the video for the recent single 'Lalisa' (2021) by Lisa from BLACKPINK, Gee Eun sourced the striking gold disc dress and headpiece from Paco Rabanne's Spring/Summer 2021 collection through an auction. In the same music video, Lisa is also dressed in six looks from Jean Paul Gaultier's archive collection: 'I saw that global pop stars were creating their own styles inspired by the high-school girl look from the film *Clueless* that is trending globally, and that made me want to present something different. It came down to what archive I was able to access and pull together. It was amazing to be able to work with Jean Paul Gaultier's team! We collaborated with the designer himself, who gave access to the full archive and carefully chose our favourite looks from years and years' worth of collections. We also dressed newbie artist Jeon So-mi

BLACKPINK's Lisa wearing the iconic Paco Rabanne disc look in the music video 'Lalisa', 2021.

in a see-through mesh look from Gaultier, and I brought out items from my own collection, like a Vivienne Westwood vintage tartan check bustier jacket and pleated skirt.'

The challenge for Gee Eun now is to source different looks. 'I have my eyes on the sweet girl vintage looks from Anna Sui or the cute flower prints from Mary Quant that I saw at the V&A exhibition in 2020. I managed to source an Anna Sui bodysuit from the London vintage shop Rellik and even reached out to Anna Sui's team but was disappointed to learn that they don't have an archive or vintage collection.'

Fashion plays an important part in the career of musicians performing onstage to audiences numbering tens of thousands. Entertainment agencies train artists from a young age, and that training often involves fashion. As an in-house director, Gee Eun has the advantage of being involved in the process from an early stage: 'Before deciding between a pair of hotpants or a skirt that will suit the artist, I focus on bringing my fashion sense to mix in and amplify the band's musical identity. I've come to learn through experience that starting early with young trainees is a key to success. We have so many conversations – from what length of socks makes their shape stand out onstage, to where they should have their first tattoo to visually appeal as part of their fashion style.'

Artists are always reviewing and trying to stay ahead even while at the top of their career and recognized for their success in music as well as fashion. Onstage, their main arena, it is all about the details. As Gee Eun explains, 'Once artists begin the tour, they are equipped with the mindset and attitude to present their work with the utmost attention to detail. For the 2017 world tour of G-Dragon's solo album *M.O.T.T.E.*, we had already worked

with global directors for choreography, production and set design to create different experiences. Together, we agreed that the stage for G-Dragon's solo tour would have a red theme and I wanted to create an entire wardrobe in different kinds of red looks, from lace and leather down to track pants. We even dressed the backing dancers in red. A red tweed coat by Chanel and Demna Gvasalia's first Balenciaga velvet suit in red were included.'

The Chanel tweed look was iconic for G-Dragon. 'The focus is always on creating a look that fits the artist comfortably anytime and anywhere, even when he is going out for a quick shop at the convenience store in his neighbourhood. To have freedom to style, G-Dragon and I agreed to buy the items, rather than entering a brand partnership straight away. This enabled G-Dragon to prove his power to create a fashion culture of his own.'

'The relationship with Chanel was organic', Gee Eun adds, 'and started with the team at the HQ studio in Paris. We met regularly, two to four times a year, which enabled an authentic and affectionate relationship. Karl Lagerfeld was really cool and welcomed the idea of attending shows by other designers as well. He was also open to the artist's own style and ideas. When we were working on the cover shoot for *Vogue Korea*, there was a moment when I realized that no matter what style G-Dragon was dressed in, Karl had perfect control over the photograph he wanted to capture. It was impressive.' The story goes that G-Dragon went on to treat his team with gifts at the Paris flagship boutique – with no discount.

Key for Gee Eun is not just working with international labels, but finding ways to bring what is most Korean to the contemporary world. 'Working with Korean designers is also

Solo artist Jeon So-mi styled by Gee Eun in Vivienne Westwood skirt and bustier, 2021.

Gee Eun styled G-Dragon all in red to match the set for his M.O.T.T.E. 2017 world tour.

G-Dragon in a Hyein Seo long fur coat chosen by Gee Eun for his 2013 'Crooked' music video.

interesting. For G-Dragon's music video "Crooked" (2013), we called in designer Hyein Seo's oversized black faux fur coat. Hyein was a fashion design student in Antwerp at the time and flew in with it. We then connected her to multi-label boutiques like IT in Hong Kong and Browns in the UK, which started stocking her collection as there was so much demand for that coat!'

Artists have an indefinable cultural value, often linked to what they wear. G-Dragon's style appealed to the world for being high-end and conceptual, while the real and tangible image of BLACKPINK's Jennie made her style approachable and relatable. She delivered fashion that was adored by and relevant to young girls today. When Gee Eun became fully involved in the music video for BLACKPINK's 'Ddu-Du Ddu-Du' (2018), her ambition was to create a platform to show the girls' full potential. 'Watching the four girls dressed glamorously in looks like the full vintage Vivienne Westwood outfit, sitting on the chairs as they started their dance moves, was electrifying! I had so much fun filling the video scenes with items I loved.'

As Gee Eun and I spoke, Jennie had just become the face for the Chanel skiwear range Coco Neige, in addition to being global brand ambassador for Chanel. (The other members of BLACKPINK are also global ambassadors for brands: Jisoo for Christian Dior, Rosé for Saint Laurent and Lisa for Celine; all work for both fashion and beauty except for Celine, which does not have a beauty range.) In 2021 BLACKPINK became officially YouTube's most subscribed artist,[1] and it has proven a successful ploy for luxury brands to tap into K-pop to reach their fans, mostly from the MZ generation: while fashion video content traditionally attracts disappointing view counts, brands saw content made with BLACKPINK quickly accumulating high numbers of views on their YouTube channels.

Gee Eun cherishes all her works with the artists she has styled for more than two decades, but she has some particularly significant memories: 'My favourite stage moment was at MAMA [Mnet Asian Music Awards] 2014, when Taeyang performed topless with G-Dragon. We really put so much thought into the style – even though it may seem like the least of work to have nothing on the top, it was one of our hardest decisions, and it really paid off. Offstage, watching Mino on the catwalk at Louis Vuitton in those Virgil Abloh designs in 2019 made me realize that a runway was nothing to an artist who performs onstage to tens of thousands. He walked beautifully with confidence and made us proud!'

'Onstage, artists perform their very best, and the energy and excitement explode. My role is to focus on the details that make the artists look fashionable in their own natural way. It can be anything from their underwear to the small brooch on a jacket or the fabric choices. It's important to me that it doesn't become work but what we enjoy doing together as a team. This involves many conversations and I'm lucky to have close contact with the artists as an in-house style director.' And what is next for Gee Eun? 'I'm scheduled to go on a trip with G-Dragon to Paris for Chanel, where the big discussions are around a big topic: what is timeless fashion?'

September 2021

Mino modelling Virgil Abloh in Paris for the Louis Vuitton Spring/Summer 2020 collection.

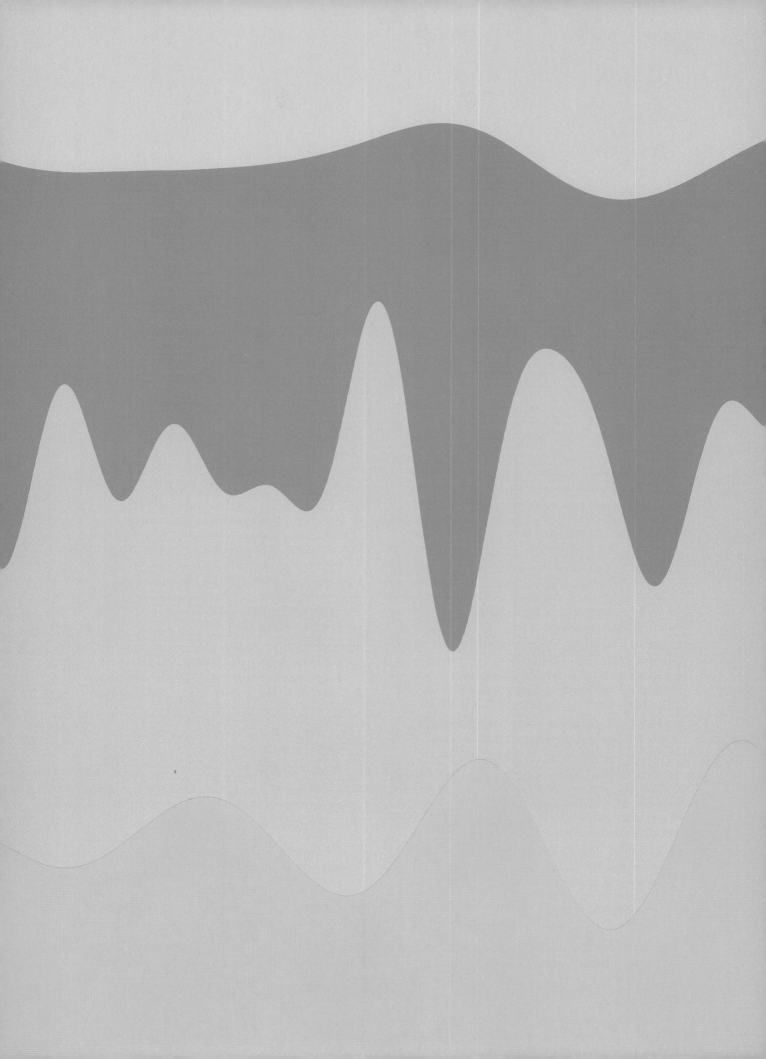

Introduction: The Hallyu Origin Story

1   Euny Hong, *The Birth of the Korean Cool* (London and New York 2014), p. 4

2   The book and exhibition delves into the performative side of hallyu only. Areas such as food and architecture, in which Korea is also making giant strides, lie sadly beyond their remit.

3   'Gangnam Style music video "broke" YouTube view limit', *BBC News*, 4 December 2014, bbc.co.uk/news/world-asia-30288542 (accessed 18 January 2022)

4   Perry Lam, 'Gangnam Style: loved by America for all wrong reasons', *South China Morning Post*, 29 October 2012, scmp.com/news/hong-kong/article/1071888/gangnam-style-loved-america-all-wrong-reasons (accessed 18 January 2022)

5   Jason Anderson, art writer and film critic for *The Grid* newspaper in Toronto, cited in Armina Ligaya, 'What's the secret to Gangnam Style's success?', *CBC News*, 28 November 2012, cbc.ca/news/entertainment/what-s-the-secret-to-gangnam-style-s-success-1.1170828 (accessed 18 January 2022)

6   HyunA, the former member of Wonder Girls who played PSY's love interest in the video, quoted in Caitlin Kelly, 'Songs that defined the decade: Psy's "Gangnam Style"', *Billboard*, 21 November 2019, billboard.com/music/music-news/psy-gangnam-style-songs-that-defined-the-decade-8544218 (accessed 18 January 2022)

7   Chang Kyung-Sup, *South Korea under Compressed Modernity: Familial Political Economy in Transition* (Abingdon and New York 2014), pp. 5–13

8   North Korea's Korean People's Army (KPA), backed by the Chinese People's Volunteer Army (PVA) and the Soviets, invaded the South (which was supported by the Republic of Korea's Army [ROKA] and the United Nations Command [UNC]), in the hope of unifying the peninsula under the communist banner.

9   On 13 December 2021, South Korean President Moon declared that South Korea, North Korea, China and the USA had reached an agreement 'in principle' to officially end the Korean War. The discussion has yet to begin as North Korea has stated it will only enter discussions once the USA ends its hostile policy towards North Korea. See Justin McCurry, 'North and South Korean agree "in principle" on formal end of war', *The Guardian*, 13 December 2021.

10 The term was used interchangeably to refer to blues, rumba, tango, jazz, etc. Western music had already been introduced on the peninsula in the late nineteenth century in the form of religious music or military marches: Michael Fuhr, *Globalization and Popular Music in South Korea: Sounding out Pop Music* (New York 2015), pp. 39–40.

11 The term *teuroteu* derives from 'foxtrot' but bears no resemblance to the original style. It was initially known as *yuhaeng changga* (trendy song) in the 1920s, becoming *teuroteu* in the 1950s.

12 Cho Junhyoung, 'Brief history of Korean cinema' in Sangjoon Lee, *Rediscovering Korean Cinema* (Ann Arbor, MI 2019), pp. 34–9

13 Kyung Moon Hwang, *A History of Korea* (Basingstoke 2010), pp. 180–2

14 Dean Chan, 'Locating play: the situated localities of portable and online gaming in East Asia' in John A. Lent and Lorna Fitzsimmons (eds), *Asian Popular Culture Now: New, Hybrid and Alternative Media* (Lanham, MD 2013), p. 18

15 Liesl Bradner, 'When Marilyn Monroe interrupted her honeymoon to go to Korea', *HistoryNet*, Winter 2020, historynet.com/when-marilyn-monroe-interrupted-her-honeymoon-to-go-to-korea.htm (accessed 18 January 2022)

16 Al Ricketts, '"Satchmo" swings at Walker Hill Resort Opening', *Stars and Stripes*, 10 April 1963, 75.stripes.com/index.php/archives/satchmo-swings-walker-hill-resort-opening (accessed 18 January 2022)

17 Jessica Prois, 'For the original K-pop stars, survival depended on making it in America', *History*, 18 March 2021, history.com/news/k-pop-origins-korean-war-kim-sisters (accessed 18 January 2022)

18 Cho (cited note 12), p. 41

19 'Which was the first color cinemascope film in Korea?', *Korean Film Archive*, eng.koreafilm.or.kr/ kmdb/trivia/funfacts/BC_0000005062 (accessed 21 February 2022)

20 Cho (cited note 12), p. 44

21 Kwan S. Kim, *The Korean Miracle (1962–1980) Revisited: Myths and Realities in Strategy and Development* (Notre Dame, IN 1992), p. 1

22 Hwang (cited note 13), pp. 225–34

23 Based on similar laws introduced in Japan in 1950.

24 'Five major problems with the statue of Admiral Yi Sun-sin in Gwanghwamun', 15 November 2010, hani.co.kr/arti/society/society_general/448754.html (accessed 13 June 2022)

25 It is interesting to note that the Ministry of Culture was associated with the Ministry of Public Information, establishing the Ministry of Culture and Public Information in 1968

26 Kim Chang Nam, *Hanguk Daejungmunhwasa* [History of Korean Popular Culture] (Paju 2021), pp. 199–201

27 All-night electricity had been available in cities since 1964. See Hwang (cited note 13), p. 231.

28 Andrei Lankov, 'Korea's TV Age Began with KBS in 1962', *Korea Times*, 17 January 2010, koreatimes.co.kr/www/news/nation/2010/01/113_59194.html (accessed 18 January 2022). In the early 1960s, TVs were mostly imported units.

29 The first TV station, HLKZ-TV (belonging to an American TV manufacturing company), was inaugurated in 1956, but due to the paucity of TV units then available and the limited broadcast times and area covered, the station did not have a lasting impact. In 1959 a fire devastated the station, bringing broadcasting to an end.

30 Kim (cited note 26), pp. 160–9

31 'K-drama: a new TV genre with gobal appeal', *Korean Culture, No. 3* (Seoul: Korean Culture Information Service 2011), p. 60, google.co.uk/books/edition/K_Drama/hhhqBgAAQBAJ?hl=en (accessed 13 June 2022)

32 'The streets were empty when 'Missi' and 'Journey' aired in the 1970s', *The Kyunghyang Shinmun*, 15 August 2010, khan.co.kr/article/201008152123185 (accessed 4 March 2022)

33 Luis Suarez-Villa and Pyo-Hwan Han, 'International trends in electronics manufacturing and the strategy of industrialization', *Economic Geography*, Vol. 66, No. 3 (July 1990), pp. 273–92 (p. 274)

34 Dr Kim S. Ran. 'The Korean system of innovation and the semi-conductor industry: a governance perspective, 1996', oecd.org/korea/2098646.pdf (accessed 4 March 2022), pp. 17–33

35 Donald N. Clark, 'U.S. role in Kwangju and beyond', 29 August 1996, latimes.com/archives/la-xpm-1996-08-29-me-38742-story.html (accessed 4 March 2022)

36 Kim (cited note 26), pp. 259–71

37 Chun's regime revived Korea's bid for the Olympic Games, which had been initiated by Park but cast aside after his assassination. Ultimately, the 1988 Summer Olympics were noteworthy for being the first to be held by a country previously thought of as 'Third World'.

38 Kim (cited note 26), pp. 264–8

39 Cho (cited note 12), p. 53

40 Yoon Min-sik, 'Cho Yong-pil, king of Korean pop music', *Korea Herald*, 18 May 2018, koreaherald.com/view.php?ud=20180518000580 (accessed 18 January 2022)

41 Park Kyung Ae, 'Women and development: the case of South Korea', *Comparative Politics*, Vol. 25, No. 2 (January 1993), p. 132

42 Darcy Paquet. *New Korean Cinema: Breaking the Waves* (New York 2009), p. 34

43 As explained in Lee Sang M., 'South Korea: from the Land of morning calm to ICT hotbed', *Academy of Management Executive*, Vol. 17, No. 2 (May 2003)., pp. 7–18

44 *The Wall Street Journal*, quoted in Ibid, p.8.

45 Kiwon Hong, 'Nation branding of Korea' in Hye-Kyung Lee and Lorraine Lim (eds), *Cultural Policies in East Asia* (London 2014), p. 74

K-CULTURE AND SOFT POWER

1 Jung Joori and Lee Hana, 'No. of hallyu fans worldwide hits 100M milestone: report', *Korea.com*, 15 January 2021, korea.net/NewsFocus/Culture/view?articleId=193943&fbclid=IwAR3ZGhi4viPJ5fW8FFHxsb_AE_3FbhhUqlm2K3ifVbg25skjhucc1lcNbE8 (accessed 20 February 2022)

2 Park Ga-young, 'K-content industry sets another export record in 2020 at $11.92 billion', *Korea Herald*, 24 January 2022, koreaherald.com/view.php?ud=20220124000809 (accessed 20 February 2022)

3 Tamar Herman, 'SM Entertainment A&R Chris Lee Talks "Cultural Technology" and creating K-pop hits', *Billboard*, 8 May 2019, billboard.com/music/music-news/sm-entertainment-ar-chris-lee-talks-cultural-technology-creating-k-pop-hits-8526179/ (accessed 20 May 2022)

4 The term metaverse first appeared in *Snow Crash*, a 1992 science-fiction novel by Neal Stephenson.

5 Virtual idols have existed since the late 1990s: see Patrick St Michel, 'A brief history of virtual pop stars', *Pitchfork*, 15 July 2016, pitchfork.com/thepitch/1229-a-brief-history-of-virtual-pop-stars (accessed 22 February 2022)

6 Kim Byung-wuk 'Games exports outstrip K-pop 10 times over: report', 8 July 2020, koreaherald.com/view.php?ud=20200708000870 (accessed 19 May 2022)

Hallyu: Soft Power and Politics

1 Youna Kim, *The Korean Wave: Korean Media Go Global* (London 2013); Youna Kim, *The Soft Power of the Korean Wave: Parasite, BTS and Drama* (London 2021)

2 Youna Kim, 'The rising east Asian wave: Korean media go global' in Daya Thussu (ed.), *Media on the Move: Global Flow and Contra-Flow* (London 2007); Kim (2013, cited note 1); Kim (2021, cited note 1)

3 Kim (2007, cited note 2)

4 Yoon Min-sik, 'Hallyu's future: limitations and sustainability', *Korea Herald*, 14 August 2017

5 Youna Kim, *Women, Television and Everyday Life in Korea: Journeys of Hope* (London 2005)

6 Youna Kim, *Routledge Handbook of Korean Culture and Society* (London 2016)

7 Kim (2013, cited note 1); Kim (2021, cited note 1)

8 Unnamed senior UN diplomat quoted in Pamela Falk, 'K-pop boy band "BTS" to give some buzz to staid United Nations', *CBS News*, 23 September 2018, cbsnews.com/news/k-pop-boy band-bts-beyond-the-scene-bangtan-boys-united-nations-general-assembly-generation-debate (accessed 31 January 2022)

9 Kim (2013, cited note 1); Kim (2021, cited note 1)

10 Haeryun Kang, '*Parasite*, Bong Joon-ho and the golden age of Korean cinema', *Washington Post*, 13 February 2020

11 Kim (2021, cited note 1)

12 Joseph Nye, *Soft Power: The Means to Success in World Politics* (New York 2004); Joseph Nye, *The Powers to Lead* (New York and Oxford 2008); Kim (2013, cited note 1); Youna Kim, *South Korean Popular Culture and North Korea* (London 2019); Kim (2021, cited note 1)

13 Joshua Kurlantzick, *Charm Offensive* (New Haven and London 2007)

14 Nye (2004, cited note 12); Nye (2008, cited note 12)

15 Kim (2013, cited note 1); Kim (2021, cited note 1)

16 Andrew Cooper, *Celebrity Diplomacy* (London 2016)

17 Kim (2007, cited note 2); Youna Kim, *Transnational Migration, Media and Identity of Asian Women: Diasporic Daughters* (London 2011)

18 Ross King, *Seoul: Memory, Reinvention and the Korean Wave* (Honolulu 2018)

19 Kim (2007, cited note 2); Kim (2013, cited note 1). Originally, the government had considered providing Korean movies, but this was changed following concerns that large numbers of moviegoers might be targets for terrorist attacks.

20 Megan Boler and Elizabeth Davis, *Affective Politics of Digital Media* (New York 2021)

21 Kim (2013, cited note 1); Kim (2021, cited note 1)

22 Roy Starrs, *Asian Nationalism in an Age of Globalization* (London 2013)

23 Jeff Kingston, *Nationalism in Asia* (Chichester and Hoboken 2016)

24 Beng Huat Chua, *Structure, Audience, and Soft Power* (Hong Kong 2012)

25 Mary Ainslie, Sarah Lipura and Joanna Lim, 'Understanding the hallyu backlash in Southeast Asia' *Kritika Kultura*, No. 28 (2017), pp. 63–91

26 Jeong Jae-seon, Lee Seul-hi and Lee Sang-gil, 'When Indonesians routinely consume Korean pop culture', *International Journal of Communication*, No. 11 (May 2017), p. 20; Park Jae-yoon and Lee Ann-gee, *The Rise of K-Dramas* (Jefferson, NC 2019)

27 Youna Kim, *Media Consumption and Everyday Life in Asia* (London 2008); Kim (2013, cited note 1); Kim (2021, cited note 1)

Digital Korean Wave: From Esports to K-pop

1 Yoon Jeongwon, 'Korean digital government infrastructure building and implementation: capacity dimensions', in Tina George Karippacheril/Kim Soonhee, Robert P. Beschel Jr. and Choi Changyong (eds), *Bringing Government into the 21st Century: The Korean Digital Governance Experience* (Washington, DC 2016), p. 46

2 Lee Kwang-Suk, 'Interrogating digital Korea: mobile phone tracking and the spatial expansion of labour control', *Media International Australia*, No. 141 (2011), pp. 107–17; Dal Yong Jin, *Smartland Korea: Mobile Communication, Culture and Society* (Ann Arbor, MI 2017)

3 Dal Yong Jin, 'The digital Korean wave: local online gaming goes global', *Media International Australia*, No. 141 (2011), pp. 128–36; Lee (cited note 2)

4 Ministry of Information and Communication, *Basic Plan for Advancing Broadband Infrastructure* (Seoul 2001)

5 Don Torrieri, *Principles of Spread-Spectrum Communication Systems* (New York 2018); Lee Gye-Pyung for LG Economic Research Institute, 'Smartphone, a new trend in the mobile phone market', 1998, lgeri.com/report/view.do?idx=3264 (accessed 4 March 2022)

6 See Jin (cited note 2)

7 Dal Yong Jin, 'Evolution of Korea's mobile technologies: from a historical approach,' *Mobile Media and Communication*, Vol. 6, No. 1 (2018), pp. 71–87

8 Stephen Temple, 'Vintage mobiles: LG Prada – first mobile with a capacitive touchscreen', *History of GSM: Birth of the Mobile Revolution*, 2007, gsmhistory.com/vintage-mobiles/#prada (accessed 31 January 2022)

9 Joyce Lee and Yang Heekyong, 'South Korea's LG becomes first major smartphone brand to withdraw from market', *Reuters*, 5 April 2021, reuters.com/article/us-lg-elec-smartphones-idUSKBN2BS032 (accessed 31 January 2022)

10 Joshua Ohsu Kwon, 'Korean webtoons go global with LINE', *Medium*, 6 March 2014, medium.com/the-headline/korean-webtoons-go-global-with-line-b82f3920580e (accessed 31 January 2022)

11 OECD, *OECD Economics Surveys Korea* (Paris 2020), p. 92

12 Stephen C. Rea, 'Chronotopes and social types in South Korean digital games', *Signs and Society*, Vol. 7, No. 1 (2019), p. 120

13 Dal Yong Jin, 'Historiography of Korean esports: perspectives on spectatorship', in Dal Yong Jin (ed.), *Global Esports: Transformation of Cultural Perceptions of Competitive Gaming* (London 2021), pp. 77–97

14 Ibid.

15 Ibid.

16 Korea Creative Content Agency, *An Analysis of the Contents Industry in the Latter Half of 2020 and the Year* (Naju 2021)

17 Dal Yong Jin and Kyong Yoon, 'The social mediascape of transnational Korean pop culture: Hallyu 2.0 as spreadable media practice', *New Media and Society*, Vol. 18, No. 7 (2016), pp. 1277–92

18 Courtney McLaren and Dal Yong Jin, '"You Can't Help But Love Them": BTS, transcultural fandom, and affective identities', *Korea Journal*, Vol. 60, No. 1 (2020), pp. 100–27

19 Julia Lee, 'K/DA, Riot Games' pop girl group, explained', *Polygon*, 5 November 2018, polygon.com/2018/11/5/18064726/league-of-legends-kda-pop-stars-video-akali-ahri-evelynn-kai-sa (accessed 31 January 2022)

20 Yoon So-Yeon, 'Virtual reality gets dose of reality as metaverse stocks drop', *The JoongAng Daily*, 28 July 2021, koreajoongangdaily.joins.com/2021/07/28/business/tech/metaverse-stock-market-fluctuation/20210728190600358.html (accessed 1 February 2022)

21 Tamar Herman, 'K-pop's virtual future: aespa, eternity, the rise of digital performers and the AI technology that allows stars to perform as avatars', *South China Morning Post*, 29 June 2021

22 Dal Yong Jin, *Artificial Intelligence in Cultural Production: Critical Perspectives on Digital Platforms* (London 2021)

Culture Technology and the Future of Hallyu

1 'Superhuman AR by Intel Studios and SM Entertainment', youtube/R3h4S7gtlul (accessed 4 March 2022)

2 Hakyung Kate Lee, 'K-pop boy band SuperM thrills fans as it performs concert online during coronavirus pandemic. Fans from 109 countries watch, recording 120 million hearts on social media', 27 April 2020, abcnews.go.com/International/pop-boy band-superm-thrills-fans-performs-concert/story?id=70362270 (accessed 4 March 2022)

3 See '"Ep.1 Black Mamba" – SM Culture Universe', youtube.com/watch?v=vbH4Lk5wYWg (accessed 4 March 2022)

K-DRAMA, WEBTOONS AND FILM

1 Meichen Sun and Kai Khiun Liew, 'Analog hallyu: historicizing K-pop formations in China', *Global Media and China*, Vol. 4, No. 4 (December 2019), pp. 419–36, journals.sagepub.com/doi/full/10.1177/2059436419881915 (accessed 20 February 2022)

2 'The "K" magic is taking over India: people find comfort in Korean dramas, music and food', *Economic Times of India*, 7 October 2021, economictimes.indiatimes.com/magazines/panache/the-k-magic-is-taking-over-india-people-find-comfort-in-korean-dramas-music-and-food/articleshow/86836620.cms?from=mdr (accessed 1 February 2022)

3 See Netflix Global Top 10 TV (non-English) chart for 13–19 September 2021 and those subsequent, top10.netflix.com/tv-non-english/2021-09-19 (accessed 20 February 2022). Netflix's metrics rank *Squid Game* its most-watched non-English language TV show of all time; see Joan E. Solsman, 'Netflix's *All of Us Are Dead* Isn't the next *Squid Game* yet, but it's big', *C|Net*, 8 February 2022, cnet.com/tech/services-and-software/netflix-biggest-shows-and-movies-ranked-according-to-netflix (accessed 20 February 2022)

4 Netflix Global Top 10 TV (non-English) chart for 24–30 January 2022, and those subsequent, top10.netflix.com/tv-non-english/2022-01-30 (accessed 20 February 2022)

5 Lee Donghu, 'The 1990s "mediatization" and the organization of the public', 2016, as mentioned in Kim Chang Nam, *Hanguk Daejung-munhwasa* [History of Korean Popular Culture] (Paju 2021), p. 301

6 Ibid.

7 A system in which each new episode is scripted, filmed and produced within a week, based on the public reaction from the episode that aired the week prior. See 'Let's talk ethics: the live-shoot system', *Seoulbeats*, 21 March 2013, seoulbeats.com/2013/03/lets-talk-ethics-the-live-shoot-system (accessed 20 February 2022)

8 Youna Kim, 'Hallyu, Korean Wave Media Culture in a Digital Age', in Dal Yong Jin and Nojin Kwak (eds), *Communication, Digital Media, and Popular Culture in Korea* (Lanham, MD 2018), p. 425

9 Once a hurdle to Korea's modernization, Neo-Confucian values are now contributing to its economic development as audiences find the traditional models comforting.

10 Koichi Iwabuchi, 'From western gaze to global gaze: Japanese cultural presence in Asia', in Diana Crane, Nobuku Kawashima and Kenichi Kawasaki (eds), *Global Culture: Media, Arts, Policy and Globalization* (London and New York 2002), p. 270

11 'Use of Korean dramas to facilitate precision mental health understanding and discussion for Asian Americans', europepmc.org/article/med/33582752 (accessed 3 March 20200) and email exchanges with the V&A in July 2021.

12 A term popularized online in around 2015 by Korean millennials to refer to their non-existent prospects due to harsh socio-economic conditions. This generation is also called the *sampo* or *opo* generation (the 3-give-up or 5-give-up generation) referring to the fact that is too expensive for them to date, marry or have children, with getting a decent job and home now added to the list: medium.com/revolutionaries/bts-hell-joseon-and-the-give-up-generations-fef9f2ba2377 (accessed 3 March 2022).

13 This unified team was not approved by all, and the issue of gender discrimination arose too.

14 Youna Kim, *The Soft Power of the Korean Wave: Parasite, BTS and Drama* (London 2021), pp. 318–21

15 Cho Junhyoung, 'A brief history of Korean cinema' (2019) in Lee Sang-joon (ed.), *Rediscovering Korean Cinema* (Ann Arbor, MI 2019), p. 55

16 Darcy Paquet, *New Korean Cinema: Breaking the Waves* (New York 2009), pp. 110–12

17 Jean Noh, 'Korean international film sales up 43% during tough 2020', *Screen Daily*, 22 February 2021, screendaily.com/news/korean-international-film-sales-up-43-during-tough-2020/5157292.article (accessed 20 February 2022)

The Road to *Parasite* (and Beyond)

1 The source for all box office statistics in this essay is the Korean Film Council. In South Korea, it is common practice to report box office performance according to the number of admissions rather than the total amount of money earned at the box office. Until the year 2000, box office figures were generally reported for Seoul only due to imprecise data collection outside the capital. From 2001, the Korean Film Council began to report nationwide admissions on a regular basis.

2 In 2001 Korean films accounted for 50.1 per cent of the market. Domestic market share would reach an all-time high of 63.8 per cent in 2006, driven by the success of films like Bong Joon-ho's *The Host* and Lee Joon-ik's *The King and the Clown*.

Webtoons: From Scrolling to Streaming

1 Patrick Frater, 'Netflix opening studio facilities to expand Korean content supply', *Variety*, 6 January 2021, variety.com/2021/biz/asia/netflix-opening-studio-facilities-in-korea-1234880370 (accessed 1 February 2022)

2 Park Dae-ui and Choi Mira, 'K-drama *Hellbound* tops Netflix' global ranking in just a day after release', *Pulse by Maeil Business News Korea*, 22 November 2021, pulsenews.co.kr/view.php?year=2021&no=1088279 (accessed 1 February 2022)

3 Nancy Miller, 'Minifesto for a new age', *Wired*, 1 March 2007, wired.com/2007/03/snackminifesto (accessed 1 February 2022)

4 Hong Nan-ji and Lee Jeong-beom, *Webtoon Seukul: webtoon changjakgwa seutori jakbeobe gwanhan modeun geot* (Webtoon School: All Things Related to the Webtoon's Creation and Story Writing) (Seoul 2021), p. 50

5 'Korean webtoon market jumps to top 1 trillion won in sales in 2020', *Korea Times*, 24 December 2021, koreatimes.co.kr/www/art/2022/01/398_321104.html (accessed 20 May 2022)

6 Defined in essence as 'stories told across multiple media' by Henry Jenkins, Katie Clinton, Ravi Purushotma, Alice J. Robison and Margaret Weigel, 'Confronting the challenges of participatory culture: media education for the 21st Century' (Chicago, IL 2006), macfound.org/media/article_pdfs/jenkins_white_paper.pdf (accessed 1 February 2022), p. 46. Quoted in Carlos Albertos Scolari, 'Transmedia story-telling: implicit consumers, narrative worlds, and branding in contemporary media production', *International Journal of Communication*, No. 3 (2019), pp. 586–606 (587).

7 Baek Byung-yeul, 'Korea's "webtoon" industry: boom or bust?', *Korea Times*, 20 February 2014, koreatimes.co.kr/www/news/culture/2014/02/203_151973.html (accessed 1 February 2022)

8 Brian Yecies and Shim Ae-gyung, *South Korea's Webtooniverse and the Digital Comic Revolution*. (Lanham, MD 2021), pp. 42–4

9 Many manga and anime were already available before then but, rather than the originals, copies created by local artists were circulated. The official recognition of those Japanese cultural materials only came in 1998.

10 Author's interview with Lee Jeong-beom, 28 December 2021.

11 Minihomepy was launched in 2002 by the social network Cyworld, which had been founded in 1999.

12 Park Kyung Ae, 'Development of ICT indicators in Korea', Service Statistics Division, Korea National Statistical Office, for the IAOS Satellite Meeting on Statistics for the Information Society, 30-31 August 2001, Tokyo: stat.go.jp/english/info/meetings/iaos/pdf/park.pdf (accessed 21 May 2022)

13 Some of the previous manhwa artists moved on to careers as webtoon artists, but the majority struggled to adjust their work to this new format, with many deciding to remain in the paper publishing field.

14 Webtoon Canvas is a Naver platform that offers to 'start your story in 6 easy steps', enabling anyone to swiftly upload their content: see webtoons.com/en/creators101/webtoon-canvas (accessed 1 February 2022). Webtoon Originals is a Naver platform that 'licenses content from the creators' and refers to contract-based commissions turning the Pro-Am into a professional.

15 Charles W. Leadbeater and Paul Miller, *The Pro-Am Revolution: How Enthusiasts are Changing Our Society and Economy* (London 2004), p. 12

16 Hong and Lee (cited note 4), p. 3

17 Today, the majority of webtoons remain free and income is also generated from the 'wait-or-pay' system whereby the viewer pays a tiny fee to read the next episode instead of waiting for its release free of charge the following week.

18 Yoon So-Yeon, 'Daum Webtoon becomes Kakao Webtoon as competition intensifies', *Korea Joon-Ang Daily*, 20 July 2021, koreajoongangdaily.joins.com/2021/07/20/business/tech/Kakao-Webtoon-Daum-Webtoon-Kakao-Page/20210720175007618.html (accessed 2 February 2022)

19 Hong and Lee (cited note 4), pp. 30–2. Today, many small and medium size independent websites such as Lehzin and Ant Studio complete the webtoon universe.

20 Studies were based on 67 webtoon companies and 710 artists.

21 *Love Story* attracted 32 million views for the first time in webtoon history, solidifying webtoons' power as a storytelling means.

22 Interview with Lee Jeong-beom, 28 December 2021.

23 Lee Jong-beom started to use QR codes in the paper book version of his webtoon *Dr Frost* back in 2012.

24 Sohn Ji-young, 'Stepping into the webtoon world, literally', *Korea Herald*, 17 December 2017, koreaherald.com/view.php?ud=20171217000267 (accessed 2 February 2022)

25 Shin Jin, '"Augmented reality" Naver Webtoon Phone Ghost is a hot topic…"Surprised by a video call from a ghost"', *Mediapen*, 7 November 2016, mediapen.com/news/view/204030 (accessed 21 May 2022)

26 Lee Jeong-beom notes that there is no real anime industry in South Korea, unlike in Japan, and so many webtoons are converted instead into films or TV dramas.

27 A recent reversal in this trend has seen the emergence of webtoons spawned from the K-drama, as in the case of *Our Beloved Summer* (2021). This time, the viewers are converted into readers, with webtoon plotlines complementing those of the K-drama.

28 Choi Min-young, 'What's the largest profit for Naver Webtoon writers? BTS and Superman webtoons are coming out too,' *Hankyoreh*, 18 August 2021, hani.co.kr/arti/economy/it/1008134.html (accessed 21 May 2022)

29 Kim Hyung-won, 'Focus on "super IP and global expansion" in the webtoon industry for 2021', *IT Chosun*, 1 January 2021, it.chosun.com/site/data/html_dir/2021/01/01/2021010100297.html (accessed 21 May 2022)

30 Chae Hee-sang, '"Story universes" for cross-media entertainment', *Koreana* (Spring 2021), p. 26

31 Natsuki Edogawa and Erina Ito, 'Fresh Korean wave sweeping world, powered by Netflix hits', *Asahi Shimbun*, 5 July 2020, asahi.com/ajw/articles/13468714 (accessed 2 February 2022); Ockoala, 'Japan confirms remake of hit JTBC drama *Itaewon Class* with male lead Takeuchi Ryoma', *A Koala's Playground*, 6 September 2021, koalasplayground.com/2021/09/06/japan-confirms-remake-of-hit-jtbc-drama-itaewon-class-with-male-lead-takeuchi-ryoma (accessed 2 February 2022)

32 Wendy Lee, 'This South Korean studio has big Hollywood plans', *LA Times*, 20 July 2015, latimes.com/entertainment-arts/business/story/2021-07-20/known-for-korean-dramas-jtbc-aims-to-be-a-bigger-hollywood-player (accessed 1 February 2022)

33 *2020 Cartoon Industry White Paper*, pp. 21–30. It should be noted that this survey includes the paper-based manhwa industry. See welcon.kocca.kr/en/support/content-news/429 (accessed 1 February 2022).

34 'Korean webtoon market jumps to top 1 trillion won in sales in 2020', *Korea Times*, 24 December 2021, koreatimes.co.kr/www/art/2022/01/398_321104.html (accessed 20 May 2022)

35 Dong Sun-hwa, 'BTS webtoon "75 Fates: CHAKHO" to be unveiled next year', *Korea Times* (4 November 2021), koreatimes.co.kr/www/art/2021/11/732_318245.html (accessed 2 February 2022); Kim (cited note 29)

The Conundrum of Global Korean Culture: On *Squid Game*

1 Irhe Sohn, 'Sacred translations: *Parasite* (2019), english subtitles, and Global Korean Cinema', virtual seminar at the *Association for Asian Studies Annual Conference* (23 March 2021)

2 *Squid Game*'s visual references to *Produce 101* also hint at how fairness can often be revealed to be a fantasy in the survivor game setting – as is portrayed in *Squid Game*. See koreajoongangdaily.joins.com/2020/11/18/entertainment/television/produce101-mnet-cjenm/20201118180500444.html6 (accessed 28 April 2022).

3 Hong Yang-ja, 'Hangukui eoriniga bureugo inneun ilbonui warabe uta' (Japanese Children's Songs Sung by Korean Children), *Minjok eumakui ihae*, Vol. 5 (1996), pp. 77–156

4 Gu Ja-chang, 'Hyangto hakja Yim Yeong-su, "il sinmun 'Ojingeogeim' bareon waegok"' (Folklore scholar Yim Yeong-su argues that

the Japanese newspaper distorts the facts about *Squid Game*), *Kukminilbo*, 11 November 2021, news.kmib.co.kr/article/view.asp?arcid=0016455773&code=61121111&stg=ws_real (accessed 2 February 2022)

K-POP AND FANDOM

1 Dal Yong Jin, 'The rise of the New Korean Wave' in *New Korean Wave: Transnational Culture in the Age of Social Media* (Chicago, IL 2016), pp. 3–19

2 The trio band was founded by Seo Taiji (former bassist of Sinawe), who was joined by top dancers and vocalists Lee Juno and Yang Hyun Suk. The latter went on to found YG Entertainment, the powerhouse behind Big Bang and BLACKPINK.

3 Park Sun-Young, 'Shinsedae: conservative attitudes of a "new generation" in South Korea and the impact on the Korean presidential election', *East-West Center*, 5 September 2007, eastwestcenter.org/news-center/east-west-wire/shinsedae-conservative-attitudes-of-a-new-generation-in-south-korea-and-the-impact-on-the-korean-pres (accessed 1 March 2022)

4 Michael Fuhr, *Globalization and Popular Music in South Korea: Sounding Out Pop Music* (New York 2016), pp. 532–5

5 Ibid., p. 55

6 While Korea is ranked as one of the most advanced OECD countries – it trails at the bottom of the list when it comes to gender equality.

7 See the high-profile cases of Britney Spears, Whitney Houston, Taylor Swift and Prince in the western music industries, or those in the world of athletics, ballet or classical music, among others.

8 Dal Yong Jin, 'Comparative discourse on J-pop and K-pop: hybridity in contemporary local music', *Korea Journal*, Vol. 60, No. 1 (2020), pp. 47–9, dbpia.co.kr/journal/articleDetail?nodeId=NODE09378564 (accessed 9 March 2022)

9 Gilbert Cruz, 'A brief history of Motown', *Time*, 12 January 2009, content.time.com/time/arts/article/0,8599,1870975,00.html (accessed 1 March 2022)

10 Mick Brown, 'Berry Gordy: the man who built motown', 23 January 2016, s.telegraph.co.uk/graphics/projects/berry-gordy-motown/index.html (accessed 9 March 2022)

11 Tomasz Sleziak, 'The role of Confucianism in contemporary South Korea', *Annual of Oriental Studies – Rocznik Orientalistyczny*, No. 66 (2013), pp. 41–3, researchgate.net/publication/272389562_The_Role_of_Confucianism_in_Contemporary_South_Korean_Society (accessed 9 March 2022)

12 A *changga* that fused the melody of the Korean national hymn with the Scottish 'Auld Lang Syne', and using new Korean lyrics praising the king, was sung for King Gojong's birthday in 1896. See Fuhr (cited note 4), pp. 39–43

13 The concepts of 'prosumer' and 'produser' were developed by Axel Bruns in 'From prosumer to produser: understanding user-led content creation', paper presented at the Transforming Audiences conference, London, September 2009; see also Axel Bruns, *Blogs, Wikipedia, Second Life and Beyond: From Production to Produsage* (New York 2008)

Beyond Appropriation and Appreciation: The Cross-Cultural Dynamics of K-pop

1 'How K-pop is responding to its longstanding appropriation problem', *Dazed Digital*, 12 August 2020, dazeddigital.com/music/article/50045/1/how-k-pop-is-responding-to-cultural-appropriation (accessed 2 February 2022)

2 Kendra James, 'Justin Timberlake has gotten away with cultural appropriation for years now', *Cosmopolitan*, 29 June 2016,

cosmopolitan.com/entertainment/celebs/a60737/justin-timberlake-cultural-appropriation (accessed 2 February 2022)

3   Claire Clements, 'Korean festival promotes unity in South Korea, United States', *Coppell Student Media*, 12 November 2018, coppell-studentmedia.com/83292/entertainment/korean-festival-promotes-unity-in-south-korea-united-states (accessed 2 February 2022)

4   Kang Myoung-Seok, '[Interview] Record producer Yoo Young-jin – Part 1', *Asian Economy*, 6 November 2011, asiae.co.kr/news/print.htm?idxno=2010061109310268065 (accessed 2 February 2022)

5   Joe Palmer, 'SM Entertainment: the "Brand"', *Kultscene*, 20 April 2015, kultscene.com/sm-entertainment-the-brand (accessed 2 February 2022)

6   Ibid.

7   Oh Ingyu, 'The globalization of K-pop: Korea's place in the global music industry', *Korea Observer*, Vol. 44, No. 3 (Autumn 2013), pp. 389–409 (p. 399)

8   Alicia Lee, 'You know your K-pop stars. Now meet the American producers and songwriters behind them', *WFSB*, 20 March 2020, wfsb.com/you-know-your-k-pop-stars-now-meet-the-american-producers-and-songwriters-behind-them/article_36191671-509f-5a25-8930-fdc1171719f1.html [limited access]

'Into The New World': K-pop Fandom, Civic Engagement and Citizenship in the Global South

1   Zoe Haylock, 'K-pop stans spammed the Dallas Police Department's app with fan cams', *Vulture*, 1 June 2020, vulture.com/2020/06/k-pop-stans-crashed-dallas-police-app-with-fan-cams.html (accessed 2 February 2022)

2   Barbara Ortutay, 'Did TikTok teens, K-pop fans punk Trump's comeback rally?', *AP News*, 21 June 2020, apnews.com/article/pop-music-music-donald-trump-us-news-united-states-2f18f18a8b40a4635fd3590fd159241c (accessed 2 February 2022)

3   '17 ways deadheads can change the world', *Headcount*, headcount.org/music-and-activism/17-ways-deadheads-can-change-the-world (accessed 2 February 2022)

4   Abby Ohlheiser, 'TikTok teens and K-pop stars don't belong to the "resistance"', *Technology Review*, 23 June 2020, technologyreview.com/2020/06/23/1004336/tiktok-teens-kpop-stans-trump-resistance-its-complicated (accessed 2 February 2022)

5   Ashley Hinck, *Politics for the Love of Fandom: Fan-based citizenship in a digital world* (Baton Rouge, LA, 2019)

6   Youkung Lee, 'How sparks at S. Korean women's school led to anti-Park fire', *AP News*, 14 March 2017, apnews.com/article/f26782acb46246a0835ecfc412ed7db1 (accessed 2 February 2022)

7   'Ewha students singing "INTO THE NEW WORLD (SNSD)" right before brutal crackdown of the police', 31 July 2016, youtube.com/watch?v=eBCBht6_C4E&ab_channel=ThinkWe (accessed 22 February 2022)

8   Tamar Herman, '9 K-pop songs that recently became part of South Korean politics', *Billboard*, 2 May 2018, billboard.com/articles/columns/k-town/8436957/k-pop-songs-politicized-south-korea (accessed 2 February 2022)

9   See 'Protest site at Gwanghwamun. Girls' Generation's "Into the New World"', youtube.com/watch?v=6Qus3mxcumQ (accessed 2 February 2022)

10 IATB, 'TWICE's "Cheer Up" used as protest song by younger Park Geun-hye protesters', *Asian Junkie*, 31 October 2016, asianjunkie.com/2016/10/31/twices-cheer-up-used-as-protest-song-by-younger-park-geun-hye-protesters (accessed 2 February 2022)

11 See twitter.com/pengjeongnam/status/795196821379293185?s=20 (accessed 2 February 2022)

12 Patpicha Tanakasempipat, 'K-pop's social power spurs Thailand's youth protests', *Reuters*, 2 November 2020, reuters.com/article/us-thailand-protests-k-pop/k-pops-social-media-power-spurs-thailands-youth-protests-idUSKBN27I23K (accessed 2 February 2022)

13 Ibid.

14 See twitter.com/BTS_algeria/status/1106621117970739200?s=20 (accessed 2 February 2022)

15 See instagram.com/p/B6bavX0J56Y/?hl=en (accessed 2 February 2022)

16 Camilo Diaz Pino, '"K-pop is rupturing Chilean society": fighting with globalized objects in localized conflicts', *Communication, Culture and Critique*, Vol. 14, No. 4 (December 2021), pp. 551–67

17 remezcla.com/music/gabriel-boric-k-pop-fans-help-chile-new-president-elected/ (accessed 2 February 2022)

18 news.abs-cbn.com/life/02/20/22/halalan2022-k-pop-fans-lead-voter-ed-efforts-fight-disinformation (accessed 13 June 2022)

19 Tamar Herman, 'Pride Month 2021: support from K-pop stars including Tiffany Young of Girls' Generation and Kevin Woo for LGBT community', *South China Morning Post*, 21 June 2021, scmp.com/lifestyle/entertainment/article/3138170/pride-month-2021-support-k-pop-stars-including-tiffany (accessed 2 February 2022)

20 Ashley Hinck, *Politics for the Love of Fandom: Fan-based citizenship in a digital world* (Baton Rouge, LA, 2019), p. 15

21 See twitter.com/BTS_EGYPT_ARMY/status/1211307807921836039?s=19 (accessed 2 February 2022)

22 Amira Mittermaier, 'Beyond compassion: Islamic voluntarism in Egypt', *American Ethnologist*, Vol. 41, No. 3 (August 2014), pp. 518–31, anthrosource.onlinelibrary.wiley.com/doi/10.1111/amet.12092

23 twitter.com/BTS_EGYPT_ARMY/status/1229420874480091136?s=20 (accessed 2 February 2022)

24 twitter.com/BTS_EGYPT_ARMY/status/1334512840603029506?s=20 (accessed 2 February 2022)

25 twitter.com/BTS_EGYPT_ARMY/status/1315649243642818560?s=20 (accessed 2 February 2022)

26 Hinck (cited note 20), p. 9

27 twitter.com/Blink_OFCINDO/status/1452265980453920770?s=20 (accessed 2 February 2022)

28 youtube.com/watch?v=MNUM88GxSWo (accessed 2 February 2022)

29 Thana Boonlert, 'Fans tuk up tuk-tuk cause', *Bangkok Post*, 5 May 2021, bangkokpost.com/life/social-and-lifestyle/2110475/fans-tuk-up-tuk-tuk-cause (accessed 2 February 2022)

30 Danial Martinus, 'People are keeping Thailand's small businesses afloat with K-pop ads', *Mashable SE Asia*, 5 July 2021, sea.mashable.com/culture/16488/people-are-keeping-thailands-small-businesses-afloat-with-k-pop-ads (accessed 2 February 2022)

31 Tamar Herman, 'BTS add date at NYC's Citi Field, become first-ever K-pop act to play U.S. stadium', *Billboard*, 8 August 2018, billboard.com/articles/columns/pop/8469396/bts-nyc-love-yourself-nyc-concert-first-ever-kpop-stateside-stadium-show (accessed 2 February 2022)

K-pop's Fictional Universe: Symbols and Hidden Clues in K-pop Music Videos

1   Great examples of Korean music videos in this category include 'Supermarket' by Pipi Band (1995), 'Magic Carpet Ride' by Jaurim (2000), 'I Know' by Seo Taiji and Boys (1992), 'Let's Ride a Horse' by Crying Nut (1998), and No Brain's 'You Have a Crush on Me' (2004).

2   In Korea in the late 1990s and early 2000s, the genre called 'music drama' was quite phenomenal. These videos were typically three- to eight-minute short films, using the music as their soundtrack. Sad and slow ballads with fierce, tragic storylines were accompanied by visuals representing fatal disease, a sad love story, war and death. Representative examples are Jo Sungmo's 'Do You Know' (2000) and 'Thorn Tree' (2002), and 'Fixing my Make-up' by Wax (2001). First-generation K-pop idol group H.O.T. illustrated the lives of wretched teenagers in the widely loved 'Hope' (1998).

3   See, for example, 'Barefooted Youth' (1997) by Buck, 'Dreams Come True' (1998) by S.E.S., 'Wa' (1999) by Lee Junghyun and 'I Don't Know' (1999) by Um Jungwha.

4   Among them 'ID; Peace B' (2000) by BoA, and 'Sky Blue Balloon' (2000) by G.O.D.

5   There are relatively few of these, but H.O.T.'s 'The Promise of H.O.T.' (1998) is an example.

6   EXO debuted as a twin group, comprising Exo-M and Exo-K, each with six members. Each member has a pair member in the other group. In 'Mama', Baekhyun from Exo-K shines a brilliant light into a mirror; on its far side, Exo-M's Lay is able to absorb and make use of this power. Similarly, each member uncovers and influences their twin member's existence and powers: in EXO's twentieth teaser video, Chanyeol discovers a stone inscribed with Suho's symbol, and in the video for 'What is Love' (2012) he finds Lay's symbol on another stone. Though several members have since left the group, the storyline accommodates these departures and continues to evolve today.

7   In 'I Need You' (2015), the teenaged BTS are abused by the brutal world. One of the members, RM, refuses to remain young and tries to become a grown-up. When RM drops his lollipop on the ground, it changes into a cigarette butt. The lollipop – a symbol for immaturity, just as the cigarette represents adulthood – recurs in many other BTS videos. Another significant symbol is the mysterious and precious imaginary flower called Smeraldo, which exists only in the BTS Universe and acts as a McGuffin to unfold their story.

8   Scenes with numerous faces surrounding Jimin, and the appearance of a giant-sized BTS, show that the members have themselves grown through self-love, proudly moving away from false happiness.

9   In the BTS Universe, BTS accomplished their growth, starting from self-love and expanding to loving and caring for one another. Now they turn outwards, to share their energy with all the people who are suffering as they once did. In the video for 'Dynamite', BTS show their will to deliver happiness and hope to people all around the world. With this song, BTS became the first Korean act to top the US's *Billboard* Hot 100, *Billboard* Artist 100 and *Billboard* 200 charts simultaneously.

10 Along with music videos, aespa use lyrics to illustrate their story. In the lyrics to 'Black Mamba', 'aespa is me, we can't be separated' indicates the strong connection between a person and their avatar. It is the advent of a new human, as 'This is the evolution'. Black Mamba feeds on people's greed and threatens the world; aespa are the warriors protecting the world from her.

11 KWANGYA is an infinite space in SM Entertainment's Fictional Universe. SM is putting together a massive story in KWANGYA, which includes all the SM musicians. At the start of 2022, a special SM concert livestreamed on YouTube showed all the K-pop groups' performances in KWANGYA. (Googling KWANGYA brings up the address of SM Entertainment's headquarters in Seoul.)

K-pop and YouTube

1   See, for example, 'Artist on the rise: aespa' (2021), youtube.com/watch?v=hmZbsfel4jM (accessed 8 February 2022)

Pretty Tough: The Aesthetics of K-pop Masculinities

1   Mark James Russell, *Pop Goes Korea: Behind the Revolution in Movies, Music, and Internet Culture* (Berkeley, CA 2012) p. 297

2   See Joanna Elfving-Hwang 'K-pop idols, artificial beauty and affective fan relationships in South Korea' in Anthony Elliott (ed.), *Routledge Handbook of Celebrity Studies* (London and New York 2018), pp. 191–201

K-BEAUTY AND FASHION

1   'YSL gets free ride on drama sensation', *Korea Times*, 24 March 2014, koreaherald.com/view.php?ud=20140324001347 (accessed 9 March 2022)

2   International Trade Administration, *South Korea – Country Commercial Guide: Cosmetics,* 13 August 2021, trade.gov/country-commercial-guides/south-korea-cosmetics (accessed 13 June 2022)

3   Valérie Gelezeau, 'The body, cosmetics and aesthetics in South Korea: The emergence of a field of research', 2015, academia.edu/27213827/ The_body_cosmetics_and_aesthetics_in_South_Korea_The_ emergence_of_a_field_of_research (accessed 3 March 2022), p. 10

4   This belief was shared by many cultures, including those of Greece, India and China.

5   Lee Soohyun and Ryu Keunkwan, 'Plastic surgery: investment in human capital or consumption?', *Journal of Human Capital*, Vol. 6, No. 3 (Autumn 2012), pp. 230–5

6   See Ruth Holliday and Joanna Elfving-Hwang, 'Gender, globalization and aesthetic surgery in South Korea', *Body Society* (May 2012), pp. 58–81

7   Ibid., p. 71

8   Park Ju-young, 'Seoul Metro to remove plastic surgery ads', *Korea Herald*, 27 November 2017, koreaherald.com/view.php?ud= 20171127000800 (accessed 10 March 2022)

9   See Monica Kim, 'The story behind seoul's latest street style staple', *Vogue*, 23 October 2015, vogue.com/article/hanbok-street-style-seoul-korean-traditional-dress (accessed 3 March 2022)

10 Lee Hyo-won, 'Renaissance of hanbok', *Korea Times*, 12 July 2007, koreatimes.co.kr/www/news/art/2007/07/203_6384.html (accessed 3 March 2022)

11 'Hanbok designer Kim Kyesoon', *KBS News*, 15 January 2007, news. kbs.co.kr/news/view.do?ncd=1283685 (accessed 3 March 2022)

12 Jang Nam-mi. '"Hanbok's modernity" by Creative Director Suh Young-hee', 26 November 2021, for *Craft+Design* No. 50, blog.naver. com/kcdf2010/222579334053 (accessed 3 March 2022)

13 Kim Bo-eun, 'Hanbok returns with modern charm, *Korea Times*, 12 August 2015, koreatimes.co.kr/www/culture/2021/11/316_184704.html (accessed 3 March 2022)

14 InHae Yeo, interview with Jeong Yun-kee, September 2021.

Formulating K-beauty: A Century of Modern Korean Cosmetics

1   Mary-Ann Russon, 'K-beauty: the rise of Korean make-up in the west', *BBC News*, 21 October 2018, bbc.co.uk/news/business-45820671 (accessed 16 February 2022); 'Exporting beauty', *Korea JoongAng Daily*, 22 June 2021, koreajoongangdaily.joins.com/2021/06/22/ business/industry/kbeauty-cosmetics/20210622165700350.html (accessed 16 February 2022)

2   Basia Skudrzyk., 'Korean beauty market is booming! Are you taking note?', *LinkedIn Pulse*, 15 June 2021, linkedin.com/pulse/k-beauty-market-booming-you-taking-note-basia-skudrzyk-mba (accessed 16 February 2022)

3   Xu Jing, *A Chinese Traveller in Medieval Korea: Xu Jing's Illustrated Account of the Xuanhe Embassy to Koryo*, trans. Se Vermeersch (Honolulu, HI 2016), p. 32

4   Yoo Seungjae, '*Bakgabun'*, *Birth of the 'Hit': 100 Years of Korean Brands*, (Seoul 2021) p. 22.

5   Korea was able to register trademarks from 1908.

6   In 1926 adverts for Japanese cosmetic products typically took up 16.3 per cent of the front-page advertising space of Korea's major broadsheet *Chosun Ilbo*.

7   The term was first used by writers Sarah Grand in 1894 and subsequently Ouida (Maria Louisa Ramé). See Sally Ledger, *The New Woman: Fiction and Feminism at the Fin de Siècle* (Manchester 1997)

8   Seop Li-gi, 'How to Look Modern', *Sinyeoseong*, p. 71

9   Cited in 'Yeopju Beauty Salon', gubo34.tistory.com/184 (accessed 13 June 2022)

10   Kim So-yeon, *Changes in Attire and Clothing* (Seoul 2006), p. 351

11   Yu Dong-hyeon. 'Incheon Story. First productions of domestic cosmetics, beauty soap... 'beauty city', birthplace of beauties', *Chosun Ilbo*, 14 September 2011, chosun.com/site/data/html_dir/2011/09/13/2011091301319.html (accessed January 2022)

12   Kyunghyang Shinmun, 1963, youtube.com/watch?v=jb79bMqXl gw&list=PLyM501lkwOfPf5Zj-_FO1pn0NRGgvX2wj&index=13 (accessed January 2022)

13   Kim Jae-hun, 'LG Household & Health Care will beat Amorepacific soon in cosmetics sector', *Korea Times*, 30 January 2020, koreatimes.co.kr/www/tech/2021/12/129_282675.html (accessed 19 February 2022). We have corrected an error in the article's currency conversion, which gives a figure of US$16.8 billion.

14   Casey Hall, 'K-beauty giant Amorepacific sees profit jump 727% in 2021', *Business of Fashion*, 10 February 2022, businessoffashion. com/news/global-markets/k-beauty-giant-amorepacific-sees-profit-jump-727-in-2021 (accessed 19 February 2022)

15   Liz Flora, 'How a hero product is born', *Business of Fashion*, 28 February 2020 https://www.businessoffashion.com/articles/beauty/how-a-hero-product-is-born/ (accessed 19 February 2022)

Hanbok: Korean Traditional, Contemporary and Fashionable Dress

1   'Interview with a hanbok designer who designed hanbok for BLACKPINK's "How you like that" music video', *HaB Korea*, 12 July 2020, habkorea.net/interview-of-a-hanbok-designer-who-designed-hanbok-for-blackpinks-how-you-like-that-music-video (accessed 1 March 2022); Susan-Han, 'Netizens are head over heels for BLACKPINK's gorgeous, modernized Korean hanbok outfits in "How You Like That"', *AllKPop*, 27 June 2020, allkpop.com/article/2020/06/netizens-are-head-over-heels-for-blackpinks-gorgeous-modernized-korean-hanbok-outfits-in-how-you-like-that (accessed 1 March 2022)

2   Hahna Yoon, 'A centuries-old Korean style gets an update', *New York Times*, 19 October 2020, nytimes.com/2020/10/19/style/hanbok-k-pop-fashion.html (accessed 1 March 2022)

3   Kyungmee Lee, 'Dress policy and western-style court attire in modern Korea' in Kyung-hee Pyun and Aida Yuen Wong (eds), *Fashion, Identity and Power in Modern Asia* (Cham 2018), pp. 47–68

4   *Twentieth Century Hanbok of Korean Women*, exh. cat., Daegu National Museum, 2018

5   Kim Hyejeong, 'A study on the customs in Han Hyungmo's film *Madame Freedom*', *Journal of Fashion Business*, Vol. 17, No. 1 (2013), pp. 98–113

6   Ryu Hui-gyeong et al., *Two Thousand Years of Korean Fashion* (Seoul 2001), pp. 142–3; *Velvet*, exh. cat., DTC Textile Museum, Daegu, 2017

7   H. Yeom, 'The style and beauty of Korean hanbok: focusing on the trend of reformed *hanbok*', *Jeontong-gwa hyeondae* (*Traditional and Contemporary*), No. 16 (2001), pp. 184–202

8   Jilkyungyee's website can be found at jilkyungyee.co.kr (accessed 1 March 2022)

9   Yunah Lee, 'Fashioning tradition in Korean contemporary fashion', *International Journal of Fashion Studies*, Vol. 2, No. 2 (2017), pp. 241–61

10   Lee Young-hee, *The Hanbok Jaengi Who Went to Paris* (Seoul 2008), pp. 15–16

11   Ibid., p. 24.

12   Sung So-young, 'Fashion's first lady focuses lens on Asia', *Korean JoongAng Daily*, 3 June 2013, koreajoongangdaily.joins.com/2013/06/03/features/Fashions-first-lady-focuses-lens-on-Asia/2972536. html (accessed 2 March 2022); Nicole Phelps, 'Carolina Herrera Spring 2011 Ready-to-Wear', *Vogue Runway*, 12 September 2010, vogue. com/fashion-shows/spring-2011-ready-to-wear/carolina-herrera (accessed 2 March 2022)

13   Kim Jae-hun, 'American designer collaborates on hanbok', *Korea Times*, 26 February 2017, koreatimes.co.kr/www/culture/2021/11/199_224720.html (accessed 2 March 2022); Rosemary Feitelberg, 'Carolina Herrera creates three customized hanboks for New York and Seoul installations', *Women's Wear Daily*, 14 February 2017, wwd.com/fashion-news/fashion-scoops/carolina-herrera-hanboks-for-new-york-and-seoul-installations-10799072 (accessed 2 March 2022)

14   Tchai Kim press package (2016)

15   Anne Marie Leshkowich and Carla Jones, 'What happens when Asian chic becomes chic in Asia?', *Fashion Theory*, Vol. 7, No. 3/4 (2003), pp. 281–300

K-pop style

1   Anna Chan, 'BLACKPINK now has more YouTube subscribers than Justin Bieber: "We will continue to bring positivity", *Billboard*, 10 September 2021, billboard.com/music/music-news/blackpink-most-youtube-subscribers-9627584 (accessed 16 February 2022)

Crystal S. Anderson is affiliate faculty in African and African American Studies and the School of Art at George Mason University. She is the author of *Soul in Seoul: African American Music and K-pop* (2020), which explores the impact of African American popular music on contemporary Korean pop, R&B and hip-hop, and the role of global fans in the music press.

Yoojin Choi is Exhibition Project Curator for Hallyu! The Korean Wave at the V&A. Previously, she was Assistant Curator in the Asian Department at the V&A, where she researched Goryeo ceramic cosmetic boxes. Her interests are in Korean contemporary art, and Korea during the period of the Japanese occupation.

Mariam Elba is a research-reporter at *ProPublica*, where she conducts research for local investigations. She is also a K-pop 'fanthropologist', looking at how K-pop fandoms around the world exercise and express identity through fan practices.

Joanna Elfving-Hwang is Associate Professor of Korean Society and Culture and Director of the Korea Research and Engagement Centre at Curtin University, Perth, Australia. Her research focuses on beauty cultures and the sociology of the body in South Korea, as well as gender in Korean society and popular culture.

Gee Eun is Visual Director at THEBLACKLABEL, having worked at YG Entertainment for over twenty years. She started out as Big Bang's personal stylist, won 'Stylist Of The Year' at the 2016 Gaon Pop Chart Awards and has gone on to style some of the biggest names in K-pop, including G-Dragon.

Dal Yong Jin is Distinguished Professor at Simon Fraser University and Global Professor in the School of Media and Communication at Korea University. He is author of *Artificial Intelligence in Cultural Production: Critical Perspectives on Digital Platforms* and *Transnational Hallyu: The Globalization of Korean Digital and Popular Culture* (both 2021).

Lia Kim is chief choreographer of 1MILLION Dance Studio in Gangnam, Seoul, whose YouTube channel has received many millions of views. She has also worked as a K-pop choreographer for JYP, YG and SM Entertainment.

Rosalie Kim is Curator of the Korean collection in the Asian Department at the V&A. With a background in architecture and philosophy, her interest lies in the making of contemporary Korean culture, craft and design in the digital age. Prior to the V&A, she worked as an architect in Korea and Europe, and led architectural studios at Kingston University in London.

So Hye Kim is Research Professor, Outreach Center for Korean Linguistic, Literary, and Cultural Studies, Korea University. Her research focuses on Korean and East Asian films of the diaspora, as well as transnational East Asian cinema and independent film movements.

Youna Kim is Professor of Global Communications at the American University of Paris. Kim was previously at the London School of Economics and Political Science where she taught from 2004, after completing her PhD at Goldsmiths, University of London. She is the author and editor of ten books on Korean/Asian media culture.

Lee Sol is a freelance writer whose interests lie in the collision of popular culture, design and technology. She is a frequent contributor to *Monthly Design* and a former Korea Foundation intern at the V&A.

Soo-Man Lee founded SM Entertainment in 1995 and still actively produces works of top artists. Called the 'father of K-pop' for his pioneering efforts to create this new genre of music, he is most recognized for the systemization of the entertainment industry, which he defined as 'Culture Technology'. He was awarded the prestigious 'Silver Crown Order' by the South Korean government in 2011 for elevating the brand image of his country with K-pop. He was the first Asian to receive US Asia Society's Asia Game Changer Award in 2016. Lee was the first Korean on the 2020 *Billboard* Impact List and has been on *Variety*'s list of top 500 Entertainment Leaders for five consecutive years.

Sun Lee is Director of Music Partnerships for Korea and Greater China & Artist Relations for APAC at YouTube. She leads business with music partners in Korea, China, Taiwan and Hong Kong and supports the promotion of Asia-Pacific (APAC) artists. Prior to her current role, she was responsible for YouTube marketing across APAC and Google marketing in Korea. In 2019 and 2021 she was recognized as one of *Billboard*'s International Power Players.

Yunah Lee is Principal Lecturer, School of Humanities and Social Science at the University of Brighton. Her work explores modernity, modernism and national identity in East Asian and British design and material culture. She co-edited *Design and Modernity in Asia: National Identity and Transnational Exchange 1945–1990* (Bloomsbury, 2022).

Darcy Paquet is author of *New Korean Cinema: Breaking the Waves* (2010). He teaches at the Busan Asian Film School and translates subtitles for many Korean films including *The Handmaiden* (2016) and *Parasite* (2019).

Song Jong-hee is an award-winning make-up director and long-time collaborator of director Park Chan-wook, working with him on films such as *Oldboy* (2003), *Lady Vengeance* (2005) and, more recently, the Palm d'Or-nominated *Decision to Leave* (2022).

Dasom Sung is an assistant curator of Korea Arts at the V&A. She was a lecturer at Seoul National University from 2020 to 2021 and is a doctoral candidate in craft theory at Seoul National University, Korea.

InHae Yeo is Senior Brand Marketing Manager at Vestiaire Collective Korea, a leading global app for desirable pre-loved fashion. She previously worked as a fashion consultant and writer for Oikonomos Club Ltd, a British Korean Communications Consultancy.

Hallyu! The Korean Wave

This book, and the exhibition it accompanies, would not have been possible without the kind support and collective effort of so many advocates and associates, from both inside and outside of the V&A, to whom I am immensely grateful.

Particular thanks go to Yoojin Choi, the Exhibition Project Curator, without whose knowledge, commitment and enthusiasm neither the book nor the exhibition would have happened. Special thanks also go to Olivia Oldroyd and Manuela Buttiglione, exhibition managers, who, together with Ruth Connolly, worked with great patience and devotion to ensure the smooth delivery of this project. I am also hugely grateful to Dasom Sung (Assistant Curator of Korean Arts), and Lee Sol and Jenny Kim (former V&A Korea Foundation interns), for their tireless efforts and invaluable support through every stage of the exhibition and publication.

I would like to thank all the authors and interviewees who contributed their time and research to this publication: Youna Kim, Dal Yong Jin, Soo-Man Lee, Darcy Paquet, Song Jong-hee, So Hye Kim, Crystal S. Anderson, Mariam Elba, Lee Sol, Lia Kim, Dasom Sung, Sun Lee, Joanna Elfving-Hwang, Yoojin Choi, Gee Eun, Yunah Lee, InHae Yeo, Van Ta Park and Jeong Yunkee. For steering the publication through to completion with great rigour and expertise, I am indebted to Rebecca Fortey, Andrew Tullis and Emma Woodiwiss in V&A Publishing, and to Marwan Kaabour for his stunning design.

Thank you also to the curators, scholars, writers, cultural commentators, business insiders, thinkers and fans who generously shared their knowledge and helped steer the curatorial conversations and content: Zara Arshad, Yunah Lee, InHae Yeo, Jiyeon Woods, Prof. Jieun Kiaer and Dr Simon Barnes-Sadler, Gwon Osang, Gee Eun, Suh Younghee, Won Seol Ran, Park Hyun Im, Alissia Hong, Lee Jong-beom, Moon Yeonsoo, Pyun Jihye, Kang Soojung, Lee Hyunju, Yang Ki, Noh Sunhee, Eunhae Lim, Bona Park, Sunok Phillips, Chan-yang Kim, and friends made at the BTS conference organized by Colette Balmain. Special thanks to my colleagues at the V&A, Anna Jackson and Hongxing Zhang for their unwavering encouragement and invaluable advice on sensitive contents for the exhibition; alongside Masami Yamada, Lydia Caston, Natalie Kane, Johanna Agerman Ross, Brendan Cormier, Kristian Volsing, Donata Miller and Jacqueline Springer.

I would like to thank all the public institutions, private collectors, broadcasting companies, music labels, entertainment agencies, creative companies, publishers, artists and designers who have so generously lent or donated their objects: 2018 Pyeongchang Winter Olympic and Paralympic Games Memorial Hall, A24, Amorepacific Archives, Amorepacific Museum of Art, Arumjigi Culture Keepers Foundation, Kim Balko, Barunson, Blizzard Entertainment, Bodleian Library, British Museum, Chanel, Chung Hae Weon, CL/Baauer Holy, CJ ENM, C-Zann E, Daegu National Museum, Lee Young-hee, Eui Jip Hwang, G-Dragon, Gee Eun, Genesis, Hanbok Advancement Center, Hanmi Semiconductors, Han Youngsoo Foundation, History of Whoo, Hwang Eui Jip, Imperial War Museum, Independence Hall Museum, Jun Min Cho, Jikji Cheongju Early Printing Museum, Jimmy Choo, Jin Teok, Jo Soon-ae, Kakao Webtoon, KBS, Kian84, Kim Hanguen, Kim Hye-soon, Kim Hyun-suk, Ko Myung Jin, Korean Film Archive, Korea Craft and Design Foundation, Korea Tourism Organization, Kukje Gallery, Kyungwoon Museum, KQ Entertainment, Lee Hajun, Lee Jinhee, Leesle, LeoJ, LG Display, LG Electronics, Louis Vuitton, Major General John Page Family, Mark Henley, May 18 Memorial Foundation, MBC, MBC Arts, Miss Darcei, Miss Sohee, Museo Nacional Centro de Arte Reina Sofia, Myung Films, Moho Films, Nam June Paik Estate, National Archive of Korea, National Gugak Museum, National Intangible Heritage Center, National Museum of Korean Contemporary History, National Museum of Modern and Contemporary Art (Korea), Naver Webtoon, Netflix Korea, OCI Museum, Oh Yoon estate, Onjium Foundation, P-Nation Entertainment, Pledis Entertainment, Pulse9 Entertainment, Riot Games, Risabae, Robert Neff Collection, Ryu Seong-hie, Samsung Innovation Museum, SBS, Scholastic, Seo Taiji, Seoul Model Factory, Seoul National University Museum of Art, Seoul Munhwasa, Shutterstock, Shin Gwang, SM Entertainment, SOAS Library, Song Jong-hee, Studio Dragon, Studio Lululala, Suwon Museum of Art, Tablo, The Black Label, Travis Wise, Twitter users (@SenyumArmy, @BTS_National, @Senyum, @Kpop4Planet, @KenyaShinee, @BtsFazkook, @BTS_ARMY_EGYPT, @filoblinksph, @armymonterrey.official), Universal Music Group, Vogue Korea, William Oldroyd, Yak films, YG Entertainment and YouTube.

This exhibition also showcased the breadth and depth of the knowledge and savoir-faire of all the V&A departments involved. For their wonderful care and amazing flair at beautifully presenting the wide range of works in the exhibition, a huge thank you to Clair Battisson, Susan Catcher, Stephanie Jamieson, Lara Meredith, Laura Ledwin, Roisin Morris, Keira Miller, Lara Flecker, Katrina Redman, Yukiko Yoshii Barrow, Dana Melchar, Nigel Bamforth and Adriana Francescutto Miró in the Conservation Departments; James McNeff and Megan Visser in Technical Services; Sarah Duncan at Photo Studio. Also thanks to Evonne Mackenzie in Design; Emma Zeitlyn and Cian Jennings in Marketing; Sophie Steel and Shannon Nash in Press; Camilla Carter, Stacey Bowles, Evelyn Curtin and Bethan Korausch in Development; Katherine Young, Asha McLoughlin, Lenny Cherry and Bryony Shepherd in Learning; Keith Hale and Tom Windross in Digital Media; and V&A Registrar Rocio Mayol Sanchez. I am thankful to Clare Inglis, Daniel Slater, Jane Lawson, Philippa Simpson, Joanna Norman, Nick Marchand, and Laura McKehan. I would also like to express my deepest gratitude to Tristram Hunt for supporting and encouraging this project from its inception.

For their innovative and immersive design of the exhibition, I would like to thank Design Lead Na Kim and her team Lee Yejou and Jeon San for the graphic design, and Alexander Turner, Graham Burn and their team at Studio MUTT for the 3D design. It was a pleasure working alongside Zelina Hughes and Saumya Monga at Studio ZNA for the lighting, and technical project managers Sarah Haines, Rebecca Derrine and Lee Starling at Fraser Randall. Special thanks also to David Hogan, Marco Carini and Simon Gross for the AV and editing, as well as to Charli Davis and her team at Luke Halls for their AV design.

Rosalie Kim

Numbers refer to pages.
Photo: V&A Photo Studio, courtesy Sarah Duncan and Kieron Boyle, unless otherwise indicated

© Courtesy Gwon Osang 5
Photo: HYEA W. KANG, courtesy Vogue Korea 7
Squid Game Artwork © 2021 Netflix. All Rights Reserved 8
© SM Entertainment Co., Ltd 10, 124–5
© Shin Gwang 14–15
Photo: Kevin Mazur/WireImage/Getty Images 17
Photo: Jun Min Cho, courtesy Museum of Contemporary History of Korea 18
© Kyungah Ham. Courtesy artist and Kukje Gallery. Photo: Chunho An 19 (above)
Photo: Archive Image/Alamy Stock Photo 19 (below)
Courtesy Seoul History Museum 20
Photo: Bettmann/Getty Images 21 (above)
Courtesy Samsung 23 (above)
Photo: National Folk Museum of Korea, Seoul 23 (below)
Photo: Lee Chang-soon, courtesy Hankook Ilbo 24 (left)
Photo: Na Kyung-taek (provided by the May 18 Memorial Foundation) 24 (right)
Photo: David Madison/Getty Images 25 (left)
Photo: Str Old/Reuters Pictures 25 (right)
Courtesy LG Electronics 28, 41 (right)
© Estate of Kim Ki Chang/Woonbo Foundation of Culture. Photo © Christie's Images/Bridgeman Images 22
© Mark Henley/Panos Pictures 26
Courtesy Museum of Contemporary History, Seoul 27
© Estate of Emil Goh, courtesy Xavier Goh 30
© CJ ENM 33
© KBS, Winter Sonata / Licensed by KBS Media Ltd. All Rights Reserved 34
Photo: THE WHITE HOUSE/ADAM SCHULTZ 35
Courtesy Korea Tourism Organisation/ HS Ad 36
Photo: REUTERS/Alamy Stock Photo 37
© sahachat/123RF 38–9
Photo: Edd Thomas 41 (left)
Blizzard Entertainment 42
Photo: Jean Chung/Bloomberg via Getty Images 43
Riot Games 45
Courtesy Pulse9 46–7
© SM Entertainment Co., Ltd 49–53
Image courtesy Curzon Film 54, 69
Photo: © Weinstein Company/Courtesy Everett Collection Inc/Alamy Stock Photo 56
Photo: Erick W. Rasco /Sports Illustrated via Getty Images 57 (above)
© Studio Dragon/CJ ENM 57 (below)
Photo: National Folk Museum of Korea, Seoul 58–9 (above)
© Nam June Paik Estate. Photo: Kristina García/Museo Nacional Centro de Arte Reina Sofia, Madrid 59 (below)
Courtesy Contents Panda 61 (above)
© 2018 2x19HD. All Rights Reserved 61 (below)
Photo: © Samuel Goldwyn Films/Courtesy Everett Collection Inc/Alamy Stock Photo 63
Courtesy MYUNGFILMS 64
ShinCine Communications 65 (left)

Photo: Photo 12/Alamy Stock Photo 65 (right)
Courtesy Next Entertainment World 67
Courtesy Lee Ha-jun. Photo: © 2019 CJ ENM Corporation, Barunson E&A. All Rights Reserved 70–1
Photo: Kyungwoon Museum, Seoul 72 (left)
Kingdom Artwork © 2020 Netflix. All Rights Reserved 73
© Kang Full published by Kakao Entertainment Corp 74
Kian84/Naver Webtoon 75
Ha Il-gwon/Naver Webtoon 76
© Studio Dragon/CJ ENM 77
Photo: Everett Collection Inc/Alamy Stock Photo 78
©Kwang jin published by Kakao Entertainment Corp 79
Courtesy Hybe Corp./Webtoon 80 (left)
© DUBU(REDICE STUDIO), Chugong, h-goon 2018/D&C WEBTOON Biz, published by Kakao Entertainment Corp. 80 (right)
Courtesy Naver Webtoon 81 (left)
© CJ ENM 81 (right)
Courtesy Song Jong Hee 83 (above right)
Courtesy Song Jong Hee 83 (below left)
Photo: AF Archive/Alamy Stock Photo 83 (below right)
© 2003 EGG FILMS Co., Ltd. All Rights Reserved 84
Courtesy Song Jong Hee 85
Photo: Photofest 87
© CJ ENM 88 (above), 89
Squid Game Artwork © 2021 Netflix. All Rights Reserved 88 (below)
Photo: Kim Dong-kyu, YONHAP/AP 90
Squid Game Artwork © 2021 Netflix. All Rights Reserved 91
Courtesy Song Jong Hee 93 (above left)
YG Entertainment 95
Photo: Philip Gowman 97
Courtesy Hybe Corp. 98–9
YG Entertainment 101
RBW Entertainment (Rainbowbridge World) 102
Photo: Newscom/Alamy Stock Photo 103
© SM Entertainment Co., Ltd 104
Photo: Estate of David Gahr/ Getty Images 105
© SM Entertainment Co., Ltd 106
Photo: Lee Young-ho/Sipa US/Alamy Stock Photo 107 (above)
Photo: Rick Diamond/WireImage for The Recording Academy - Grammy Foundation/Getty Images 107 (below)
Photo: Scott Gries/Getty Images 107 (middle)
Source: Instagram, @filoblinksph 109
Source: Twitter, @Kpop4Planet, accessed on 19/09/2021 110 (above left)
Source: Twitter @BtsFazkook, accessed on 19/09/2021 110 (above right)
Source: Twitter, @BTS_ARMY_EGYPT, accessed 19/09/2021 110 (below left)
Source: Twitter @KenyaShinee, accessed on 19/09/2021 110 (below right)
Source: Twitter,@BTS_National/@SenyumArmy, accessed on 19/09/2021 112 (left)
Photo: Chalinee Thirasupa/Reuters Pictures 112 (right)
Source: Facebook, Tuk-up, accessed on 19/09/2021 113 (left)